Philosophy Looks at Chess

Philosophy Looks at Chess

Edited by

BENJAMIN HALE

OPEN COURT
Chicago and La Salle, Illinois

To order books from Open Court, call 1-800-815-2280, or visit
our website at www.opencourtbooks.com.

Open Court Publishing Company is a division of Carus Publishing
Company.

Printed and bound in the United States of America.

Library of Congress Cataloging-in-Publication Data

Philosophy looks at chess / edited by Benjamin Hale.
    p. cm.
   Includes bibliographical references and index.
    Summary: "A collection of essays exploring philosophical
themes at work in the game of chess. Topics addressed include
the intersection of chess and technology, the difference (or lack
thereof) between Artificial Intelligence and human intelligence,
the nature of games, and cultural aspects of chess strategy"
—Provided by publisher.
   ISBN 978-0-8126-9633-2 (trade paper : alk. paper)
   1. Chess—Philosophy. 2. Games and technology. I. Hale,
Benjamin, 1972-
GV1314.7.P45 2008
794.1—dc22
                       2008024385

Contents

Introduction   vii

1. To Know the Past One Must First Know the Future: Raymond Smullyan and the Mysteries of Retrograde Analysis
BERND GRAEFRATH   1

2. A Deep Blue Grasshopper: Playing Games with Artificial Intelligence
ANDY MIAH   13

3. Playing Chess in the Chinese Room
TAMA COUTTS   25

4. Garry Kasparov Is a Cyborg, or What ChessBase Teaches Us about Technology
JOHN HARTMANN   39

5. Chess-Playing Computers and Embodied Grandmasters: In What Ways Does the Difference Matter?
EVAN SELINGER   65

6. The Difficult Ways of God and Caïssa: Chess, Theodicy, and Determinism in Gadamer
BILL MARTIN   89

7. Who Plays Games in Philosophy?
AHTI-VEIKKO PIETARINEN   119

8. Hip-Hop Tactics: A Culturalogic Expression of the African Aesthetic's Role in Determining the Basis of Creativity on the Sixty-Four Squares of Warfare
TOMMY J. CURRY   137

9. Quiet, Please! There's a Game Here: Discourse and
   Silence in the Formal Pragmatics of a Chess Match
   BENJAMIN HALE   157

10. Casuistry and Chess: Some Methodological Lessons
    for Ethics
    PETER MORRISS   171

11. Chess Is Not a Game
    DEBORAH P. VOSSEN   191

12. The Reviled Art
    STUART RACHELS   209

Contributors   227
Index   231

Introduction

A great many papers in philosophy begin with a problem. "Imagine," they beseech, "that there is a trolley, or a violinist, or a teletransporter, or a planet just like our own in every salient way but one." "Suppose," they importune, "that everything else being equal, some very minor something is different." Consider the following: You have picked up a book titled *Philosophy Looks at Chess*. You are in a store, or a library, or a coffee shop. The shelves are festooned with other intriguing volumes: *Chess Strategy*, *Chess Openings*, *Chess for Dopes*; or, on the other side of the room, *Leviathan, Zarathustra, The Republic, The Meditations*. You must decide: What is this?

When you first read the title of this book on chess and philosophy, you certainly conclude that the book relates to some deep problem in chess. You may be thinking that this must be a book on Kasparov's challenge to Deep Blue or on the relationship between chess and the meaning of the life, or on strategy, broadly conceived. But this book—the book you have in your hands—is nothing of the sort. Its contents could never be so neatly captured by a single question or problem, and its title could never be so easily comprehended by reference to a single chess event or an approach to strategy. Such inherent confusion over the contents of this book may explain why I generally avoid talking about the chess essays I've collected at the philosophy cocktail parties and black-tie soirées that pepper my busy social schedule. Philosophical questions surrounding chess are thought by some to be too pedestrian to crowd out the otherwise pressing philosophical debates on four-dimensionalism, anarcho-syndicalism, and desire satisfactionism. Nevertheless, the content of this collection of essays never fails to spark a discussion.

Contributions to this volume span a wide range of topics related to chess, and diverge from most philosophy volumes in that the approaches of each author are guided by no standard methodology.

Some authors write whimsically, while others write with gravity; some speak with authority, while others speak with the sheepish humility of a self-loathing woodpusher. This volume includes essays from so-called analytic philosophers, enamored as they are with concision, logic, and compartmentalization, and so-called Continental philosophers, driven as they are by a flair for the literary and the dramatic. It includes essays from aestheticians and from philosophers of sport, from students and professors, from Grandmasters and grand-patzers. For this reason, this volume, to my mind, functions in the true spirit of both philosophy and chess. There is no clear approach, there is no distinctive doctrine. Instead this volume offers a gallimaufry of writings and musings that relate playfully to the game of chess, written by people who play chess, who like chess, who love chess, and who are addicted to chess.

I have selected most essays for their readability and breadth. Some deal with extraordinarily difficult topics in professional philosophy, while others simply scratch the surface on superficial matters. In this short introduction, I would like to give you a brief overview of each reading and offer, where I can, some justification for my ordering the contents in the way that I have. At the end of the day, the collection is intended playfully, so those who seek to make too much sense of the ordering will find themselves at a loss.

First, the lay of the land: we begin the volume by asking about what it is to "understand" chess; from "understanding" or "knowing" we move into "being," into questions about what chess is, and whether chess is an apt metaphor for life; from "being" we round our task out by moving to "doing." This is a natural progression, echoing intuitions from ancient philosophers. Our safari through philosophy and chess takes us from the moment at which we *see* to the point at which we *do*.

Bernd Graefrath, a professor at the University of Duisburg-Essen, offers the first chapter. Graefrath provides an illuminating discussion of a type of chess problem for the puzzle-driven player: a "retrograde analysis." Where most traditional chess problems present a player with a forward-looking board arrangement and require that the player determine the correct or the best next move or series of moves following from that arrangement, retrograde analysis turns the traditional approach to chess problems on its head. A retrograde analysis calls upon the player to analyze *what has already happened* in a game, and not what *should* happen. This breed of chess problem gained popularity with the widely published chess problems of Raymond Smullyan, which Graefrath covers in his piece. For those unfamiliar with retrograde analysis, the four puzzles that Graefrath offers may provide entertainment in themselves. However, there is more at play in Graefrath's piece than meets the eye. He seeks the unifying philosophical principle that guides Smullyan's many books on retrograde analysis. In his essay, Graefrath not only provides intelligent commentary on these few puzzles, but he concludes that one can tease out two important philosophical insights from Smullyan's work. The first is what Graefrath calls "cognitive optimism": that given even some of the seemingly most intractable puzzles, our powers of cognition can lead us to unravel the puzzles of the universe. And the second relates to the limitations of cognitive optimism: Smullyan shows that, despite our best abilities, there are many puzzles for which we will never have an answer.

Turning further toward questions of understanding and intelligence, Andy Miah draws on the philosophy of artificial intelligence (AI) to wonder what kind of knowledge we can legitimately call "intelligence." To do so, he utilizes the writings of two famous theorists, Alan Turing and John Searle, both of whom reappear in several subsequent chapters. Miah challenges a fundament of computer programmers the world over: that chess-playing computers provide a good model of intelligence. He argues that chess does not make such a great model of artificial intelligence as is often thought. Instead, he reasons, there are many other games and sports that provide sufficiently more stringent tests of intelligence. To draw this conclusion, he introduces yet a third theorist, Bernard Suits, and borrows heavily from his view of game playing. Suits's view emphasizes not only an ability to reason out strategies and tactics, but also some affinity for creativity, spontaneity, and arbitrariness in game playing.

Tama Coutts contributes a lively essay in a similar vein that offers a brief overview and criticism of John Searle's "Chinese room argument." He argues, very much in opposition to Andy Miah's position, that chess-playing computers, in fact, *understand* chess in the relevant manner. His argument proceeds straightforwardly: he introduces Searle's Chinese room argument and then modifies it to ask whether it can adequately suit the case of chess. He then commandeers two replies to the argument that Searle himself addresses in his own work: the "systems reply" and the "robot reply." Coutts argues that the "robot reply" is successful, particularly in the case of chess. To support this claim, he returns to the case of chess and reasons that it is feasible and permissible to attribute *understanding* to chess-playing computers. Oh to sit him down across a board with Andy Miah! Perhaps they might best battle out their differences with figurines.

John Hartmann broadens this discussion considerably by addressing the relation between humans and technology. In an exhaustive and fascinating case analysis, he covers American master Tim Mirabile as he prepares for a match using ChessBase. This case, he believes, holds enlightening answers to the question that has surely been whispered in hushed tones by many a chess enthusiast: *Is Garry Kasparov a Cyborg?* Hartmann's strategy is to ask questions about how Kasparov came to master the thinking of Deep Blue, his competitor for several famous matches during the mid-1990s. He details the organization and structure of a chess program, crawls into the mind of a master as he prepares for a match, and rounds it out with a discussion of Kasparov's own preparations. As much an exploration of the educational use of ChessBase as it is a criticism of the prominent philosopher Hubert Dreyfus, a professor at UC Berkeley, Hartmann advances an account of technology that understands computers as working in concert with players. In the end, he argues that Fritz and Junior, two chess engines, worked effectively as unacknowledged members of Team Kasparov.

Furthering this discussion, Professor Evan Selinger's piece integrates a somewhat different point from the philosophy of technology. He investigates two *existential* depictions of chess—one from Hubert Dreyfus, mentioned above, and the other from the film director Ingmar Bergman. He seeks to unpack what it would mean for computers to play chess like humans. Selinger's claim is that "as a matter of contingency, human interaction is, de facto, interaction between agents in *culturally marked bodies.*" He believes that those who emphasize the way in which chess-playing computers are similar to humans overlook a crucial, and in many ways obvious, difference between the two: humans have bodies, and play games through them. In this case, Selinger's target is Hubert Dreyfus, whom he accuses of advancing a personal theoretical agenda and neglecting the human elements of those who actually play chess. Specifically, he believes that Dreyfus has gone too far in defending his now famous article "What Computers Can't Do" by unwittingly creating an arrangement in which *eros* and *prejudice*, aspects of humanity critical to his own view, are *incapable* of influencing a Grandmaster's perception. All this to say: even though Dreyfus himself notes the importance of "embodiment," according to Selinger, Dreyfus's own account is riddled with disembodied images.

Ahti Pietarinen wonders aloud whether "the chess/language analogy is worthy of serious philosophizing." He does so by taking us on a brisk jaunt through the history of game theory. His superbly researched and historically rich piece may be heavy going for the casual reader of philosophy, but those interested in game theory and its relation to chess will find much to enjoy in this history. In particular, Pietarinen walks us through the uses of chess in Charles S. Peirce, Edmund Husserl, Ferdinand de Saussure, Ludwig Wittgenstein, L. E. J. Brouwer, Paul Grice, and Jürgen Habermas. A fascinating jaunt for sure!

Philosopher Bill Martin strikes a similarly historical chord, though this time in a very different manner. Pietarinen's piece was centered on the philosophy of language and chess as an analogy for language. Martin seeks to unearth an argument that a benevolent God can still exist in a world permeated with evil and tragedy. He does so by exploring Hans-Georg Gadamer—a German philosopher of language, seated prominently in the branch of philosophy known as hermeneutics—who has used chess to argue on behalf of such a theodicy.

On a different and more whimsical note, Tommy Curry's essay on the sixty-four squares of chess warfare is fantastically rhythmic. It evokes all at once the lyrical poetry of Gil Scott-Heron, the political beats of Public Enemy, and the hard-edged scrap of the Washington Square Park chess hustler. If chess is often understood as a battle between rival factions, this revolution will not be televised. Curry himself has a provisional chess rating over 2000, which, for those in the know, places him in the "exceptional" category. While the content of his piece diverges considerably from most of the other essays in the volume, I think you'll find his conclusions provocative. Contrary to most thinking about chess, he reasons that when one plays chess, one plays the player, not the board. He focuses on the psychological and sociocultural elements in human interactions to reason that Black (Africana) players play chess differently than white (Caucasian) players. Such a generalization seems illegitimate—indeed, sweeping. But Curry offers a compelling case that the attitude (or the "negritude," as he calls it) of Black players is intimately caught up in their play. Whether you buy his argument or reject it wholesale, his essay, to my mind, brims with enthusiasm both for the game of chess and for his rich Africana history.

In my own piece I employ the case of chess to reason that strategic moves in chess maintain a formal structure that suggests that at least one player invokes an interactive and intentional attitude with regard to the moves of the other player. I use the example of the chess game to rebut a generally accepted claim in a branch of ethics called "discourse ethics." The claim I attack is that communicative interaction is one of two variants of action that uniquely and necessarily carries with it the presupposition that one must "take the perspective of the other." Typically, discourse ethics is thought to pertain only to those entities that can reciprocally engage one another in a conversation about needs, requirements, desires, and harms. But in the case of chess, interaction need not be linguistically mediated. In fact, etiquette dictates that players do not speak to one another, which, I try to show, provides an important countercase of non–linguistically mediated interaction. I extrapolate from the chess game to argue on behalf of entities that cannot speak. The aim in my chapter is to investigate whether discursive decision-making needs to be accompanied by moral authority on the part of the opposing interlocutor. Specifically, my intent is to investigate the issue of whether interaction requires at least two language-capable agents in order to be rule-governed. I argue that it does not; that anticipating what another player is doing is more than simply a matter of understanding the words that he uses to describe his position: it is also a matter of understanding the moves that he will make. This analysis therefore shows that discourse ethics applies to games with nonhumans as well as to games with humans.

Pete Morriss discusses an area of ethics called "casuistry" to reason that games of chess are not as revealing about ethical dilemmas as they might at first seem. He begins from the natural comparison between life and chess. He reasons that many philosophers are drawn to the idea that ethical problems are just like chess problems: just as one cannot uncover universal principles that should guide one's chess game, so too can one not uncover ethical principles. Ethical problems, these philosophers reason, are best taken on a case-by-case, or casuistic, basis. But Morriss argues that it is potentially a mistake to be drawn to this view. Chess players don't simply approach chess from the bottom up: they learn through doing, by comparing themselves to better and worse players, by challenging one another—they gain feedback. Ethical problems are not like this. There is no paradigmatic feedback loop in ethics. There's a lot more fumbling. As a result, it is very easy to fall into lockstep with external authority, instead of challenging this authority, as one might do in chess. Hence, the relationship between chess-related problem solving and ethical problem solving, so trumpeted by the casuist, is not as perfect as it first seems.

Deb Vossen asks whether chess can rightly be considered a game in the first place. She concludes, much to the surprise of many readers, that chess is *not* a game. Her evocative claim turns on a distinction between *a game* and *the idea of a game*, which evolved out of Bernard Suits's phenomenally underappreciated work *The Grasshopper: Games, Life and Utopia*. She advances this position by way of a technical argument that employs Suits's discussion of "prelusory" goals and "lusory" attitudes. The word "lusory" generally means sporty or playful; and in Suits's sense, it means that when we engage in the play of chess, we must enter the lusory attitude. She uses the notion of a prelusory goal to argue that such goals exist in a game (in this case, a game of chess) but not at all in the idea of the game (in the idea of chess).

Stuart Rachels, IM, provides a dramatically different and welcome voice to the final chapter in the volume. Often we catch only momentary snippets of philosophical insight from chess players as they shuffle away from the game table, granting throngs of sportscasters brief interviews between sleep and study. Boris Spassky, Garry Kasparov, Judit and Susan Polgar, and Greg and Jennifer Shahade, among others, have all offered insightful, and sometimes philosophical, comments about chess. But Rachels is a rare breed: he is both an accomplished philosopher and an accomplished chess player. He holds the title of youngest chess master in American history, he is a professor of philosophy at the University of Alabama, and he is the son of one of my favorite authors, the well-known James Rachels, who himself was an accomplished chess player and philosopher. What is refreshing about Rachels's contribution is that it rests squarely in a tradition of *rumination* about the game of chess. It recounts intelligently his relationship to the game, his thoughts on its status in popular culture, and his frustrations as a fledgling player. While it is considerably less theoretical than some of the other pieces in this volume, it is an absolute joy to read, and if you play chess, it will inspire you to think differently about the intellectual aspects of the game.

For me, editing this volume has been illuminating and inspiring. I've discovered new theorists, thought differently about chess, and learned of areas of philosophy otherwise unknown to me. I had the good fortune to be introduced to Bernard Suits's work while editing this book. I picked up *Grasshopper* in the fall of last year, and only found time to read the fantastic volume while rocking my newborn son to sleep at our local coffee shop. Perhaps most importantly, for the first time in my life, I was excused of guilt. I needn't consider my many-times-daily diversions to play a game of bullet chess diversions at all. I could justify my procrastination, I could justify my obsession, by appeal to a commitment that I'd made with this publisher.

I should hope that the reader derives the same enjoyment exploring the diverse essays in this volume that I have enjoyed editing them. My own chess is outrageously lackluster. I am humbled by the quality of chess experience prevalent among many of the contributors to this volume. I was however motivated to do this volume for the same reasons that inspired so many of the other authors in this volume to improve their games—at some point in my life, I grew obsessed with chess. In particular, chess provided for me the worst kind of distraction from writing my dissertation; and now it provides for me a similar distraction from doing the work that I know I must do. While others I have known have lost themselves in bridge, poker, Scrabble, drinking, drugs, and even, in one case, manically purchasing and wearing items made of velour, chess became my sanctuary. These games we play, these games that we use to keep our minds whirring while we think through difficult questions, these are the playground of thought. They offer amusement when we are down, they offer play when we must labor, they offer sanity when we are about to lose our minds, but most of all, they keep us thinking. And that, my dear reader, is what this volume is about.

1

To Know the Past One Must First Know the Future: Raymond Smullyan and the Mysteries of Retrograde Analysis

BERND GRAEFRATH

Some philosophers have a second field of interest to which they are at least as dedicated as to their profession. For most of them, these two fields, even when both taken seriously, are not related to each other. Thus, when the philosopher Michael Dummett published his monumental book *The Game of Tarot*, playing-card historians regarded it at once as a standard work, about not only the history of tarot cards and the games played with them, but also the history of playing cards in general (Dummett 1980). However, this subject has no thematic relation to philosophical discussions (except for a general critique of a modern type of obscurantism which misrepresents an entertaining card game as a source of ancient wisdom). With Raymond Smullyan, the case is different. Already in his puzzle books, such as *Forever Undecided: A Puzzle Guide to Gödel* (1987), logical riddles abound which illustrate deep philosophical themes. In his two books of chess problems, *The Chess Mysteries of Sherlock Holmes* (1979) and *The Chess Mysteries of the Arabian Knights* (1982), this connection is not so obvious; but a closer look may reveal a hidden connection to his philosophical world view, which he develops and discusses in his philosophical book *The Tao is Silent* (1977) and in his autobiography *Some Interesting Memories: A Paradoxical Life* (2002).

As could be expected, Smullyan's chess problems are not of the usual kind, in which you have to find the only way in which White could mate Black in a stipulated number of moves. Rather, he specializes in problems in which you do not explore the future, but the past. These problems in "retrograde analysis" ask the potential solver to look backward to the history of the imaginary game which led to the given diagram position. These problems are artfully composed in a way so that there is only one correct answer. In a special area of retrograde analysis, it is even possible to reconstruct every single move of this imaginary history, in a so-called proof game. But Smullyan only deals with traditional retros, in which one particular question has to be answered, and for reasons of logical necessity, the solution can be found. The solver has to become a detective who collects the evidence of the game position and then proceeds according to Sherlock Holmes's maxim: *When one has eliminated the impossible, then whatever remains, however improbable, must be the truth.*

The stipulation of a retro problem asks questions of the following type: Which side can still castle? (This is not allowed if either the king or the rook must have made a move sometime in the past.) Can a player now capture *en passant*? (This is only allowed if the pawn which is about to be captured must just have made a double step on the previous move.) Did a particular piece come into existence by the promotion of a pawn, while its original predecessor was captured? In some cases, it is even possible that a mate in a precise number of moves can be forced, but the exact mating move cannot be played on the board: White may have a decisive attack against every possible black defense, but the particular move to be chosen depends on White's and Black's possible resources (i.e., castling and taking *en passant*), and these in turn depend on the history of the game and can only be known when we see the next moves. So in this case, "to know the past one must first know the future" (an intriguing sentence for which Smullyan is indebted to Jack Kotik).

In every case of a good retro, it turns out that something unexpected must have happened in the past in order to explain the diagram position that, until one has found out the solution, appears to be impossible or so chaotic that no precise answer seems to be possible. This procedure may contain a deep analogy to the creation of a philosophical world view. Although answering big questions is not popular among contemporary philosophers, one might try to develop a comprehensive view of the world that is more plausible than all its rivals. However, there will be no logical proof, because— different from a chess position—there is neither complete knowledge of all the given facts nor a priori knowledge of the original position. The chess detective is in a position that for a philosopher is an unattainable dream: He can give deductive proofs as answers to questions about which others can only speculate inductively.

The Birth of Retrograde Analysis

Sam Loyd, the great puzzle king, may also have given birth to retro problems. His following chess problem may look, at first sight, rather normal, because its stipulation asks the reader to find a forward play by which White can force a mate against a defending black side:

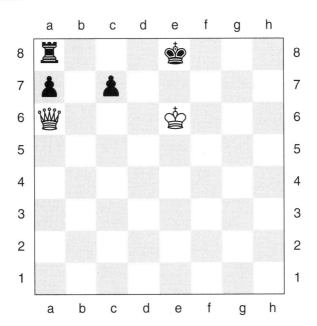

Sam Loyd
Musical World 1859 (?)
Mate in 2 moves

A solver who is familiar only with this traditional type of chess problem could come to the conclusion that the problem does not have a solution, because against many white moves, Black can escape by castling to the queenside. But Loyd has excluded this defense by widening the horizon of chess problems: He views them as having a past that leads back to the initial starting position, from which it developed legally; that is, according to the rules of playing a game of chess. Once this perspective is accepted, one is allowed to question whether Black may castle. And in this case, it can be proven that (if the diagram position arose from a regular game) either the black king or black rook must already have moved, thus forfeiting the right to castle. This is done by asking a simple question: If it is White's turn to move, then what was Black's last move? The two black pawns are still on their original squares, and so White mates by (1) Qa1 and (2) Qh8#.

What began as a side issue later gave rise to an independent type of chess problem. Exploring the past of a diagram position is no longer a method subservient to the aims of forward play, but itself moves into the center of attention. The solver is now asked a question which directly asks about the fictional history of a chess game, or even about some eccentric aspects of a given position which, quite surprisingly, can be answered for certain with the help of pure logic. Raymond Smullyan became fascinated by this type of problem when he was a teenager, and although he composed more than a hundred retro problems later on, he still thinks that the best of them is one he composed when he was only sixteen years old.

Smullyan's Best Retro Problem

An extensive discussion of the following problem (Smullyan 1979) can give an idea of the intricacies that one must go through in order to give a sufficiently detailed solution by retrograde analysis. Nowadays, even more complex retro problems are composed, but already Smullyan's problem clearly shows a philosophically interesting point: Given data may look extremely chaotic, but could nevertheless arise from hidden regularities. For example, a list of numbers may seem totally irregular, like a product of random variation; but, as we learn in elementary mathematics, such seeming irregularity can well be the result of a short and elegant algebraic formula when 1, 2, 3, and so forth, are inserted in place of an X. A similar explanation can be given about the way of establishing a natural law: a vast amount of evidence is elegantly explained by a basic principle that is applied to various empirical circumstances. The metaphysician may then be viewed as someone who tries to establish an even more basic principle from which the natural laws can be deduced. Similarly, a police detective will presuppose that all the evidence gathered at a scene of crime can be rationally explained by a plausible or even unique story that can convince a jury in a court of law. In this way, the tasks of the police detective and of the metaphysician may be motivated by a similar approach, although their optimistic hopes may sometimes lead them astray. Sometimes, an unknown third party has "framed" an innocent suspect; and sometimes, the most elegant metaphysical systems may be wide of the mark. In these cases, the simple and most economical explanations are not the best.

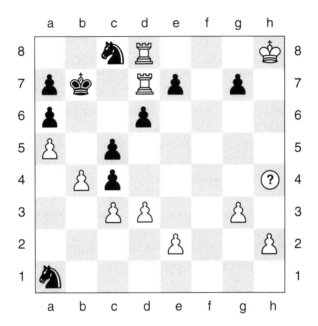

Raymond Smullyan
The Chess Mysteries of Sherlock Holmes (1979)
What is the missing piece? (What does the
    question mark stand for?)

The black king is in check from the white rook d7. So White must have made the last move. The only legally possible move must have been a capture by a white pawn from c7, promoting to a rook at d8. What has become of the other white pieces? An original white rook, the white queen, two white bishops and two white knights have not been accounted for yet. But the position of the black pawns tells us about four captures on white squares (from b7 to a6 and from f7 to c4). The white bishop starting on c1 only moves on black squares, so the black pawns captured four of the other five pieces. Consequently, a white piece could be the missing piece (but not the white bishop which only moves on white squares). Now we can start from a different angle: Could the missing piece be black? It could not be a black queen or rook, because then the white king at h8 would be in check, which would be illegal, because both kings cannot be in check simultaneously. But how about a black pawn, knight or bishop? In order to answer this, we have to explore the history of the white rook d8. It evolved from a white pawn at c7; but this must have come from f2, capturing four black pieces: from the f-file to the c-file, and then to d8. The following black pieces are not accounted for yet: a black queen, two black rooks, two black bishops, and one black pawn, which is sufficient to explain the captures, but still does not give us a definitive answer. Have we reached a dead end? We can learn that on its last move, White did not capture a black queen or rook at d8, because these could not have moved to this square legally, because the white king at h8 would already have been in check previously. So a black bishop or black knight was captured at d8. But can we go further than that?

A little detail that may seem unimportant comes to the rescue: Since two black pawns are at e7 and g7, this proves that the black bishop at f8 never left its home square, but was captured there. Both black knights are still around, and this forces us to conclude that the missing black pawn must have promoted to an additional black knight or bishop, because there is no other possibility for a black piece to be captured at d8 on White's last move. The promoted black pawn must have come from h7; but how did it get to White's home base? It had to make at least one capture to get around the white pawn h2. But can we know (in the strict sense of proving it) where this capture to the g-file took place?

Now we have to take another step back. Since the black pawn h7 that promoted was later captured, and a black queen or rook cannot legally be placed at h4, it is impossible that the piece at h4 is black. But since it is white, the possibilities for the capturing of white pieces by black pawns become rather restricted. There are ten plus one white pieces in the diagram position, only five are left, and all of these were captured by black pawns: bxa, fxexdxc, and hxg. So the black pawn h7 can only have captured once on the way to its promotion square. But then how did it get around the white pawn g3? If this pawn could have come from f2, then a definite solution of the problem would be impossible. But there are not enough black pieces available to allow such a capture, because then the original white pawn from g2 could not have reached d8 via c7. So only one possibility remains: The black pawn h7 captured a white piece at g2 and promoted at g1. And now the mystery finally dissolves: All black pawn captures happened on white squares: a6, e6, d5, c4, and g2. This only leaves one white piece, namely, the black-squared white bishop from c1, and consequently, it is the missing piece at h4.

A Problem of Forking Paths

Can there be a solution which, nevertheless, cannot be shown? A logical positivist[1] who defends a strict verificationism[2] would regard this as an absurdity. But Smullyan is emphatically not such a type of positivist. In his book *Some Interesting Memories: A Paradoxical Life* (2002), he writes: "A word about logical positivism: This doctrine regards as meaningless any statement that is incapable of verification or refutation. [. . .] Almost all of metaphysics goes out of the window according to logical positivism. [. . .] I have always regarded logical positivism as ridiculous!" This view is relevant for Smullyan's philosophy of God, religion, and the Tao. One of his retro problems may be viewed as an illustration of his antiverificationism (see page 8).

Regardless of what happened in the past of the fictional game that led to the diagram position, White can always force a mate in two moves. But this cannot be demonstrated by making a move, because there are two possible histories with different consequences for the entitlement of the players in the given position. What was Black's last move? The black pawn cannot have moved e6-e5, because then the white king would illegally have been in check. But Black could have played e7-e5, or some move by the king or rook. If Black moved his king or rook, he has lost the right to castle, and White mates in two moves by playing 1. Ke6. But if he makes this move, Black will save his life by playing 1. . . . 0-0-0. So White may prefer to play 1. d5xe6, capturing *en passant*, and Black will be mated on the next move, regardless whether he castles or not. But if White tries to make the *en passant* capture, Black will protest, claiming (correctly!) that White would have to prove that Black's last move must have been e7-e5, and this cannot be done. So here one might say that in order to know the past one must first know the future: Black's defense depends on White's

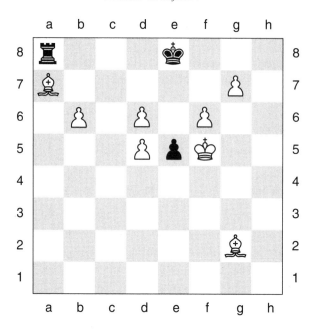

Raymond Smullyan
The Chess Mysteries of Sherlock Holmes (1979)
Indemonstrable mate in 2 moves

first move; and Black's claim about the past can only be known after White has already made his try.

Limits of Objectivity

Readers may wonder about Smullyan's simultaneous fascination by both strictest logic and Eastern mysticism. But these two sides of his life may well be complementary, although it really is surprising to see a philosopher and logician praised by Rudolf Carnap write something like the following in his autobiography: "To me, the atheist is blind, whereas the religionist is sighted, but his vision is distorted. I believe that all of the existing religions are full of false-hoods, but they are dynamic and progressing and nearer to the truth than atheism, which is static and going nowhere." In the final chapter of *The Tao Is Silent*, Smullyan presents a dialogue in which a metaphysician and a mystic develop a view that may be most attractive for someone with a high regard for logic, mathematics, and the sciences, but still thinks that the area of meaningful discourse is not restricted to this area. They may not even cover the most important questions! And even if no metaphysical proofs can be given, this does not make the project of metaphysics meaningless. Wittgensteinian in spirit, Smullyan justifies running against the limits of what can reasonably be said, because this will teach something and may even lead to a deeper insight. Some may fear that with a world view like this, Smullyan is opening the doors for an unenlightened obscurantism; but he would defend himself by saying that one should be open-minded rather than skeptical like a logical positivist who throws the baby out with the bathwater.

Retrograde Analysis and Philosophy

Problems of retrograde analysis can lead to two quite different philosophical insights. One is cognitive optimism: At least in some fields of human inquiry, our rational capabilities can lead us to discoveries where one might have doubted that knowledge could ever be available. A seeming chaos could be the result of a strict application of an elegant law, and definitive knowledge can sometimes be reached even under most unpromising circumstances (like in the chess problem of the missing piece). In a closed system, such a law could even be proven to cover all possible cases. Unfortunately (for the cognitive optimist), the big questions of traditional metaphysics cannot be answered in such a reliable way, because not all relevant data are given. And even if they were given, there still might be absolute limits for the knowledge of the truth (as Gödel taught us). Thus, Smullyan's logical puzzles (like the chess problem with a certain but indemonstrable mate) also illustrate the limits of cognitive optimism. But Smullyan remains an optimist, albeit of a more sophisticated type than the merely cognitive one. He does not defend a traditional kind of metaphysics, as we know it from the rationalist systems. His approach is rather reminiscent of what could be called "hypothetical metaphysics," with Arthur Schopenhauer's philosophy as a paradigm example.

Further Prospects: Time Will Tell

With only some small additional piece of information, even complete knowledge of the past is possible—in the closed system where all the laws are known, although the quasi-Laplacian demon only catches a glimpse of one particular moment of the game. This point can very well be illustrated by a modern branch of retro problems, namely that of exact proof games. A diagram position is given with a stipulation that it has been reached in a regular game of chess in a specific number of moves. This is all the information one gets, but it is sufficient to deduct the most wonderful occurrences of the past in every detail with absolute certainty. The following proof game was jointly composed by three masters of this field:

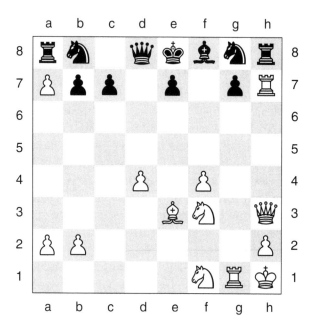

Reto Aschwanden, Michel Caillaud, and
Gerd Wilts
The Problemist 2004, 1st Prize
Proof Game in 18.5 moves

"In 18.5 moves" means that the diagram shows the position after White's nineteenth move. When analyzing the diagram position, it soon becomes clear that White needs nearly all his moves to get his pieces from the initial game array to their specific end position. But then all the missing black pieces must have moved to squares that were on the way of the white pieces. Only eighteen black moves are to be made, and it turns out that these have to be used to promote two black pawns, which are afterwards captured. But before this happens, they have to perform a great (so-called Indian) maneuver in order to make White's castling possible. And they even return to their promotion square and are finally captured there. The rest of the black pieces still are on their home base, leaving no obvious traces of the past. Nevertheless, this past can be known, and nowadays there is even computer software available that can prove that the following solution is correct and unique: 1.c4 d5 2.Qb3 Bd7 3.Qh3 Bb5 4.cxb5 d4 5.b6 d3 6.bxa7 dxe2 7.d4 f5 8.Be3 f4 9.Nd2 f3 10.Rc1 fxg2 11.f4 exf1B 12.Ngf3 g1R 13.Rc6 Rg5 14.Rh6 Ba6 15.Rxh7 Rb5 16.0-0 Rg5+ 17.Kh1 Rg1+ 18.Rxg1 Bf1 19.Nxf1. Everything must have happened in exactly this sequence: an evolutionary scientist's dream, based on few fossils and a precise knowledge of available time. Perhaps philosophers should also have such dreams. After all, G. E. Moore wrote that "the first and most important problem of philosophy is: To give a general description of the *whole* Universe."

NOTES

1. Logical positivism is a philosophical school of the twentieth century that combines traditional empiricism with the tools of modern logic. It takes the natural sciences and their methods as the paradigms of acquiring knowledge. In its most extreme form, it denies the existence of anything that cannot be known by the natural sciences, and it regards only those statements as meaningful the truth of which can be determined by empirical means.

2. According to the principle of verifiability, the meaning of a statement is its method of verification. If some sentences contain propositions that cannot be verified empirically (such as those of traditional metaphysics or of normative ethics), then they are regarded as being without cognitive content, only expressing some subjective feelings or attitudes.

REFERENCES

Dummett, Michael. 1980. *The Game of Tarot from Ferrara to Salt Lake City.* London: Gerald Duckworth.

Smullyan, Raymond M. 1977. *The Tao Is Silent.* San Francisco: Harper and Row.

———. 1979. *The Chess Mysteries of Sherlock Holmes.* New York: Knopf.

————. 1982. *The Chess Mysteries of the Arabian Knights.* New York: Knopf.

————. 1987. *Forever Undecided: A Puzzle Guide to Gödel.* New York: Knopf.

————. 2002. *Some Interesting Memories: A Paradoxical Life.* Davenport, IA: Thinkers' Press.

2

A Deep Blue Grasshopper: Playing Games with Artificial Intelligence

ANDY MIAH

> But perhaps this has nothing to do with chess, but is a game to the death between two forms of intelligence—the bounded field of postmodern intelligence and the unbounded vectors and virtualities of digital intelligence. A game of symbolic exchange in which Kasparov as the last chess player needs not only to be defeated, but humiliated by his own imaginary catastrophe. And he was.
>
> —DAVID COOK and ARTHUR KROKER,
>   "The Digital Prince and the Last Chess Player"

Can a machine think as you and I do? Can a machine have consciousness, feelings, or knowledge, rather than just simulate these capacities? These are the interests of artificial intelligence (AI) research and these questions have been asked for over half a century. The philosophy of AI is far reaching and continues to be fuelled by the early ideas of Alan Turing (1950) and his contemporary John Searle (1980). The critical questions remain the same as they always have been: Are the kinds of capabilities demonstrated by machines an indication of intelligence and, if so, is this kind of intelligence similar to that of sentient beings, such as humans?

Various authors have questioned this approach to philosophizing AI, asking whether the comparison between "wetware" and "hardware" is appropriate. Does it matter if machines have the same form of intelligence to humans? Does this manner of framing the question limit our conceptualization of intelligence? Indeed, if one models AI on sentient beings, does this constitute an unexplained speciesistic move? These questions about intelligent life are integral to broader philosophical inquiries into the nature of being. Modeling intelligence on biological life raises doubts about the existence of the soul or the spiritual, since the ends of this research have the potential to explain away these concepts, reducing being human to "mere" physics.

Various defenses of wetware's superiority consist of claims about some spiritual, soulful, or simply intangible biologic quality that cannot be operationalized and replicated by computing (Haldane 1997). Others consider this discourse to be speciesistic in that it unreasonably measures nonbiological matter in terms of the specific biological capacities of humans. On this view, the response might be that, it is not that the human being has a unique quality, but merely that it has not yet been shown how human cognition is entirely a mechanistic process.

Traditionally, the method through which AI has been tested is game theory, or, more accurately, through the creation of closed-system games, which do not require participants to encounter any of the more morally problematic choices that face people in real-life situations (Luger and Subblefield 1998). As Lee explains:

> Games such as chess, go, and drafts (or checkers) are ideal games for computerization. This is partly because they are games of perfect information as all the pieces are visible to both players and there is no element of chance or probability. This means that it should be possible to calculate the ideal move for any given situation, and hence, in theory at least, a computer should be able to play perfect chess. (1989, 108–9)

Yet, while a considerable amount of work has sought to propose games that test for intelligence, few take into account what it means to play a game. I will argue that the game playing of AI theory functions as mere algorithm rather than game playing and that further thought is needed. Moreover, I will argue that, contrary to Lee (1989), the specific game of chess is not the best game we might utilize to test for the comparative intelligence capacity of humans and machines.

Within the philosophy of AI and the related cultural discourse surrounding it, chess occupies a privileged position as a measure for understanding how close machines have come to reaching the intelligence capabilities of humans. A significant amount of media attention and research has been focused on creating computers that can beat Grandmasters of chess. In this respect, chess has been afforded a rather privileged game status, for the considerable intellectual capability that is required of its players.

Opinions vary about what kind of intelligence is required for being good at chess. From one perspective, Grandmaster status is an indication of intellectual superiority just as capability in chess is a measure of one's mind. Such a view would conclude that the great human minds can be found sitting across a checkered board, busily thinking through move possibilities. Chess is a game that involves creative thought, imagination, the possibility of abstraction, and thinking ahead. For others, chess is merely a computational form of knowledge, a specific kind of knowledge that allows one to consider a number of complex options at the same time, as well as to think laterally. From this perspective, being good at chess is certainly some measure of intellect, but it does not approximate the richer and wider construct of human intelligence, as it is simply not measuring other kinds of knowledge.

It is for this reason that the present chapter wishes to inquire into the suitability of chess as an indication of machine intelligence. At this juncture in the developing philosophy of information, it seems pertinent to reconsider this enduring debate. Specifically, this chapter will argue that other kinds of games are more suitable than chess to serve as a measure of machine intelligence compared with human intelligence. This is reflected in the title, "A Deep Blue Grasshopper," which elaborates on the notion of game playing and endeavors to consider whether Deep Blue (and its subsequent incarnations) responds to such an idea. It suggests that the privileged status of chess has been largely unwarranted, in part deriving from the cultural significance of chess as a game for intellectuals. Instead of wondering what the implications of a machine playing chess are, a more interesting question to ask would be "can a machine play soccer?" The example of soccer is relatively arbitrary and serves simply to illustrate that research into the philosophy of AI has appropriated a relatively biased notion of knowledge, which is premised wholly upon discrete and *relatively* uncomplicated logic.

In contrast to the rationale of using chess playing as a measure of intelligence, I suggest that our criteria must encompass broader characteristics of human knowledge than is demonstrated solely through the linear tests of Turing. A more suitable measure of human intelligence will be to reveal whether machines are able to exhibit the characteristics of play activity, which are present in a number of physical games.[1] Importantly, the reverse of this is not true—human play is not merely the replication of patterned behaviors. Nevertheless, it is first necessary to articulate the artificial-intelligence position and its limits.

Contextualizing AI

The work of Alan Turing became widely known through his famous Turing test and Turing machines. The former entails a proposition for considering how one might conclude that computers have intelligence comparable to that of humans. Through his imitation game, Turing argued that if it is possible for a computer to fool a human being into believing that it is human (through conversing with one another on a computer screen), then it can be concluded that the computer has the same degree of intelligence as a human. The implications of this hypothesis were far reaching, since the possibility of the two being indistinguishable aspired to collapse the special status of humans as defined by a Cartesian view. The possibility that humans are not defined or, at least, not unique because of their mental capabilities had threatened significant scientific research that endeavored to speak the contrary. If a computer could be passed off as a human, then, Turing argued, for all intents and purposes, a computer should be regarded as human. After all, our only way of interacting with other humans is through language, which is precisely what the Turing test measures.

In contrast, Searle (1980) considers that Turing's test is misleading and, instead, analogizes it to his famed "Chinese room argument." Here, Searle argues that even if the computer were able to fool another human into believing that it was talking to another human, this would not connote its having intelligence. Searle's Chinese room and his extended version, named the Chinese gym, describes how a computer program might be able to demonstrate its syntactic grasp and thus, provide the appearance of intelligence through a comprehensible conversation. However, Searle contends that it would lack any comprehension of the semantic quality of words, including those ascribed to the emotions, which are considered as constitutive of that which defines human intelligence.

Searle asks that we imagine a room with a person in it who receives Chinese symbols through a slot in a door. The person has a manual that allows him or her to match up the Chinese symbols with the English counterpart and thus, the person can output the translation. To anyone outside of the room, it would appear that the person has translated the Chinese words and thus understands what they refer to. In actual fact, the person has demonstrated merely a capability for pattern matching and has no real understanding of the meaning of the Chinese symbols (Searle 1990).

The example reveals a disparity within research about AI that is premised upon its artificiality standing against some, supposedly, natural intelligence. Furthermore, such natural intelligence tends to be directed towards that exhibited by a human being. Thus, it implies that if anything should be considered intelligent, then at least we must grant that humans are. Consequently, it is possible to identify two assumptions and thus distinct pursuits of AI research:

Strong AI: That intelligence is entirely algorithmic and can be formalized through the kinds of computer programs that we currently use. The aims of such research are to determine what degree of intelligence can be held by a machine and to what degree such intelligence can be used.

Weak AI: That intelligence is comprised partly, if not largely, by the semantic, nonalgorithmic characteristics of information that are not accessible to the syntactically defined computer programs. The aims of such research are to determine whether this degree of intelligence is comparable to the intelligence of a human being and could, in any way, exceed the capabilities of human intelligence.

These two perspectives about intelligence are united in their wanting to understand whether it is possible to replicate the intelligence of a human being—or at least to replicate the affective mental processes of animals. The former claims that such an end goal for AI research is possible, even though the computing power does not yet exist. Conversely, the latter is more interested in harnessing the ways in which artificial intelligence can be used. Weak AI acknowledges that the limitations of AI do not necessarily reduce its significance but is cautious about claiming that such findings represent intelligence, since it identifies intelligence as including semantic qualities that cannot be formalized.

Turing's work set about to assert a strong AI thesis, where the machine was able to appear convincingly human. In contrast, Searle argues for weak AI and rejects the possibility that a machine could possess nonalgorithmic aspects of intelligence. For this reason, Searle's position has provoked a broader interest in researching AI that acknowledges that quantifiable measures of intelligence are not sufficient.

Deep Blue

In 1997, IBM's famous machine Deep Blue successfully conquered Grandmaster Garry Kasparov at chess after a arduous battle. As Moravec (1998) describes, "Kasparov won a long first game against Deep Blue, but lost next day to masterly moves by the machine. Then came three grueling draws, and a final game, in which a visibly shaken and angry Kasparov resigned early, with a weak position. It was the first competition he had ever lost" (1998). The discourse surrounding the capabilities of Deep Blue must thus be seen from these two different perspectives. For proponents of weak AI, Deep Blue reflects a measure of only one aspect of mind functioning, which does not lead to the conclusion that a machine is comparable to a human mind. Indeed, this is the view of its creators, who claim no level of intelligence within the machine (Moravec 1998).

For those who consider chess-playing capacity as reflective of some special intellectual capacity, the symbolic significance of Deep Blue beating Garry Kasparov is the rise of machines and their capacity to surpass the capabilities of humanity's self-described superiority. As Cook and Kroker (1997) identify, the cultural significance of chess means that the contest between Kasparov and Deep Blue was not simply a matter of experimentation. Indeed, it defined the struggle between human and automaton, a theme that underpins many dystopian visions of the future, which is framed by a presumption that machines will make people redundant. Thus, chess represents the last stand for humans against machines. Its appeal functions on a number of levels. The claims are impressive and startling, though, I suggest, contingent upon how one understands intelligence and the special cultural value of chess.

I argue on behalf of the latter of these possible claims over artificial intelligence, though the basis for rejecting the possibility of strong AI is based less on the impossibility of a machine's capacity to adequately replicate a human mind. Rather it concerns the inadequacy of the tests that have been used to make such conclusions. In short, on the current, traditional model of AI research, the kind of AI that can be built does not permit the realization of strong AI. In accordance with Bringsjord (1998), I believe that "chess is too easy," so even if we succeed in beating the human, the claim does not allow us to conclude that this constitutes human intelligence. Admittedly, this seems a particularly unforgiving reaction to the very impressive capabilities of Deep Blue and the research that has led to its success as a chess player. Yet, to infer from this megamachine's success that it is now comparable to a mind is not accurate. However, there is something crucial about the role of chess in society and what expertise in chess conveys philosophically about intelligence that should not be neglected. I will propose that chess is the wrong kind of game and that strong AI seeks a more complex and sophisticated but closed game system.

To elaborate on this, it is necessary to consider further the development of chess-playing machines and how they work. Deep Blue operates in a sequential manner and, when faced with its move in chess, it must analyze every possible move before being able to determine which is the better. This constant "trial and error" strategy contrasts with the human method that appears to involve learning which available moves are worthy of consideration and choosing from competing moves of significant value. Thus, humans are said to possess an intuition that computers can never gain. Such systems as Deep Blue and its offspring represent tentative efforts at creating a much broader, autonomous intelligence that is of interest in Artificial Life (AL) research. Evidence of these crucial differences is found in the stories surrounding the Kasparov versus Deep Blue contests. As Moravec (1998) explains, "The event was notable for many reasons, but one especially is of interest here. Several times during both matches, Kasparov reported signs of a mind in the machine. At times in the second tournament, he worried there might be humans behind the scenes, feeding Deep Blue strategic insights!" It is interesting that this event should lead the world's greatest chess player into an accidental Turing test admission. Yet, even if we discount Kasparov's response as a mere psychology of impressions, as opposed to something more profound about what took place, these ways of talking about the computer's actions allude to the requirements of intentionality.

The development of AL (in contrast to AI) offers a perspective on intelligence that can enrich this suggested "presence" of a mind that was discussed in the Deep Blue stories. AL is inspired more by biological traditions than the linearity of Turing's imitation game (Mainzer 1998). It is this approach that speaks to the present critique of AI research. Aspiring to a different model for replicating biological systems avoids the assumed importance of algorithmic knowledge. However, I do not wish to pursue any further the recent achievements of AL. Rather, I want to suggest that one important dimension of AL's foundation must involve the pursuit of game-playing more broadly. Thus, it is important not to neglect what has been achieved in the context of chess, but it is necessary to extend what is relevant about this kind of test.

A similar idea is found in Bringsjord (1998), who suggests that a "storytelling" test rather than a Turing test should be used to measure computational intelligence. Bringsjord considers that stories constitute a significant (and even dominant) aspect of human communications. People make sense of the world by creating stories, which entail the creation of characters and identifying with them to assimilate their perspective. While Bringsjord's strategy is novel and plausible, it omits an important aspect of the mind/machine test that is an integral part of chess—that of game playing. The importance of chess being a gamelike activity seems to have been taken for granted. Yet, it does not seem that chess aspires to anything gamelike at all and, thus, its claims to creative, spontaneous, or strategic play do not ring true. Deep Blue cannot be strategic since it does not know it is playing a game. Thus, to extend the relevant aspects of the chess-intelligence test, it is necessary to pursue further the construction of game playing.

Grasshoppers

AI research has neglected to undertake a critical consideration of the meaning of game playing, which is surprising since the complex human interaction that we might typically identify as the richness of intelligence closely relies on playfulness. Thus, AI developers must seek a test that is more broadly reflective of humanness if the aspiration is to claim that machines exhibit humanlike intelligence. The importance of game playing is reflected in Johan Huizinga's classic text *Homo Ludens*, which, coincidentally, was published in 1950, the same year that Alan

Turing delivered his seminal paper "Computing Machinery and Intelligence" in the renowned journal of psychology and philosophy *Mind*. The salience of Huizinga's work is brought alive in Bernard Suits's tale in *The Grasshopper* (1978). Within his manuscript, Suits develops a unitary notion of game playing through the story of the Grasshopper, a character who seeks to spend his entire life playing games convinced that only activities with intrinsic value—games—can be a good life.

Suits suggests that the distinct value of being human involves the propensity to play games and that we find the richest conceptualization of humanness through this form of activity. From this, I argue that game playing embodies qualities that reflect what might be termed *broad intelligence* or *artificial general intelligence* (AGI). Suits's Grasshopper knew that intelligent animals spent as much time as possible playing games, rather than working or engaging with any form of instrumental activity. The characteristics of game-playing behavior thus include such examples as disinterestedness and a feeling of being distinct from ordinary life. Additionally, Suits stipulates:

> To play a game is to attempt to achieve a specific state of affairs [prelusory goal], using only means permitted by rules [lusory means], where the rules prohibit use of more efficient in favor of less efficient means [constitutive rules], and where the rules are accepted just because they make possible such activity [lusory attitude]. I also offer the following simpler and, so to speak, more portable version of the above: playing a game is the voluntary attempt to overcome unnecessary obstacles. (Suits 2005)

From *The Grasshopper* and his more formal models of games, Suits notes that game playing entails formal and informal elements that encompass both aspects of the game's structural limits *and* a game-playing attitude that must be observed by the game player (Suits 1969, 1967, 1977). Yet, within Suits's work, he emphasizes concepts that we would not typically identify as machinic, such as agency. To this extent, one might consider that my claim to pursue Suits's game-playing characteristics as tests for human intelligence are, again, speciesistic. Yet, the kind of agency associated with other types of games is, nevertheless, still a form of closed decision-making. To illustrate, we might consider the game of soccer where a player must undertake a series of closed decisions that can be easily transformed into algorithms. For instance, the set of options available to a player when a goal is scored, or when a whistle is blown. Yet, players also exhibit what appear to be "open" system decisions. For instance, the split-second decision-making that constitutes the way a player kicks the ball—the angle of the foot, the timing, and so on. In sport, it is common to describe such intuitions as talents, which are possible to teach only up to a point.

So, what would it mean if a computer could play soccer effectively? What kind of claim about intelligence could be made? Chess seems to lack a number of the types of the decisions that face a soccer player and, for this reason, I suggest tests for human intelligence must develop into other kinds of games, which have the advantage of being mixed-space—both real and yet closed. Crucially, understanding the sociohistorical development of chess as a test for intelligence informs this proposal. Indeed, it is precisely the presence of a sociocultural context that allows chess to appear as a persuasive test for intelligence. However, it is necessary to develop a test that involves a broader range of decision-making actions. Thus, my thesis is that chess is the wrong kind of game to test for intelligence, rather than a criticism of game playing generally as our form of measurement. Chess is certainly the right kind of test since it is gamelike, but it is not the kind of game to reveal whether a machine has humanlike intelligence. Other kinds of games, such as those that more closely approximate sportlike games, where creativity and spontaneity adopt a more complex variation, are more useful to study. Within such activities, opportunities for nonlinear decision-making and deviance from preconceived strategic patterns exist. The temporal element of such activities demands of its players a different kind of knowledge than that of chess playing.

From this perspective, there is an expectation that machines must appropriate some level of facility for reflexivity that goes beyond following preprogrammed moves available in a chess game. The possibility for deviating from one's strategy or losing concentration in chess is what makes a human player different from a machine. Being able to play a game in the Suitsian sense, thus, would allow the fulfillment of such conditions. In short, one might describe the flaws in Deep Blue's intelligence as an inability to know when to break the rule. Yet, such capacities are not unreasonably demanding in the sense that expecting a computer to "enjoy" a game might be. Instead, a broader range of game-playing characteristics develops the achievements of AI research through such tests as playing chess, without asking too much of a machine's capabilities.

NOTES

1. This proposition does not neglect the playfulness of games like chess, but aims to establish how such an activity is distinguishable from the physical games I propose.

REFERENCES

Bringsjord, Selmer. 1998. "Chess Is Too Easy." *Technology Review* 101, no. 2.

Cook, David, and Arthur Kroker. 1997. "The Digital Prince and the Last Chess Player." CTheory. Event-scene e042, May 20 1997. www.ctheory.net/articles.aspx?id=175.

Haldane, J. 1997. "Could the Soul Be Software?" *Ends and Means: Journal of the University of Aberdeen Centre for Philosophy, Technology, and Society.*

Huizinga, Johan. 1950. *Homo Ludens.* London: Routledge and Kegan Paul.

Lee, Mark H. *Intelligent Robotics.* New York: Milton Keynes / Open University Press, 1989.

Luger, G. F., and W. A. Subblefield. 1998. *Artificial Intelligence: Structures and Strategies for Complex Problem Solving.* Reading, MA: Addison-Wesley Longman.

Mainzer, Klaus. 1998. "Computer Technology and Evolution: From Artificial Intelligence to Artificial Life." *Techne: Society for Philosophy and Technology* 4, no. 1.

Moravec, Hans. 1998. "When Will Computer Hardware Match the Human Brain?" *Journal of Evolution and Technology* 1.

Searle, John R. 1980. "Minds, Brains, and Programs." *Behavioral and Brain Sciences* 3.

———. 1990. "Is the Brain's Mind a Computer Program?" *Scientific American* 262.

Suits, Bernard. 1967. "What Is a Game?" *Philosophy of Science* 34.

———. 1969. "Games and Paradox." *Philosophy of Science* 36, no. 3.

———.1977. "Words on Play." *Journal of the Philosophy of Sport* 4.

———. 2005. *The Grasshopper: Games, Life and Utopia.* Ontario: Broadview Press. Orig. pub. 1978.

Turing, Alan M. 1950. *Programmers' Handbook for the Manchester Electronic Computer.* Manchester, UK: University of Manchester Computing Library.

3
Playing Chess in the Chinese Room

TAMA COUTTS

This is a chapter about computers, understanding, and chess. It will focus on the issue of whether computers can be said to have an understanding of a language or a game, and the lens that allows this focus is a famous thought experiment of the philosopher John Searle. Searle makes a distinction between strong Artificial Intelligence (strong AI) and weak Artificial Intelligence (weak AI). Weak AI presents a fairly uncontroversial thesis—according to weak AI, computers are useful tools for studying minds, in part because computers can *simulate* many of the cognitive processes of a mind. According to strong AI, on the other hand, something is a mind or has a mind in the case that it instantiates the right program (see Searle 1987, 18). From this claim it follows that human minds are just the right programs being "run" in biological matter. Searle takes aim at the thesis of strong AI with his famous Chinese room thought experiment. I will reconstruct his thinking in order to argue that chess-playing computers actually *understand* chess in a way not importantly different from humans. I do so by changing the thought experiment slightly, so as to make it about chess-playing machines.

First, I clarify the kind of understanding the debate centers around and the key terms "Turing machine," "computer," and "program." Next, I explain the "Chinese room" thought experiment and Searle's accompanying argument, and offer two replies to Searle. I claim that the second of these, the so-called robot reply, is successful. However I don't argue for this in detail, because while something more than the systems reply is needed in the natural language case, it is not needed in the case of chess. Finally, I look at a chess version of the thought experiment, and argue that, barring a further argument, there is no reason not to ascribe understanding of chess to computers. An interesting *suggestion* that follows from this discussion is that some things may have understanding but lack other cognitive processes that we commonly attribute to minded beings, such as beliefs and desires.

Understanding, Computers, and Turing Machines

Presumably there are certain cognitive processes that a thing must maintain, be, or be capable of if it is a mind or has a mind. Indeed, some think that we are well on the way to developing computers with minds, and that chess-playing machines are an important step towards this goal because they can carry out certain cognitive processes. Searle tries to show that computers do not and cannot have any cognitive processes. His argument is presented in the next section, but in order to understand it we need to get clear what Searle means by *understanding*, the cognitive process that he focuses on. Also we need to get clear what his target is in the thought experiment, what he means by "computer" and "program," which in turn requires a discussion of what a Turing machine is.

When Searle argues that computers lack understanding he is using the term "understand" in the sense it is used when one says of a native speaker, "Tim understands English but he doesn't understand German." He attempts to show that a computer cannot understand an arbitrary natural language.

This takes us to the second terminological question: what does Searle mean by "computer"? In order to answer this question we need to know what a Turing machine is.[1] Roughly, a Turing machine is a mathematical or logical object which satisfies the following:

a) It has a finite number of states.
b) It has a read/write head that can read/write a finite number of symbols.
c) It has an ordered list[2] of symbols that the read/write head can read, write on, and move along.

d) It has instructions: at any point in time, on the basis of the current state of the machine and whichever symbol the read/write head is reading, the machine performs at least one (but possibly all) of the following:

   i)   Writes a symbol.
   ii) Moves its read/write head so that it is reading a different symbol.[3]
   iii) Changes its state.

Whatever else is true of mathematical objects, one cannot have face-to-face encounters with them. So, for instance, one never encounters the number 1. To be sure, one sees "1" regularly. But this is not the number 1; it is a name of that number in the same way that "Tim" is a name of Tim. Turing machines, like numbers, have an interesting relationship to the physical world. A Turing machine can have one or more physical instantiations,[4] each of which is an object or group of objects that plays the roles of the constituents of the machine. So, for instance, an instantiation of a Turing machine must have something that plays the role of the list, something that plays the role of the read/write head, and so forth. A desktop computer, which is the sort of thing Searle has in mind when he uses the term "computer," is nothing but an interesting instantiation of a particular Turing machine, in part because it operates so quickly. A program is just the instructions mentioned in (d) above.

An important point for my purposes is that any *thing* is an instantiation of at least one Turing machine[5] and of at least one program: "I am, I suppose, the instantiation of any number of computer programs," remarks Searle (1987, 33). So, for instance, according to these criteria, my desk is an instantiation of a Turing machine. The role of an ordered list is played by its surface and it reads that surface. We can simply stipulate that whatever is on it (including nothing) plays the role of having an input of 1 and give it one simple state, STATE 1. Our instructions for STATE 1 are something like this: if the machine is reading a 1 it must halt (terminate). The machine "starts" in STATE 1 and immediately halts. Similarly, we can define an instantiation of a Turing machine in which the desk is the instantiation of that machine's program. A program that does similarly little will do the trick.[6]

The Chinese Room Thought Experiment

With this explained, the thesis Searle is attacking can be made clear. He is *not* attacking the thesis that a mind is an instantiation of a program.[7] As we've seen, any physical object at all is an instantiation of some Turing machine's program. Rather he is attacking the thesis that any object can be a mind *just by* instantiating the right program, that is to say by being an instantiation of a Turing machine with a particular program. Earlier we supposed that if a thing is a mind then it must maintain, be, or be capable of certain cognitive processes. Searle argues that a computer cannot have these processes. We can set out the reasoning as follows:

> **Premise 1:** To have a mind a thing must maintain, be, or be capable of certain cognitive processes $c_1, c_2, \ldots, c_n$.
> **Premise 2:** One of the cognitive processes a thing must maintain, be, or be capable of, which we'll call "c_u," is understanding.
> **Premise 3:** Computers lack c_u, that is to say, they lack understanding.
> **Conclusion:** Therefore computers cannot have minds.

This is a valid argument.[8] Presumably if we restrict our attention to *human* minds premise 2 is trivial[9] and the Chinese room thought experiment is supposed to support premise 3. Premise 1 is an attempt to supplement premise 2 and premise 3 so that they yield the conclusion. Searle never makes it clear how exactly we are to get from premise 2 and premise 3 to the conclusion but it seems that he must accept something like premise 1. Let us now see how his argument for premise 3 works.

Searle wants to show that instantiating *any* program is not sufficient for understanding. So how can he show this? We can roughly reconstruct his thinking as follows: consider a thing that lacks understanding of some natural language. Now suppose that that thing instantiates some Turing machine, and hence some program. We suppose that doing this allows the thing under consideration to take in similar inputs and give similar outputs to a thing that we *know* understands. The inputs and outputs in this case would be the sentences of some natural language. If it *still* seems that the thing doesn't understand the natural language then instantiating any program at all isn't sufficient for understanding that language.

The Chinese room is a thought experiment along these lines.[10] Imagine that there is a room with a little slot in the wall and that the room contains a whole heap of books and a person, Sally. Let us also suppose that Sally speaks (and reads) English but not Chinese. There is a Chinese speaker outside the room who writes down Chinese sentences on pieces of paper and pushes the pieces of paper through the slot into the room. Sally's task is to look up, in the books, whatever is written on each piece of paper and follow instructions written there that tell her what to write down on another piece of paper. So, although she does not know this, she is looking up strings of Chinese characters and copying out strings of Chinese characters on the second piece of paper. Once she has followed all the instructions that are given for a certain input (i.e. for a given piece of paper) she pushes the second piece of paper out of the room through the slot. Also, unbeknownst to her, she is copying out sensible responses to the sentences written down by the Chinese speaker outside the room.[11] In addition there is an English speaker outside the room, whom Sally is engaged in a conversation with by similar means. She receives bits of paper with writing (in English) on them and responds by writing down English sentences and pushing the bits of paper through the slot, out of the room.

Searle observes that in the Chinese room thought experiment, Sally, with respect to Chinese writing, acts very like a native speaker: she takes the same stuff as input and produces the same stuff as output. Yet Sally obviously does not understand Chinese. Equally obviously she does understand English and it is precisely *because* of this that she can carry on the conversation with the English speaker. Note that the details of the Turing machine that Sally is instantiating are *arbitrary*—all that matters are the inputs and outputs. Hence instantiating *any* program is not sufficient for understanding a natural language. Since we supposed that one thing a mind must be able to do is understand a natural language we reach Searle's conclusion: instantiating any program is not sufficient for being a mind (or having a mind) and thus there must be more to human minds than just instantiating a particular Turing machine.

Two Responses to the Chinese Room

Suffice to say, this argument is a source of great controversy; some think it a stroke of genius, and others think it a regrettable piece of

philosophical conjuring. Given limitations of space, I will only consider two replies, called the "systems reply" and the "robot reply,"
both of which Searle addresses himself.

According to the systems reply, Searle is correct: *Sally* indeed
does not understand Chinese. Rather, *the whole system* understands
Chinese; it is the room plus the books plus Sally that understands
Chinese. Searle proposes a simple response. Let us revise the original thought experiment—instead of Sally in a room with some
books, let us suppose that she has memorized the contents of the
books. So, in the revised thought experiment, the Chinese speaker
writes out some characters on a piece of paper and hands them to
Sally. She then recalls the characters and matching instructions and
writes out whatever characters the instructions tell her to on a second piece of paper before handing it to the Chinese speaker. In the
revised version of the thought experiment there is nothing apart
from Sally for the system to be. Yet, Searle claims, we still don't
want to say that she *understands* Chinese.

As far as I can see the only response available to the proponent
of the systems reply is to say that Sally indeed understands Chinese,
but the mechanics of her understanding of Chinese are very different from those of her understanding of English. (To put it another
way—there is an English subsystem and a Chinese subsystem in
Sally's mind and they function very differently.) But this response
is hopeless, for it explicitly concedes that whatever Sally's understanding of English consists in is very different from whatever is
allowing her to produce Chinese characters. So the latter cannot
explain the former. Note that the conclusion reached is consistent
with the suggestion that something could understand a language
just by instantiating the right program. It is just that such a program
can't explain *human* understanding of natural languages.

A second response to the systems reply bears brief discussion
and leads naturally into the robot reply. This objection depends on
what philosophers sometimes call "intentionality." This is a rather
mysterious concept that perhaps can be glossed as *aboutness*. The
idea roughly is that certain mental states, such as beliefs and
desires, are *about* objects. So my belief that Australia is in the
Southern Hemisphere is a belief *about* Australia. Likewise, if I see
a salami at the supermarket and desire it then my desire is *about*
the salami. According to Searle a system like the one under discussion has no intentionality—so, for instance, no noises such a
system makes are *about* anything. If we take intentionality seriously

then lacking it would seem to rule out having understanding. Presumably when someone or something understands a language, its speech acts[12] and mental states are about things. Hence if this is not the case then the language-using thing or person doesn't understand. Searle's own view is that intentionality is the product of certain physical systems—it is an empirical question whether a certain physical system has intentionality. According to him it just happens to be the case as a matter of empirical fact that brains have intentionality and digital computers don't. But he concludes, as presumably he must, that there *could* be other physical systems very unlike human brains that have intentionality. Rather than go into a long discussion of this mysterious concept, which anyway there isn't space for, let us turn to the second reply, which tries both to answer this objection and avoid Searle's response to the systems reply.

The second reply to the Chinese room thought experiment is called the "robot reply." As with the systems reply, according to the robot reply, Sally does not understand Chinese. Proponents of this response suggest that we put the Chinese room inside something that can have inputs that mimic the senses of a human, like a robot. The robot resembles a human in most outward functions: with cameras for eyes, speakers for a mouth, microphones for ears, and so on. The input received by the robot through these various devices is turned into Chinese characters which are processed by Sally, who sits inside the Chinese room, which sits inside the robot, at superhuman speed. The characters she writes down cause the robot to respond to the input it receives. To bring linguistic interaction back into view, let us suppose that the robot is conversing with a Chinese speaker. Searle has two things to say about this reply. First, he points out that this response concedes that pure symbol manipulation alone is not sufficient for understanding—embodied experience (or something like it) is required too. Secondly, he claims that this response fails in exactly the same way as the systems reply. In her room copying out symbols Sally has no understanding of Chinese, and presumably, according to Searle, neither does the robot. In addition, Searle claims that the robot also has no *intentionality*, which would rule out it having understanding in the manner sketched above.

Before responding to Searle, let me concede him his claim that pure symbol manipulation is not sufficient for understanding. It is also, I agree, a matter of having the correct input and output. But such a concession shouldn't dismay supporters of AI. Rather this conclusion can be viewed as a step toward building a thinking machine—thanks to Searle, we now know a bit more about what such a thinking machine would have to be like. With this concession, it is hard to see what Searle's argument is; it appears to rely only on a strong intuition that the robot has no understanding or intentionality. Clearly the robot reply rules out the first response made to the systems reply, since a move analogous to the suggestion that Sally could memorize the books is now impossible. There is no sense to be made of memorizing a robot. So that problem is overcome, leaving the question of intuitions about intentionality and understanding.

When an argument seems to boil down to the "dull thud of intuitions" it is often unclear how to proceed. Rather than just stating that I don't share Searle's intuitions I'll try to undermine them.[13] Regarding intentionality: Suppose that the robot asks the Chinese speaker in Chinese: "Can you pass me the tasty sump oil?" The Chinese speaker responds "What do you want me to pass you?" The robot then points *at the oil* and says "that." Cases like this don't support the intuition that the robot has no intentionality. Indeed, one might wonder why even something utterly inanimate such as a sentence on a piece of paper can't be *about* something. In a different vein one might think that there is no such thing as "aboutness" and that it was confusion that first led to it being taken seriously.

As regards understanding—here's a counter–thought experiment. Searle's thought experiment seems to depend on us having the intuition that if we knew that the robot with whom we were conversing had a little man inside it manipulating symbols we would decide that it was not a minded thing but that rather it was an "ingenious dummy." To put it another way: certainly the robot might *fool* us into thinking it had a mind, but once we had a separate complete account of the robot's behavior we wouldn't be tempted to say it had a mind. Suppose then that we discovered that inside every neuron in a speaker's head was a tiny person who had a set of instructions telling her how to direct electrical impulses the neuron received. Would we then be inclined to withdraw our ascription of a mind to the speaker? Surely not. Hopefully these remarks have gone some or all of the way to dissuading you from sharing Searle's intuitions and hence some or all of the way to convincing you that the robot response is a quite sufficient response to Searle, albeit one that makes important and instructive concessions.

Chess in the Chinese Room

Let us turn from the complicated phenomenon that is language to the much more simple chess case. It is the aim of this section to demonstrate that a Turing machine can understand chess in a way that is not significantly different from how a human understands chess. Additionally, I want to at least put forward the idea that a thing can have understanding but not beliefs, desires, and whichever other cognitive capacities constitute agency.

Earlier we decided that the sense of "understanding" we were interested in was the sense in which "understands" is being used in a sentence such as "Tim understands English." Let us then suppose that, in this section, the sense of "understands" we are interested in is the sense in which "understands" is used in a sentence such as "Tim understands how to play chess."[14]

Now, going back to the original thought experiment, suppose that Sally (inside her room) is being given chess positions on bits of paper, by someone who believes they are playing chess against her. To preserve the analogy with the original thought experiment, let us also suppose that Sally knows nothing about chess or chess notation. To her there are just some letters, numbers, dashes, and the like on a piece of paper. Her task is to follow certain instructions given the position she has received in the room and to produce a chess move written in algebraic notation. This she writes on a piece of paper and passes out of the room. The claim analogous to Searle's original claim is this: although Sally is consistently writing down legal (and mostly good) chess moves, she understands nothing whatsoever of chess. We also suppose that she is playing draughts (also known as checkers), which she knows how to play, against someone outside the room. She is given draughts moves written on bits of paper, and she plays the move she receives on a board she has set up inside the room. She considers her reply, and makes her move, on that board, before writing it down on a piece of paper, and passing the piece of paper out of the room through the slot. In this latter case, it is in virtue of her understanding *how to play draughts* that she produces legal (and mostly good) draughts moves.

This variation on the thought experiment is interesting because, given that what has been argued thus far is correct, an adequate response can be given to it without having to invoke an analogue of the robot reply. Why? Because, in the chess case, it's not the case that (something like) embodied experience or (something like) intentionality is required for understanding.[15]

Consider a systems-style reply. The claim made is, as in the case of the systems reply, that Sally indeed does not understand chess—but that the *whole system* does. Suppose then that, as before, one suggests that we revise the thought experiment so that Sally internalizes the whole system, by memorizing symbols and rules. Now, according to someone wanting to defend the systems-style reply, such as myself, Sally has two subsystems in her mind for processing positions given to her. (One for chess and one for draughts.) To be sure they are different. But they don't seem to be anything like as different as the subsystems for English and Chinese in the original thought experiment. In the case of Sally's draughts subsystem, presumably she picks a few promising-looking moves and analyzes them for a while before choosing a move. In the case of her chess subsystem she grinds through many millions of positions before picking a move. It is true that there is a vast difference in the *number* of positions analyzed but does this disqualify the chess subsystem from understanding? Certainly some further argument would be required for such a claim. The existence of two different subsystems in no way conflicts with the claim that both understand. Unlike in the original thought experiment, however, it doesn't even seem obvious that there is a deep difference between the subsystems—perhaps they not only both understand, but understand in the same way. Recall, *en passant*, that when discussing the systems reply to the original thought experiment, we noted that the systems reply seemed unable to account for *human* understanding of a natural language. Yet it seems that in the chess version of the thought experiment a similar reply *can* explain human understanding of chess.

One might try to demonstrate some deep difference between the workings of the subsystems. For instance, one might claim that in the case of the draughts subsystem, Sally knows that she is playing a game of draughts, that she is thinking about moving pieces, trying to win, and so forth, but the other subsystem does nothing but process symbols; when Sally (internally) manipulates these symbols she know nothing about any game, any pieces or any objective. The only (but sufficient) response on behalf of the systems-style reply is to deny that these things matter *when it comes to understanding a game*. An interesting question as to which side the burden of proof falls on now arises. Does one side have to show that these things matter or does the other have to show that they don't?[16] I'm not at all sure how to answer this question, so I shall just say that I am *not* claiming that the chess-playing computer is an agent with beliefs, desires, or intentionality. Hence any request that requires the production of such things can go unanswered. My claim is precisely that there could be a thing that has only some of the stuff an agent has—namely, understanding. Furthermore it is understanding of a very limited kind, of one game only. To claim that (for example) the computer doesn't *believe* that it's playing chess is to miss the point completely. I am not claiming that the computer *believes* anything. So it turns out that the claim needed to make this challenge worrying is that things like having beliefs, desires, and intentionality are somehow *prerequisites* for understanding chess, or understanding anything at all. This is something that certainly isn't established by the Chinese room thought experiment.

Barring some further argument I conclude that a Chinese room–style argument fails in the chess case. The difference between the chess case and the original thought experiment is worth emphasizing. In the original thought experiment Searle was challenging the claim that computers could have minds as humans do, that computers could be agents, with beliefs, desires, intentionality, and so forth. Such a claim is much harder to defend than the claim that computers only understand a language, which is in turn much harder to defend than the claim that computers only understand one game. It is for this reason that my defense of one of the simplest responses was successful against the chess version of Searle's thought experiment.

Conclusion

This chapter has galloped across a great deal of philosophical terrain at breakneck speed. Hopefully it stimulated the interest of the reader in at least one of the topics discussed. I attempted to at least weakly argue for the conclusion that a computer with the right inputs that produced the right outputs should be considered to have understanding of a natural language, but my main contention was that the very machine on your desk should be considered to understand chess in a way not importantly different from a person. The latter conclusion relied on my unargued suggestion that perhaps things can have understanding without having beliefs, desires, or other cognitive processes.[17]

NOTES

Thank you to everyone who read earlier versions of this paper and gave me feedback. In particular I'd like to thank Zach Weber, Matt Carter, Conrad Asmus, Elena Walsh, Sam Gates, Ross Barham, Michael Ashcroft, and Ben Hale.

1. Named after the English philosopher, mathematician, and logician Alan Turing, who played an important role in the creation of modern computers by inventing Turing machines. A polymath, he also played a key role in cracking the Germans' Enigma code during the Second World War. The interested reader is directed to Hodges 2002.

2. "Ordered" here is meant in the logician's or mathematician's sense. That is to say that there is some two-place relation such that for any two symbols either the first stands in that relation to the second or the second to the first, but not both of these. One might think of the relation as "left-of" or "above" or something similar.

3. "Moves" needn't be taken literally here. The thought is just that the machine is now taking a different symbol as its input. The symbols it can change to having as its input given that it *had* a certain symbol as its input depend on the ordering of the symbols.

4. Henceforth "instantiation" will be a shorthand for "physical instantiation."

5. Some subtleties regarding quantification: this claim is ambiguous like Russell's famous "everyone loves someone." The claim is not that there is a single machine, and that of this single machine every physical object is a physical instantiation. Rather the claim is that for any physical object there is a machine that it is a physical instantiation of, although each physical object may be an instantiation of a different machine.

6. There are many good introductions to Turing machines that treat the technical details with rigor. For instance, see the excellent book by Boolos, Burgess, and Jeffrey 2002, chapt. 3. I don't bother, in later discussion, with the subtle differences between a Turing machine and a program *of* a Turing machine. Since there are no programs without machines and vice-versa there doesn't seem a need: any *instantiation of* a program must be an instantiation of a machine and vice-versa.

7. The same subtleties about quantification apply here as earlier. Searle is very skeptical about this claim when the quantifiers are reversed, that is to say, he is very skeptical about the suggestion that there is a single program or machine that all minds must be instantiations of, although he doesn't rule it out.

8. "Valid argument" is a term of art. If an argument is valid then *if* the premises are true the conclusion must be true.

9. This raises the interesting question as to what Searle thinks about animal minds, although there is not space to discuss it here.

10. I am aiming to present the thought experiment as simply as possible. For this reason my formulation differs a little from Searle's. Hopefully I have preserved all the essential points faithfully.

11. Note that to say that the thought experiment is impossible in the strongest sense is to play into Searle's hands. If one were to say we couldn't have some kind of mechanical procedure that yields sensible responses to sentences of a natural language (regardless of the physical stuff that the procedure is taking place in) then Searle would already have his conclusion.

12. Their assertions anyway. I suppose that one *might* want to say that orders or questions aren't about things.

13. I don't claim that there are any *arguments* in this paragraph or the next. My hope is just to prompt some different intuitions.

14. Apologies are in order for the uncritical evocation of senses. I must beg a lack of space.

15. In case the reader found the discussion of the robot reply utterly unconvincing, the point here is that *nothing more than* an analogue of the systems reply is needed. But in the natural language case something more *is* needed. (Whether or not it is what the robot reply provides.)

16. For instance, philosopher Michael Dummett seems to think that having "concepts" such as "lawful move," "winning," and "losing" are prerequisites for being able to play a game. Presumably he doesn't think that these claims need argument, since he provides none. See Dummett 2003, 103–4.

17. It is worth pointing out two corollaries of the discussion in the text. If one accepts that understanding requires other cognitive capacities or states, then one must deny that a desktop computer can understand chess; and if one accepts that a desktop computer can understand chess without other cognitive capacities or states then one must deny the view that having such states is necessary for understanding.

REFERENCES

Boolos, George, John Burgess, and Richard Jeffrey. 2002. *Computability and Logic*. 4th ed. Cambridge: Cambridge University Press.

Dummett, Michael. 2003. "What Do I Know When I Know a Language?" In *The Seas of Language*, edited by Michael Dummett. Oxford: Oxford University Press, 2003.

Hodges, Andrew. 2002. "Alan Turing." In *The Stanford Encyclopedia of Philosophy*. http://plato.stanford.edu/entries/turing/.

Searle, John R. 1987. "Minds, Brains, and Programs." In *Artificial Intelligence: The Case Against.* Edited by Rainer Born. London: Croon Helm.

SUGGESTED FURTHER READINGS

Carter, Matt. 2007. *An Introduction to Artificial Intelligence.* Edinburgh: Edinburgh University Press.

Cole, David. 2004. "The Chinese Room Argument." In *The Stanford Encyclopedia of Philosophy.* http://plato.stanford.edu/entries/chinese-room/.

Hauser, Larry. 2001. "The Chinese Room Argument." In *The Internet Encyclopedia of Philosophy.* http://www.iep.utm.edu/c/chineser.htm.

Penrose, Roger. 1989. *The Emperor's New Mind.* Oxford: Oxford University Press.

Searle, John R. 1984. *Minds, Brains & Science.* New York: Penguin Books, 1984.

———. 1999. "The Chinese Room." In *The MIT Encyclopedia of the Cognitive Sciences*, edited by Robert Wilson and Frank Keil. Cambridge, MA: MIT Press.

4

Garry Kasparov Is a Cyborg, or What ChessBase Teaches Us about Technology

JOHN HARTMANN

With the possible exception of the 1972 Fischer-Spassky match, chess has never captured the public imagination as it did when man met machine in the mid-1990s. The Kasparov–Deep Blue matches were portrayed in the mass media as the fundamental battle between human creativity and the cold powers of the calculating machine. When Kasparov defeated Deep Blue in 1996, the world celebrated with him. When he lost the 1997 match with his famous *fingerfehler*, it was headline news around the globe.

Sadly, much of the public discourse about these matches obscures the most interesting philosophical aspects of the human encounter with technology. Hubert Dreyfus, one of the few philosophers to comment on Kasparov's loss, believes that because the computer is not intelligent—because it is not an embodied being operating at an expert level of intelligence—humans have nothing to fear (Dreyfus 1992). After the match, he said that while Deep Blue's play was impressive, "in a world in which relevance and intelligence play a crucial role and meaning in concrete situations, the computer has always behaved miserably, and there's no reason to think that this will change with this victory" ("Big Blue Wins"). One of Dreyfus's students makes much the same point when he claims that because chess programs feel no emotion, "they are mere simulations of intelligence" (Carman 2006, 9).

Certainly Deep Blue did not rejoice when it beat Kasparov—but its creators did. One of Dreyfus's underlying presuppositions is that he casts technologies such as Deep Blue as autonomous entities, abstracting from them everything that went into their construction.[1] But Deep Blue did not spring full-grown from the head of Feng-hsuing Hsu! In reifying technologies such as Deep Blue, Dreyfus seems to be carving out a safe space for human ingenuity. In truth, he ignores all of the human (and nonhuman!) ingenuity that went into the creation of the machine.

If we are to view chess as a kind of lens for understanding human-technology relations, the matches with Deep Blue may not be our best laboratory. Deep Blue only played a handful of games against limited competition in its career, and was retired by IBM after defeating Kasparov. Meanwhile, thousands of players use computers every day to study and play against both humans and machines. Surely any understanding of human-machine relations would be better modeled on common, everyday interactions rather than the dusty games of a defunct machine.

In this chapter, we will examine the human relation to technology by using our interaction with chess technology as a case study. As we will see, the question of technology has not escaped the attention of philosophers, and we will find many of their concerns and insights embodied in the way chess players relate to chess technology. We will follow chess players into their "chess laboratories," and learn how they use chess technologies to bolster or deaden their play. Ultimately, we will see that the question of technology turns on what it is that technology *does*, and a thorough understanding of how technology affects human experience is the goal of this chapter.

Heidegger and the Crafty Clones

In order to explain the role played by chess software in contemporary chess, we need some definitions. We can point out three aspects of chess software for the purposes of this chapter.

First, there is the database program itself. This is the program used to access saved data. Users can search by player, position, annotator, or opening. Second, there is the playing program or the engine. This is the software "brain" that actually plays chess, and these same engines can also plug into the database programs. Finally, there is the chess data, which comes in three main varieties. There are game databases, or collections of complete games. There are opening databases, or "opening books," which are used by engines to play the openings. Last but not least, there are "tablebases," or specific databases for different types of endgames.

Chess enthusiasts have a number of options when it comes to their software needs. Chess Assistant© is popular with Russian players and émigrés, while SCID© is a freeware alternative. But the leader in the field of chess technology is without question ChessBase GMBH©, who develops and markets the flagship ChessBase chess database, the Fritz© family of playing programs, and a host of data products and educational modules. ChessBase is used by most of the world's best players, and no less an authority than Kasparov himself described ChessBase as "the most important development in chess since the printing press."[2] Some of the ChessBase stable of engines—most notably, Fritz, Junior, and Shredder—have become "silicon seconds"[3] for modern players, and their evaluations are cited in annotations by Grandmasters around the world. Because of the hegemony of ChessBase products in modern chess, we will use ChessBase and Fritz as our case studies when possible.

How do people use chess technology? How do they use ChessBase and Fritz in their chess activities? On a superficial level, this is a simple question to answer. Chess players now have strong analytic engines running on incredibly powerful hardware. Fritz and friends are seen as the silicon oracles residing in our computers that can be consulted about the "truth" of a position or new idea. They "look over our shoulder," silently assessing each move we enter into the computer, instantly registering their approval or disagreement. Chess technology is commonly taken to provide an irrefutable, immutable source of chess truth and knowledge—after all, a computer is objective and *never* miscalculates. . . .

Perhaps this seems overly dramatic. But one only need observe the behavior of chess software users on chessclub.com or play-chess.com during the broadcast of an international event to understand this claim. On these sites, the age-old tradition of kibitzing is translated into cyber-chatter, and master-level players offer their evaluations of the position for all observers. Most players do not listen, however, preferring to cut and paste the evaluation and main variations from their chess engine into their kibitzes to others. Other observers will request computer analysis from those equipped with the newest engines and fastest hardware, refusing to analyze the position themselves. Instead of kibitzing our lines and engaging in communal analysis, we tell each other what our versions of Fritz have to say.

This fetishization of silicon intelligence manifests itself in a number of ways. As we have just noted, kibitzers fix their engines on an observed game, and armed with computer analysis, they feel as if they are experts. Their engines see a complex tactical continuation that eludes most of the human observers, and they waste little time in trumpeting their engine's brilliant "discovery." As Jennifer Shahade notes, this is slightly rude. "If someone wants to use computers to analyze top level live games, that's fine, but why not be courteous? . . . Others might even want to train their own [sense of] tactics rather than have Fritz force-feed them variations" (Shahade 2005).

Another aspect of this fetishization is the proliferation of chess engines playing against one another on the Internet. For some reason, many chess players like to set up a computer account on chessclub.com or playchess.com and match their chess engine against other players.[4] This phenomenon really took off with the so-called Crafty clones—a number of computer accounts that used the open-source engine Crafty to generate moves. For years, one could log onto chessclub.com and find a dozen different versions of Crafty to play against. The Crafty clones were not accounts created by the author of the engine to test his creation;[5] rather, these accounts seem to have been created solely for the entertainment of their owners.[6] Some accounts would only play other computers, while others would take on all comers. Most fascinating, however, was the personal stake that every account owner seemed to have in the success or failure of "his" Crafty. The typical "clone owner" crowed about his engine's rating, or about the latest Grandmaster that her engine has slain, instead of taking pride in his own chess prowess.

Such reliance on chess technology seems, well, *strange.* In the first case, the computer thinks for us. In the second, it (literally) plays the game for us. What is it about technology that seems to compel us to defer to its superiority? Shouldn't this worry us? Why doesn't it? It was something of this concern, I think, that drove the first sustained philosophical engagements with technology. Beginning early in the twentieth century, thinkers such as Jacques Ellul, Karl Jaspers, and Lewis Mumford began to articulate a dystopian vision of technology as dangerous and dehumanizing. This "classical" or "substantialist" philosophy of technology reached its zenith in the work of Martin Heidegger, and it is to his work that we will now turn.

In "The Question Concerning Technology" (Heidegger 1977b), his most focused effort on the topic, Heidegger tries to draw a distinction between the commonplace or "correct" definition of technology and its essence. The correct definition of technology is the one that we normally presuppose in our everyday activities. For us, technology is (1) something we "do" and (2) the tools we use. Technology is the means to our various ends—we want to drive across the country, so we hop in our cars, fuel up at the local gas station, and we're off.

This instrumental definition of technology deeply permeates our age. Consider the scare over bagged spinach in the fall of 2006. *E. coli* bacteria contamination was traced to cattle feces from nearby feedlots, which was transferred to the spinach farms via water runoff. The simplest means of overcoming this continuing threat to public health is to alter the diet of the cattle—as it turns out, grass-fed cattle do not harbor this particularly virulent bug. Instead, as Michael Pollan notes, the food industry appears to be leaning towards the irradiation of the food supply. "It's easier to find a technological fix than to address the root cause of such a problem. This has always been the genius of industrial capitalism—to take its failings and turn them into exciting new business opportunities" (2006, 17).

On the face of it, irradiation seems a dramatic overreaction to the problem. Why not alter the setup of the cattle feedlots?[7] Instead of treating manure as a nuisance, why not change the diet of the cattle, thus allowing the harvesting of all that manure for fertilizer? For Heidegger, there is something intrinsic to our age that forces us to see nature as something to be technologically managed. The world appears to us as a series of raw materials that require our irradiating machines and food processors. This, according to Heidegger, is the essence of modern technology. It is a historically conditioned "enframing" (*Gestell*) of our meaningful experience of the world and its contents. Under the sway of the *Gestell*, everything appears as a raw material for consumption, or as "standing-reserve." Trees have only the sense of harvested wood for us, and undeveloped lots of land have no meaning in themselves save their potential for development.[8] Our manner of thinking is determined by the *Gestell*—we cannot think outside of *this* box. Even we ourselves appear as "standing-reserve." We meddle with our genetic code without concern, and we entrust our labor to human resources departments. We understand ourselves only as resources to be manipulated and managed, and not as persons with integral value.

What is most frightening from the Heideggerian perspective is the ease with which we accept this. Certainly, as in the case with the "Crafty clones," we feel as if there is something amiss. But we shrug and move along. As Heidegger puts it, "everything works. That's what's uncanny, that it works, that it leads to further functioning, and that technology continues to rip and uproot man from the earth" (1977a, 17). The computers hum and churn out predigested moves. Many software users are so impressed by Fritz and friends that they begin to let them dominate their game. In their rush to have the fastest computer or own the highest rating, they defer to the engines completely, even (as with the Crafty clones) letting them play their games for them.

Nonetheless, one wonders here whether Heidegger is doing full justice to the role these technologies play in our lives. Do all technologies dehumanize us? Are all technologies equally dangerous? Many philosophers have come to question Heidegger on precisely this point, where critics have characterized Heidegger as either a nostalgic romantic or a Luddite.[9] We can clearly understand these concerns when we examine the role that new technologies play in chess. While many people allow their engines to think for them, there are no small number of chess players who take up a productive relation with chess technologies. It is no coincidence that we have witnessed an explosion in the number of young Grandmasters across the globe.[10] With the proliferation of chess technologies—particularly the ChessBase line of products—modern chess players have incredible amounts of information at their fingertips. Chess technology opens up new possibilities for chess practice and understanding when used judiciously. It is this careful use of technology that Jennifer Shahade has in mind when she says, "Much of using Fritz well is knowing when to turn it off" (2005).

In order to assess this challenge to Heidegger's analysis, we need to understand how a strong player uses chess technology "judiciously." For this reason, we will follow a chess master into his chess laboratory, and watch him use ChessBase and Fritz to prepare for an important game.

Mirabile's Novelty

Let us begin by peering over the shoulder of a master-level player as he prepares for a game using ChessBase. In this case, the player is the American master Tim Mirabile, and the occasion is the 2002 Nassau Chess Club Championship. We will join him as he prepares for his fifth-round game with Grandmaster Igor Novikov.

How does a modern player like Mirabile, armed with ChessBase, prepare for a game? He knows he will have the white pieces in his game with Novikov, so he must locate all of Novikov's games with the black pieces. In the past, this would have meant culling the pages of printed materials, that is, magazines, opening books, and the Informant series. This is a time-consuming process, and one that requires the presence of a large, specialized chess library—a near impossibility for someone who might have traveled to play in a large tournament.

Armed with a computer and ChessBase, however, Mirabile can locate Novikov's previous games fairly easily. Using a large reference database, such as MegaBase from ChessBase, he can search for Novikov, and filter the games so as to locate only those games in which Novikov had the black pieces.

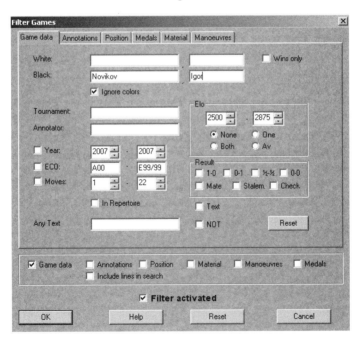

In order to further aid his research, he copies all of the filtered games to the "clip database," which serves as a temporary storage unit. What now? Using one of the numerous sorting capabilities of ChessBase, he orders these games according to ECO code[11] by clicking on that column heading.

Clip Database: 699 Games

File Edit View Tools Window Help

Text | Games | Openings | Themes | Tactics | Strategy | Endgames

Number	White	Elo W	Black	Elo B	Result	Moves	ECO	Tournament	Date	VCS	P
411	Nataf,I	2553	Novikov,I	2610	1-0	76	B87	Montreal-A 5th	04.08.2004	rCS	
493	Repkova Eid,E	2330	Novikov,I	2580	½-½	21	B87	Cairo-A	1997		
496	Robovic,S	2410	Novikov,I	2580	0-1	34	B87	Vienna op	1995		
617	Trindade,S	2305	Novikov,I	2460	0-1	30	B87	WchT U26 Mendoza	1985		
662	Yakovich,Y	2450	Novikov,I	2480	0-1	34	B87	Uzhgorod	1987		
673	Yudasin,L	2495	Novikov,I	2495	½-½	42	B87	URS-ch FL54 Kujbyshev	1986		
674	Yurtaev,L	2455	Novikov,I	2490	0-1	29	B87	Agzamov mem Tashkent	1986		
250	Karklins,A	2287	Novikov,I	2598	0-1	38	B90	Levy mem Denver	20.09.2003		
249	Karklins,A	2384	Novikov,I	2588	0-1	36	B90	King's Island op 10th	10.11.2001		
235	Ivanov,A	2525	Novikov,I	2540	½-½	51	B91	New York op	1993		
252	Kekelidze,M	2445	Novikov,I	2610	1-0	49	B91	Graz op-A	1999		
267	Kholmov,R	2465	Novikov,I	2420	½-½	39	B91	Yerevan	1984		
603	Svidler,P	2650	Novikov,I	2585	½-½	11	B91	Yerevan ol (Men)	1996		
9	Ambarcumjan,A		Novikov,I		0-1	32	B92	URS-ch U20 Daugavpils	1979		
128	Dvoirys,S	2445	Novikov,I	2465	1-0	46	B92	URS-ch FL53 Kharkov	1985	VcS	
126	Dvoirys,S	2485	Novikov,I	2420	½-½	34	B92	URS-ch U20 Vilnius	1984		
284	Korzubov,P	2470	Novikov,I	2420	0-1	59	B92	URS-ch U20 Vilnius	1984		
606	Sznapik,A	2480	Novikov,I	2500	1-0	47	B92	Tbilisi	1988		
621	Tseshkovsky,V	2490	Novikov,I	2420	1-0	28	B92	Yerevan	1984		
679	Zaichik,G	2420	Novikov,I	2280	1-0	42	B92	URS-ch sf Volgodonsk	1983		
3	Ahmed,E	2395	Novikov,I	2580	½-½	8	B93	Cairo-A	1997		
8	Almasi,Z	2580	Novikov,I	2545	1-0	56	B93	Cattolica op	1993		
116	Dolmatov,S	2550	Novikov,I	2280	½-½	22	B93	URS-ch sf Volgodonsk	1983		
127	Dvoirys,S	2470	Novikov,I	2490	½-½	86	B93	Rubinstein mem	1989		
168	Gavrikov,V	2485	Novikov,I	2385	½-½	37	B93	URS-ch U26 Jurmala	1983		
210	Hazai,L	2465	Novikov,I	2480	½-½	21	B93	Cemauiev A	1987		

1.e4 c5 2.Nf3 d6 3.d4 cxd4 4.Nxd4 Nf6 5.Nc3 a6 6.Bc4 e6 7.Bb3 b5 8.Bg5 Be7 9.Qf3 Qc7 10.0-0-0 0-0 11.e5 Bb7 12.exf6 Bxf3 13.fxe7 Bxd

Filter | Copy | Edit | Clip | Delete

Done - Choose Font   100%

Immediately, Mirabile sees something important. While some players vary their openings often, making themselves harder to prepare for, Novikov takes the opposite approach. His opening repertoire is narrow, but quite deep. He plays the same openings again and again, and while this makes him easier to prepare for, it gives him the advantage of great familiarity with the ideas and themes in the position.

Mirabile now knows with a fairly high degree of certainty what Novikov will play against him. Mirabile almost always plays 1. e4, and Novikov almost always responds with the Sicilian Najdorf. This information narrows the field of research considerably. Mirabile need only look up what Novikov plays against his favorite line—the Sozin variation (6. Bc4)—to prepare for his game with confidence.

In looking through Novikov's games, Mirabile learns that Novikov had defended a sharp variation that he (Mirabile) had played against another player.[12] Given that Novikov tends to play a very narrow range of openings, he might play into this line again, given the chance. So Mirabile decides to check Novikov's decisions in this game from 1987. He opens the game in his database and turns Fritz on in the background. Has Novikov overlooked something? Let's put ourselves in Mirabile's shoes:

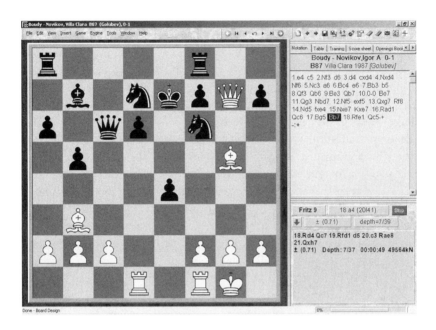

Almost immediately, we see that White has pressure for the sacrificed material. Black is tied in knots. His pawn on e4 is weak and subject to attack. Further, Black's king is precariously placed on the e-file, and he must take care to avoid problems with his rooks if the king is forced to the back rank. Can Black hold on?

In the stem game, Boudy played 18. Rfe1. This pressures the e-pawn, but is slow. Novikov's response, 18 . . . Qc5!, unhooks the queen from defending the e-pawn, and allows him to hold the position. A modern engine like Fritz or Junior will quickly tout 18. Rd4!, and with good reason. White attacks the e-pawn directly, and threatens either Rfd1 (eyeing the d6 pawn) or Re1 on the next move. After 18. Rd4, Black's game is difficult. He can try to hold with 18 . . . Rae8, but after 19. Re1!, White has a definite advantage.

As he arrives at this position on the screen, Mirabile sees that Fritz favors this new move, and notes the spike in its evaluation. But he also knows that the computer is not always correct. For many reasons,[13] it sometimes evaluates difficult positions improperly. Certainly Fritz's suggestion merits investigation. In order to deem the move worthy of being played in an important game, however, more work is needed.

Mirabile thus begins to test Fritz's suggestion, inputting sample variations into the computer, and watching to see if Fritz's evaluation of the position matches his own. He is not merely relying on Fritz to "tell him what to play"; rather, he is using Fritz as something akin to the spell-check feature in a word processor. The engine is running in the background, watching to see if Mirabile makes any gross (tactical) errors. In the event that he overlooks some tactical shot, Fritz will alert him to his oversight. It does not "think" for him, just as a spell checker does not spell for a writer. For a strong player (and a ChessBase poweruser) like Mirabile, the engine is merely one tool among many used in the pursuit of chess truth.

The rook move works. Mirabile saves his work, and adds this idea to his opening repertoire. He cannot stop here, however; there is no guarantee that Novikov will play into this trap. So Mirabile continues his preparation by investigating other lines that Novikov has played in the past, and refreshing his own memory regarding his preferred methods of attack.

Sympathetic readers may wonder at this point about the outcome of Mirabile's novelty. Was it successful? Did Novikov play into Mirabile's hands? Happily for Tim (and for us!), he was able to spring this surprise upon his esteemed opponent and beat the Grandmaster in forty-four moves. The novelty did not suffice to win the game in itself, of course, but it did give Mirabile a strong advantage that he drove home with excellent technique.[14]

Actors, Actors Everywhere

The example of Mirabile and his novelty provides us a useful case study of how strong players use chess technology. In this light, we can begin to see both the value and the limitations of Heidegger's philosophy of technology. There is some reason to think that we remain dominated by technology to this day. The case of the Crafty clones shows us how some people become entranced by technology. On Heidegger's account, all technology works in this way, dominating and enslaving us. Careful consideration of Mirabile and his novelty, however, exposes the limitations of Heidegger's analysis. Not *all* technologies enslave us. On the contrary, we find in the case of Mirabile and his novelty the possibility of a productive interaction with technology.

Technology, then, does not always dominate us. But what does it *do*? If there is no essence to technology, how should we understand it? The limitations of the classical approach to technology have prompted more recent thinkers to focus less upon technology in the abstract and more upon the diverse technologies themselves. It is no accident that this shift is described by Hans Achterhuis as an "empirical turn" (1997, 6ff)—by focusing on the use of specific artifacts by real people in real situations, we avoid the pitfalls of substantialism, and arrive at a philosophical position that does justice to the technologies themselves.

An adequate understanding of technology must also avoid the pitfall of instrumentalism or "neutralism,"[15] which is the idea that technological artifacts have no meaning or import outside of their use. Such an approach might seem sound if we consider Mirabile and his relation to technology, but it becomes problematic when we remember those poor souls who are so dazzled by Fritz and friends. Much of the difficulty in articulating an adequate philosophy of technology is the need to do justice to both substantialism and neutralism, while avoiding the rigidity of either position.

An interactionalist position represents a "middle ground" approach to technology. More importantly, however, it directly tackles the problem of just what it is that technology does. In human-technology relations, agency is traditionally understood to be a human property. The nonhumans involved (the material artifacts) are not conscious entities and possess no intentions to be enacted.[16] If we consider how people interact with technology, however, it quickly becomes clear that the nonhumans *do something*—they possess something like agency as it is commonly understood.

In order to help explain this claim, let me offer another example. The National Rifle Association has long marketed its anti-gun-control position with a famous slogan: "guns don't kill people; people kill people." The idea is clear. Gun control legislation is unnecessary, since people, and not guns, are the real problem. The gun, after all, can't pull its own trigger.

What does a philosophical analysis of the interaction between human and gun reveal? Don Ihde and Bruno Latour, two thinkers associated with the "empirical turn," have independently analyzed this interaction and come to similar conclusions (Ihde 1990, 27; Latour 1999, 176–93). For Ihde and Latour, both gun control and right-to-bear-arms partisans maintain untenable presuppositions about the human-gun nexus. Gun control advocates implicitly understand technology in a substantialist manner, where the artifact (the gun) bears within itself all the conditions necessary to determine human action. Here artifacts are reified to the point that they are believed to exert definite control over users. As Latour puts it, "on account of the gun the law-abiding citizen, a good guy, becomes dangerous" (Latour 1999, 76). Right-to-bear-arms advocates, on the other hand, implicitly understand technology in a neutralistic manner. All artifacts are thoroughly innocuous in themselves on this reading, and take on normative significance only when they are put to some use by a human actor.

Why do the substantialist and the neutralistic understandings of technology fail? Let's return to the human-gun relation. In this case, we have an angry human, and a gun on a table. How does the situation change when the human picks up the gun? As should be fairly obvious, this interaction considerably alters the situation. Suddenly the human actor can do new things—he can compel assent by waving his gun, or he can force someone to stop doing evil.

But it is not only the human who gains new powers in this interaction. By virtue of being picked up, the gun takes on new properties as well. Instead of lying inert on a table, the gun becomes a weapon in the hand of an angry human. Alternatively, it becomes an iconic representation of the peace movement when someone puts a flower in its barrel. One of the key insights of an interactionalist approach to technology is that both humans and nonhumans are transformed through their relations.

The human-gun example helps us to underscore the limitations of both the substantialist and neutralistic interpretations of technology. Both are versions of an untenable essentialism—either technology is essentially dangerous (Heidegger), or technology is essentially neutral (instrumentalism). The interactionalist approach of Ihde and Latour makes clear the variability or "relativism"[17] of technological mediation. Technologies are "multistable" (Ihde 2002, 33–34, 106–7), meaning that they bear within themselves certain trajectories for use. They are nonneutral in that they transform situations through their use, but they can also take on different meanings in different contexts. A gun "acts" differently when it has a flower in its barrel, and when it is being held by a criminal. In an interactionalist approach to understanding technology, agency is spread across all actors in interaction. Humans and nonhumans exert agency upon one another, transforming one another[18] by means of technical mediation.

We see this best when we return to the example of Mirabile and his novelty. Who, we might wonder, is responsible for the creation of the novelty? Who should get the credit for the victory over the Grandmaster? Arguments could be made for either the human or the nonhuman receiving credit for the star move. In a substantialist framework, responsibility would be attributed to Fritz and ChessBase. It was the chess engine that first suggested the move, after all, and Mirabile had only to play the move on the board to gain a powerful advantage. From a neutralist perspective, it would be Mirabile who was the true author of the move. ChessBase and Fritz were merely the tools used to find the move, and of course, he still had to outplay his opponent over the board without silicon assistance.

Our examination of the process that led Mirabile to play Rd4 requires us to reject both the substantialist and the neutralist interpretations. Neither Fritz nor Mirabile are responsible for the novelty—*both* are responsible. We cannot attribute responsibility to Fritz alone. Fritz could not sift through Novikov's games on its own, and Fritz did not choose the position after 17. . . . Bb7 for careful analysis. We cannot attribute full responsibility to Mirabile, either. Fritz pointed the novelty out, and worked in the background while Mirabile examined the position so as to ensure the tactical validity of his variations. Both the human and the nonhuman are thus responsible for the creation of the novelty.

What about the victory itself? Recall what happened—Mirabile sprung his novelty on the Grandmaster, and proceeded to take the full point in forty-four moves. Can we give the human full credit for the moves after 18. Rd4? According to Mirabile himself, he had studied numerous continuations with Fritz, and was "in book" until 21. Qxh7.[19] Is the human then solely responsible for moves 21–44?

One of the consequences of an interactionalist approach to technology is the recognition that nonhumans possess some kind of agency. As we saw with the human-gun example, the human actor is altered by means of his or her interaction with nonhumans. The same holds for the human-Fritz relation. Given his expertise in using ChessBase, and his habitual use of chess engines in his study, it would be hard to believe that Mirabile would not be influenced by the "thinking" of the machine. We would have no trouble describing its pedagogical influence if Fritz were a human study partner; why should we ignore its contributions because of its non-human status?

Strange as it may seem, we must attribute responsibility for the novelty and for all the remaining moves to both Mirabile and the computer. Better yet, there are *numerous* actors, humans and non-humans, that should receive some credit for the victory. Consider all of the actors that contributed to the creation of 18. Rd4: the books and magazines that Mirabile read, the opponents he played and studied, the authors of Fritz and ChessBase, the hardware man-ufacturers, the Internet providers that allowed Mirabile to down-load new games for his database, the Fritz engine, and Tim himself! Agency is not a property of any actor in particular; rather, it is an attribute of the entire network of actors that contributed to the cre-ation of 18. Rd4.

This is why we must see Mirabile himself as a cross between the human and the computer; he is, practically speaking, a *cyborg*. Donna Haraway, author of "A Cyborg Manifesto," understands the cyborg to be "a cybernetic organism, a hybrid of machine and organism, a creature of social reality as well as a creature of fiction . . . we are all chimeras, theorized and fabricated hybrids of machine and organism; in short, we are cyborgs" (Haraway 1991, 149–50). Although her idea sounds fanciful, she is making much the same point we make here. One of the consequences of our analy-sis is a blurring of the line between the human and the nonhuman. A blind person "sees" through a cane, extending the range of her senses beyond the "purely human." Advances in medical technolo-gies, from eyeglasses to antibiotics to artificial joints, effect a simi-lar effacement. Antibiotics aid our immune systems, and eyeglasses normalize our failing eyesight. This is what Ihde terms the extendibility of the human subject (Ihde 1990, 39)—our interaction with technology means that we are all cyborgs. The chess cyborg is but one species among many.

If we are correct in our description of the modern chess player as a cyborg, we should find confirmation of our thesis in modern chess practice. If interaction with chess technology has created a new kind of player—a player with "Fritz in his head," as Gurevich says (2005)—then we should see the concrete effects of this interaction in the very moves these players make. Such evidence, and such differences, are the theme of the final section.

The First Chess Cyborg

So what is "modern" chess? What differentiates it from classical chess? The following game from 1994 provides a useful example.

1. e4 c5 2. Nf3 e6 3. d4 cxd4 4. Nxd4 Nf6 5. Nc3 Nc6 6. Ndb5 d6 7. Bf4 e5 8. Bg5 a6 9. Na3 b5 10. Nd5 Be7 11. Bxf6 Bxf6 12. c3 Bb7 13. Nc2 Nb8 14. a4 bxa4 15. Rxa4 Nd7 16. Rb4 Nc5?! [16. . . . Rb8 or even Ra7 avoids the following shot]

17. Rxb7!

According to John Nunn, this is "an extraordinary idea" (2005, 153). White sacrifices an exchange to solidify his grip on the d5 square and attack the light squares. In itself, however, this seems to be insufficient compensation for the exchange. As John Watson notes, "material is somewhat reduced and White doesn't have much development, the two bishops, or other traditional compensation for the exchange" (Watson 2003, 228). There is no immediate, tactical route to a decisive advantage. What makes White's idea so extraordinary?

17. . . . Nxb7 18. b4!

"Terrific!," says Watson (2003, 228), and with good reason. Here is the justification for White's play. With this quiet move, White is able to stop Black's knight from returning to c5 and fighting for the light squares, and this is Black's most obvious plan for contesting White's control of the center. The position is objectively unclear, but as Igor Stohl points out, White has the initiative and much easier play (Stohl 2006, 44).

White's play is exemplary, according to three leading theoreticians. And yet, notice how many basic points of classical chess strategy were broken in the execution of this "extraordinary idea." White ignores castling. The dictum that states you shouldn't move the same piece twice in the opening is cast aside—the knights have moved seven times, and the light-squared bishop not at all! And White's queenside rook, which should be developed to a center file according to classical principles, has been developed to a4, b4, and b7, at which time it was exchanged for a bishop![20] So why is White's play considered so successful in light of these obvious rule violations? Nunn offers the following explanation:

> much top class chess is incomprehensible when viewed in terms of the principles formulated in contemporary textbooks. Whereas chess has advanced greatly in the last half-century, much of the instructional material has not kept up with these advances. It is impossible to explain White's play in this game in terms of the old ideas: "rooks belong in the center," "don't move the same piece twice in the opening," and so on. In order to make sense, the game has to be viewed in modern terms: White's play is founded on the creation of a strategic plan and the single-minded execution of that plan [control of d5 and the light squares], based on the specific requirements of the position. (2005, 154)

Modern chess only makes sense, according to Nunn, if we recognize that it has exposed the limited validity of all strategic principles. A lack of dogmatism, combined with an emphasis on concrete analysis, is at the heart of modern practice. Nimzovichian principles are true insofar as they work, but they must be jettisoned as soon as the position on the board demands it.

White's play is not chaotic in our example. He does break three cardinal rules of opening play, but he does so in order to achieve more useful goals in the position. With 17. Rxb7 and 18. b4!, White is able to cement his superiority in the center, entomb Black's knight, and control the light squares. In this position, these goals are more important than rapid castling or complete piece development.

Ideas like these have led John Watson to describe the paradigm of modern chess strategy as "rule-independence." Rule-independence is "the gradual divestment on the part of chess players of the multitudinous generalities, rules, and abstract principles which guided classical chess, and which still dominate our teaching texts. Furthermore, a rejection of the very notion of the 'rule' has taken place, in favor of a pragmatic investigation of individual situations" (Watson 1999, 97). Rules, on Watson's account, really are made to be broken. They provide the basis for chess knowledge, but real understanding only comes when we know where and when to ignore them.

Watson's characterization of rule-independence has not been without controversy; in particular, Jacob Aagaard has challenged Watson on this point.[21] For our purposes, however, it is enough to note that both authors end up describing modern chess as pragmatic[22] in nature. Both authors also highlight the role played by chess technologies in the fashioning of rule-independence or pragmatism in modern chess.

According to both Watson and Aagaard, it is because of the modern player's interaction with the computer—his ability to test moves against the computer, to find antipositional moves that work nonetheless—that the concrete, pragmatic character of modern chess has emerged. Watson makes this point very clearly in *Chess Strategy in Action*: "Players on all levels are able to try out seemingly risky, paradoxical, and "unprincipled" moves and strategies on a computer. . . . Contemporary play has thus been marked by greater openness towards positional and attacking strategies that were previously considered anti-positional and/or unsound" (2003, 9). And Aagaard's newest work, *Practical Chess Defense*, is inspired by the new possibilities opened up through careful use of chess technology. "Most of the prominent players consult chess-playing programs, so they cannot help adapting their thinking methods, as inspired by the machines" (2006, 7). Aagaard points out two instances of this influence. Modern players more easily see "Fritz-moves," or the sort of strong, antipositional moves that the computer excels in finding. But "more important," says Aagaard, is the transition towards a pragmatic understanding of chess truths (2006, 7).

If this is correct, White's play in our example should not surprise us. Garry Kasparov was certainly a strong player before the introduction of ChessBase, and his demolition of Alexei Shirov in our example occurs at the beginning of the ChessBase era. But Kasparov has repeatedly described the importance of chess technologies in his progress, and he identifies his play in 1999 and 2000 to be his best from a competitive perspective.[23] The reason for this characterization, I think, is simple. Kasparov had thoroughly integrated chess technology into his preparation by 1999, while his opponents lagged behind to varying degrees.[24] Kasparov's opening preparation, already dangerous, became legendary for its depth and breadth, and he used the computer as a partner—not an oracle—in analysis. This integration of the computer into his training, coupled with a healthy skepticism regarding its veracity, reshaped Kasparov's game. For all intents and purposes, Garry Kasparov was the first chess cyborg.

If we must view Kasparov's encounters with the computer as emblematic of human-technology interactions, it is *this* image that we should focus upon. Certainly the balance of Kasparov's interaction with chess technology must tip in the favor of his productive, as opposed to destructive, use of the computer. We could tally this balance by simply noting that Kasparov played a total of fourteen games against Deep Blue,[25] while he used ChessBase on a daily basis for nearly twenty years. More telling, however, is the influence each technology had on Kasparov's chess and chess career.

It is not coincidental that Igor Stohl uses the year 1994 for the transition point between his twin volumes on Kasparov's best games. In 1994, chess technology came of age. Kasparov publicly lost rapid games to Fritz 3 and Chess Genius. Fritz and its "colleague" Doctor?, newly integrated into the ChessBase database program, allowed players to "check" the games of the masters for blunders and improvements. And Kasparov, who suggested the idea of a chess database to Frederic Friedel, the founder of ChessBase GMBH (Mohite 2004), was among the first to take full advantage of chess technology.

There are numerous examples of this influence on Kasparov's play after 1994. One of the first was the famous rook sacrifice sprung on Anand in the tenth game of the 1995 World Championship match. On Stohl's account, "this was the first time that Kasparov had stated he had used a computer extensively as an analytical tool" (Stohl 2006, 9). This is not to say that Fritz understood Kasparov's idea on its own. In fact, according to Stohl, the computer could not understand the key move in the variation (17. Qg4!) and had to be "convinced" of its strength through extended analysis (Stohl 2006, 78).

In Kramnik-Kasparov (Linares, 1999), Kasparov used the computer to analyze positions deep into the middlegame, and hold a draw because of his ability to locate and make use of the blind spots in computer analysis. Kasparov allowed Kramnik to achieve a position that the computer deemed a near win. Having seen more deeply into the position, however, Kasparov prepared a rook sacrifice that forced a draw.

Perhaps the most telling instance of Kasparov's studied interaction with chess technology is his 2005 encounter with Kasimdzhanov.[26]

1. d4 d5 2. c4 c6 3. Nc3 Nf6 4. e3 e6 5. Nf3 Nbd7 6. Bd3 dxc4 7. Bxc4 b5 8. Bd3 Bb7 9. 0-0 a6 10. e4 c5 11. d5 Qc7 12. dxe6 fxe6 13. Bc2 c4 14. Nd4 Nc5 15. Be3 e5 16. Nf3 Be7 17. Ng5 0-0!N

Kasparov had prepared the Meran with White for his 2003 match with Deep Junior, and in the midst of his preparation, he noticed that the computer would allow White to win the exchange in this position. In fact, Deep Junior would evaluate the position as favoring Black, despite the material deficit! This led Kasparov to more thoroughly investigate the idea, and he concluded that the computer had stumbled upon a rather remarkable positional sacrifice of material. While the position did not arise in the 2003 match, it did become part of Kasparov's opening database. Kazimdzhanov was unaware of this, and played into Kasparov's analysis. After

18. Bxc5 Bxc5 19. Ne6 Qb6 20. Nxf8 Rxf8

Kasparov had full compensation for the exchange and went on to win the game in fine style.

What, in contrast, was the influence of the Deep Blue matches on Kasparov? In my opinion, surprisingly little. Kasparov exhibited no major traumas from his loss to Deep Blue, and in fact, went on to draw his matches against Fritz and Junior in 2003.[27] If anything, the fact that Kasparov's best chess[28] came after the Deep Blue matches suggests that the loss served as a "wake-up call" for Kasparov. Instead of turning away from chess technologies after the Deep Blue matches, Kasparov embraced them, deeply integrating them into his study and preparations. In preparing for an ill-fated match against Shirov in 1998, for example, Kasparov and his team made extensive use of analysis engines in their preparations. Stohl writes, "Together with his team, [Kasparov] undertook the arduous task of electronically checking, updating, and overhauling most of his repertoire" (Stohl 2006, 12). But the computer's influence was not limited to the opening phase of the game. In the 1999 match against the "World Team," Kasparov counted on his ability to integrate the engine into his study of middle and endgame positions to grind out a victory. In these years, Fritz and Junior became full-fledged members of Team Kasparov.

To a casual reader opening to this page, this last point must seem like madness. Fritz and Junior were Kasparov's seconds? They "trained" him? If our analysis is correct, however, it's not so far fetched. Technologies do not always dominate us, and they aren't neutral tools awaiting our use. Technologies—nonhumans—possess agency too. They are multistable, as Ihde puts it—they can do different things in different contexts. Fritz and Junior have become oracles of chess truth because of Kasparov's endorsements, and Kasparov was "trained" by Fritz and Junior to see chess differently, to play in a new way. Deep Blue was just another IBM supercomputer before it beat Kasparov. Today it is a symbol of all our fears about technology.

Can we thus say that the machine "won" in 1997? Kasparov didn't come to the board alone—he was the product of human and nonhuman actors, a cyborg in the truest sense of the term. Deep Blue, too, was a tangled web of humans and nonhumans, having been tuned and tweaked by humans to play like a human Grandmaster.[29] Deep Blue was a cyborg just as surely as was Kasparov, and each combatant bore the traces of carbon and silicon based influences. We have seen in this chapter that human and nonhuman can be difficult to separate by following the actors and their associations. Can we then say that human lost to machine when Deep Blue defeated Kasparov? Or are "human" and "machine" now so intimately intertwined that any attempt to differentiate between the two must be seen as untenable?

NOTES

Acknowledgements: I would like to thank Anna Forslund, Tim Mirabile, Jacob Aagaard, and Don Maddox (ChessBase USA) for their assistance with this project.

1. Evan Selinger makes this point in two recent essays. See Selinger 2006 and Ihde and Selinger 2005. Incidentally, Selinger ends his contribution to this volume by noting the need for an in-depth study of the relation between humans and technologies in chess competitions. (See p. 83.) My chapter can perhaps be seen as a companion piece to Selinger's for this reason.

2. This quote comes from ChessBase advertising, as well as an interview with Frederic Friedel (Mohite 2004).

3. A "second" is akin to a chess research assistant. Most Grandmasters will hire a second for important events if they can afford it, but with the proliferation of notebook computers and chess software, the need for human assistance can be somewhat mitigated.

4. In the interest of full disclosure, I had a computer account on chessclub.com that was used to test a lesser-known engine called Little Goliath.

5. In fact, Bob Hyatt (Crafty's author) had to ban most of these clones from playing against the official Crafty account so that his testing of engine modifications would not be skewed.

6. I should note that not all computer accounts are created for these odd purposes. Some computer accounts are designed to test opening theory, for example, while others are configured to allow humans to practice against them. It is the case of the Machiavelli-wannabe who lives vicariously through his or her engine that I attempt to understand here.

7. As Pollan notes, "To think of animal manure as pollution rather than fertility is a relatively new (and industrial) idea" (2006, 17)

8. Some may argue that the environmental movement is one that precisely does not understand trees and wooded lots in this way. But what are the environmentalists trying to "save" but our "natural resources?" The trees must be saved because we might need them later (to provide oxygen, etc.), and not because they are valuable in themselves. What makes Heidegger's analysis so disturbing is that no one is exempt from the *Gestell*.

9. For a fairly typical critique of Heidegger's philosophy of technology, see Verbeek 2005, 61–75.

10. Bobby Fischer was the youngest Grandmaster on record for approximately thirty-three years. He earned his title in 1958, and his record was broken by Judit Polgar in 1991. There have been fifteen players since 1991 who would have broken Fischer's record. The current record holder is Sergey Karjakin, who attained the title at the age of twelve years and seven months in 2002 (Friedel 2006).

11. ECO stands for Encyclopedia of Chess Openings. It is part of an international, "languageless" system of chess notation developed by the Yugoslavian company Sahovski Informator, which publishes the afore-mentioned Informator series of books.

12. Mirabile, T-Berg, G, 41st Nassau Futurity (2002), 1–0.

13. There are many reasons that a computer may misevaluate a position or a move. The engine may be buggy; that is to say, it may contain gross programming errors that cause it to offer bad advice. It may have a poor evaluation function, in which case the engine works as it is supposed to, but simply lacks the knowledge to discern the finer points of the game. Finally, the solution to a specific position or problem may lay too far ahead in the game for the computer to see. This last problem, called the "horizon effect," is particularly problematic in quieter positions where long-range planning trumps short-range tactical maneuvers. While most amateurs believe that the engines are objective and almost infallible, smarter players (as we will see) take note of their blind spots and compensate accordingly.

14. For those hardy souls who want to see the whole game, here it is: Mirabile–Novikov, NCC Championship (2002). 1. e4 c5 2. Nf3 d6 3. d4 cxd4 4. Nxd4 Nf6 5. Nc3 a6 6. Bc4 e6 7. Bb3 b5 8. Qf3 Qb6 9. Be3 Qb7 10. 0-0 Be7 11. Qg3 Nbd7 12. Nf5 exf5 13. Qxg7 Rf8 14. Nd5 fxe4 15. Nxe7 Kxe7 16. Rad1 Qc6 17. Bg5 Bb7 18. Rd4 d5 19. Bxd5 Qxd5 20. Rxd5 Bxd5 21. Qxh7 Rac8 22. Rd1 Rxc2 23. Qf5 Be6 24. Rxd7+ Kxd7 25. Qxf6 Kc6 26. h4 Rc5 27. Qe7 Rg8 28. Qa7 Rcxg5 29. hxg5 Rxg5 30. Qxa6+ Kc7 31. Qa7+ Kc6 32. Qe3 Rg4 33. b4 Kb7 34. Qc5 Bd7 35. Qd5+ Kc7 36. Qxf7 e3 37. fxe3 Rxb4 38. Kf2 Ra4 39. Kf3 Kd6 40. Qf8+ Ke6 41. e4 Bc6 42. Qf5+ Kd6 43. Kf4 Rc4 44. g4 b4 1–0

15. This is Ihde's term. See Ihde 1990, chap. 1.

16. Part of the problem with Dreyfus's understanding of Deep Blue and chess computers in general is that it renders the computer in precisely this way.

17. Ihde's term; see Ihde 1990, chap 1.

18. Due to space constraints, I cannot fully delve into the transformations undergone by Fritz. However, let me briefly suggest how Fritz is transformed via its interactions with human players. As more and more human players use Fritz, and as more and more strong players publicly validate Fritz's analysis through citing it in their own work, Fritz takes on new properties. It "becomes" more correct, a stronger player. Fritz

becomes what Latour calls a "Black Box"—we now take for granted the fact that the computer plays strong moves without considering the origins of the program or the various iterations that it underwent before achieving Grandmaster strength. Fritz is constructed by a network of actors as a "silicon oracle." In this way, it is transformed through interaction.

19. Mirabile e-mail interview. My thanks to Tim for his willingness to answer questions for this chapter.

20. See Nunn 2005, 153, and Watson 2003, 228, for a more thorough accounting of these violations.

21. In *Excelling at Chess*, Jacob Aagaard explains that chess is "a large collection of rules that constantly interact, with some of them having greater importance in this or that specific position" (2002, 51). Here Aagaard affirms the validity of basic strategic rules, but with an important addendum—different rules "have greater importance in this or that position." In other words, some rules must be flouted in certain positions in the interest of other rules and goals. White temporarily ignores some basic principles in our example, but he does so that he might achieve more useful goals in the specific position. Rule-independence may be too strong a term for this phenomenon in modern chess; perhaps "rule-flexibility" may better capture it. Much more could be said about the Watson-Aagaard debate, but in the final analysis, I do not think the two disagree as much as their writings would have us believe. Aagaard himself acknowledges this in *Excelling at Chess Calculation* when he says that "the antithesis of what I am saying [i.e. Watson's 'rule-independence'] is not its direct opposite. . . . [M]y belief that such things as rules and guidelines are practical tools a tournament player can use to his advantage, does not mean that I disparage calculation" (2004, 43).

22. By pragmatism, I mean that the rules of chess strategy are valid only insofar as they provide a satisfactory outcome to a problematic situation. I am consciously putting this in Deweyian terms, partially because I think Dewey's notion of warranted assertability sheds much light on the pragmatism that Watson and Aagaard discuss. On this point, and for a broadly Deweyian account of technology, see Larry Hickman's *Philosophical Tools for Technological Culture* (2001).

23. "And of course 1999. I think that was probably my best year. The quality of my decision-making and energy, I think it was the highest ever in the history of chess. Wijk aan Zee, Linares . . . I was well ahead of the rest with new ideas, and with more determination. I think my all-time peak was in Frankfurt, 1999, winning the rapid chess. That was the peak" (Greengard 2005b).

24. This is not to say that other chess players were ignorant of the benefits of human-silicon interaction. Vishy Anand is reported to be among the most expert of ChessBase users, for example. But Kasparov believes that others only began to really use computers for preparation after 1999 (Vasiliev).

25. This would include two games against Deep Thought in 1989 (2-0, Kasparov), six against Deep Blue in 1996 (4-2, Kasparov), and six in 1997 (3.5-2.5, Deep Blue).

26. Both Stohl (2006, 336) and Mig Greengard (2005a) tell the back-story of this novelty. I have been told that Kasparov related the tale in a New in Chess column, but I have not seen the text in question.

27. Stohl believes that Kasparov exhibited excessive caution in his matches against X3D Fritz and Deep Junior in 2003 (Stohl 2006, 10), but this is a misunderstanding of Kasparov's strategy. Because Kasparov was provided with copies of the engines he would be facing before the match, he was able to probe the engines for flaws and opening problems. His repeated attempts to sacrifice the g-pawn in the Semi-Slav reveals Kasparov's belief in his superior ability to play unbalanced positions, and his play bore no traces of the "anticomputer" strategy he employed against Deep Blue in 1997.

28. See note 25.

29. Consider the constitutive actors in the construction of Deep Blue: Hsu, Tan, et al., Carnegie Mellon University, IBM, the various hardware manufacturers, the Grandmasters hired to refine Deep Blue's positional play, etc.

REFERENCES

Aagaard, Jacob. 2002. *Excelling at Chess*. London: Everyman Chess.

———. 2004. *Excelling at Chess Calculation*. London: Everyman Chess.

———. 2006. *Practical Chess Defense*. Gothenburg: Quality Chess Books.

Achterhuis, Hans, ed. 1997. *American Philosophy of Technology: The Empirical Turn*. Translated by Robert P. Crease. Bloomington: Indiana University Press, 2001.

"Big Blue Wins." 1997. *Newshour*. PBS. May 12. http://www.pbs.org/newshour/bb/entertainment/jan-june97/big_blue_5-12.html.

Carman, Taylor. 2006. "Letter to the Editor." *New Yorker*, Feb. 6.

Dreyfus, Hubert. 1992. *What Computers "Still" Can't Do: A Critique of Artificial Reason*. Rev. ed. Cambridge, MA: MIT Press.

Friedel, Frederic. 2006. "Chess Prodigies and Mini-Grandmasters." Chessbase.com. Jan. 10. http://www.chessbase.com/newsprint.asp?newsid=2858.

Golubev, Mikhail. 2001. *The Sicilian Sozin*. Great Britain: Gambit Ltd.

Greengard, Mig. 2005a. "How the Pros Do It." chesscafe.com. March 21. http://www.chesscafe.com/text/mig23.pdf.

———. 2005b. "The Garry Kasparov ChessBase Interview, Part 2." ChessBase.com. April 14. http://www.chessbase.com/newsdetail.asp?newsid=2326.

Gurevich, Mikhail. 2005. "There is Nothing to Be Done—Computers Beat Us." ChessBase.com. December 17. http://www.chessbase.com/eventarticle.asp?newsid=2805.

Haraway, Donna J. 1991. "A Cyborg Manifesto: Science, Technology and Socialist-Feminism in the Late Twentieth Century." In *Simians, Cyborgs, and Women: The Reinvention of Nature.* New York: Routledge.

Heidegger, Martin. 1977a. "Only a God Can Save Us Now." Trans. D. Schendler. *Graduate Faculty Philosophy Journal* 6 (Winter): 5–27.

———. 1977b. "The Question Concerning Technology." In *The Question Concerning Technology and Other Essays,* translated by William Lovitt. New York: Harper and Row.

Hickman, Larry. 2001. *Philosophical Tools for Technological Culture.* Bloomington: Indiana University Press.

Ihde, Don. 1990. *Technology and the Lifeworld.* Indianapolis: Indiana University Press.

———. 2002. *Bodies in Technology.* Minneapolis: University of Minnesota Press,

Ihde, Don, and Evan Selinger. 2005. "Merleau-Ponty and Epistemology Machines." *Human Studies* 27, no. 4: 361–76.

Latour, Bruno. 1999. *Pandora's Hope.* Cambridge: Harvard University Press.

Mohite, Manisha. 2004. "Software that Keeps Chess Players Going." *Deccan Herald.* January 21. http://www.deccanherald.com/deccanherald/jan212004/ss5.asp.

Nunn, John. 2005. *Grandmaster Chess Move by Move.* London: Gambit Publications.

Pollan, Michael. 2006. "The Vegetable-Industrial Complex." *New York Times Magazine.* October 15.

Selinger, Evan. 2006. "Normative Phenomenology." In *Postphenomenology: A Critical Companion to Ihde,* edited by Evan Selinger. Albany: SUNY Press.

Shahade, Jennifer. 2005. "Fritz Control." Chessninja.com. http://www.chessninja.com/dailydirt/2005/08/jen_shahade_fritz_control.htm.

Stohl, Igor. 2006. *Garry Kasparov's Greatest Chess Games.* Vol. 2. London: Gambit Publications Limited.

Vasiliev, Yuri. "Garry Kasparov: 'Chess Has Given Me Everything!' [Interview with Garry Kasparov]." Translated by Ravi Abhyankar. chesscenter.com. http://www.chesscenter.com/twic/kasvas14mar.html.

Verbeek, Peter-Paul. 2005. *What Things Do: Philosophical Reflections on Technology, Agency, and Design.* Translated by Robert P. Crease. University Park: Penn State University Press.

Watson, John. 1999. *Secrets of Modern Chess Strategy: Advances Since Nimzovitch.* London: Gambit Publications.

———. 2003. *Chess Strategy in Action.* London: Gambit Publications.

5

Chess-Playing Computers and Embodied Grandmasters: In What Ways Does the Difference Matter?

EVAN SELINGER

As a theorist, I find chess interesting even though I do not play the game more frequently than once or twice a year. Chess narratives are seductive because they convey four recurring motifs concerning how people fundamentally use artifacts:

1. *Humans versus Machines.* The fascination with computers competing against humans at chess attests to longstanding fears about artificial intelligence being superior to human intelligence, and algorithmic processing replacing intuitive judgment. As concern builds over the possibility that a "posthuman" future might arise, both religious and secular discussions express a palpable yearning for evidence that human excellence exists and can be recognized during the moments in which the so-called human spirit triumphs over its technological replacements.

2. *Humans versus Other Humans.* The fascination with chess competition attests to perennial interest in how and why humans try to establish self-worth by besting other humans in games that require equipment to play.[1] Whether or not chess is an actual "sport" is irrelevant as far as this matter goes. The crucial point is that chess is an adversarial endeavor, and it cannot be engaged without using the pieces and a board.

3. *Humans versus Themselves.* Fascination with chess competition demonstrates our deep interest in how and why humans try to

transform themselves by cultivating discipline in practices that require equipment to participate in. Chess is a potent example of this phenomenon because game play does not revolve around the contingent conditions that influence how other competitions are conducted (e.g., unfair referees, weather-tarnished fields, unlucky dice or cards). In this sense, players assume direct responsibility for their conduct, including their improvement, decline, and stagnation.

4. *Humans versus Nature.* How much transcendence is the human mind capable of? Not only do novices play the game in a wholly different manner than Grandmasters (the highest-ranking international chess title), but chess is a domain that offers a symbolic glimpse into indefiniteness—new tensions and ideas always lurk on the horizon. No matter how well one plays, there is always more to learn.

The purpose of this chapter is to contrast two different *existential* portrayals of chess. One is provided by Hubert Dreyfus, a highly regarded philosopher of technology. The other comes from renowned director and screenwriter Ingmar Bergman, as expressed in his cinematic masterpiece *The Seventh Seal* (1957). Although Dreyfus focuses on motifs 1–4, and Bergman's exploration privileges the fourth issue, juxtaposing both treatments can shed light on the question: *What would it mean for computers to play chess like humans do?*[2]

My central claim will be that, as a matter of contingency, human interaction is, de facto, interaction between agents in *culturally marked bodies.* Not only is Dreyfus insensitive to this point, but so too are chess commentators who fail to emphasize that computers do not currently play chess like humans do because their strategy and tactics are not influenced by perceptions of culturally embodied persons who signify as perceived bodies—in terms of age, race, and gender, for example—and who signify performatively as they play—concentrate, deliberate, and make moves, for example. What I will show, therefore, is that under the guise of rigorous phenomenological description, Dreyfus becomes blinded by a normative agenda that prejudices his account of what it is like for Grandmasters to play chess. By trying to establish why it is dangerous to replace human judgment with computerized processes, Dreyfus surreptitiously projects a *fantasy* in which *eros* and *preju-*

dice—two hallmarks of human disposition—fail to be capable of influencing how the Grandmaster perceives a move. In this respect, despite rhetorically touting the importance of "embodiment," Dreyfus unwittingly infuses his account with disembodied images of chess players who more closely resemble affectless computers than flesh-and-blood agents.

Before discussing Dreyfus, however, our attention will turn to Bergman. The cinematic analysis that follows will be largely symbolic, and as such, is presented in order to orient the reader to some of the basic issues concerning embodiment. The main point, which will be clearer as the essay progresses, is that Bergman highlights the problem of bodily limitations more explicitly than Dreyfus does. Indeed, I will make the case that if Dreyfus attended to embodiment as closely as Bergman does, then he would be better positioned to present an accurate account of perception as employed by human chess players.

Bergman: Chess against Death

When Dreyfus analyzes how Grandmasters determine where to move their chess pieces, he relies upon insights from a philosophical tradition called existential phenomenology.[3] Existential phenomenologists attempt to provide an account of the invariant structures of experience—structures of experience that apply to all (or, at least, to all "typical") human beings by virtue of a shared human condition that underlies all cultural differences. Bergman's *The Seventh Seal* is a cinematic expression of just such a philosophical ambition.

While Bergman uses many images to explore philosophical themes in the film, the now-iconic motif of chess is, perhaps, the most important. It serves as the central window through which the viewer can engage with Bergman's metaphysics—a reality in which coming to grips with God's absence is tormenting, and playing the game of chess is not a distraction from life, but rather a symbolic confrontation with the meaning of *finitude*.

Set in the Middle Ages when the ravages of the plague made it commonplace to think about mortality, the film opens with Antonius Block, a knight returning from the Crusades, challenging Death's personification to a chess match. Because Death concedes that, as the paintings and legends attest, he has a predilection for chess and is a rather skilled player, Block's request is readily accepted. Block may live for the duration of their game, and he may go free if he wins the game.

Rather than completing their contest in a single temporal sequence, Bergman's elaborate choreography allows for the allegorical quality of chess to linger throughout the film's duration. As each move unfolds, and as Block's early success turns into inevitable defeat, the viewer is provoked to consider mortality. In this context, two scenes deserve to be highlighted. In the first, Block informs a priest that he plans on besting Death only to learn that the priest is, in fact, Death himself in disguise. The second is a sequence towards the end of the film, in which Block distracts Death by knocking the pieces of the chessboard over in order for a family of actors to escape undetected. We will return to both of these scenes shortly.

Considering the depth of Bergman's themes, one might wonder why he emphasizes chess.[4] As Woody Allen's short story "Death Knocks" cleverly shows, far from always suggesting profundity, it can be comical to imagine game playing as the defining test that determines whether one's life can be bargained for (Allen 1978). In homage to Bergman, Allen describes a man trying to extend his life by playing Gin Rummy with Death. And yet, without being anachronistic, this parody (and the subsequent ones) can be viewed as evidence that it is unlikely that Bergmann expected the cliché of "life as a game" to suffice as a resonant expression of existential insights. Parodies tend to create comic effect only when they subject substantive ideas to imitation mixed with revision.

The power of Bergman's choice, then, likely depends upon viewers perceiving chess to be a unique activity—an archetypical bridge between Eastern and Western histories that occupies a special niche in the collective imagination. Like Bergman, numerous artists and thinkers have appropriated the motif of chess to explore fundamental dualisms: life and death, success and failure, active and passive comportment, defensive and offensive posturing, day and night, sacrifice and repayment, etcetera. For present purposes, however, the most relevant view that Bergman evokes is that to play chess skillfully is to call forth intellectual powers that *define our humanity—both our singularity and our commonality with other natural beings*. To clarify these points, let us begin with the first, humans' singularity.

Chess playing requires foresight, and this, in turn, requires players of varied levels of skill to consider *all three tenses of time*: not only present moves, but past and future ones as well. This simple observation can remind us of criteria that demarcate humans from other beings, both organic and inorganic ones.[5]

The first demarcation at issue is one that separates humans from things. Like human chess players, inanimate objects, ranging from chess pieces to chess playing computers, have temporal existence; but unlike humans, objects do not experience temporality as a theme for reflective contemplation. Indeed, inanimate objects have no sense of how they were created.[6] Neither do they have beliefs or desires about how to best spend the time that will elapse before they malfunction and ultimately disintegrate. For reasons such as these, the German phenomenologist Martin Heidegger calls things "world poor."

The second demarcation at issue is one that separates humans from animals. Like chess players, other animals have temporal existence; but unlike them, animals cannot experience the past and future as objects of critical reflection. To be sure, many animals have some sense of the past. In addition to evolutionary proclivities, direct experience with previously encountered predators, food sources, communal norms, and, in some cases, tools, influence how they currently perceive other creatures and beings. Moreover, some animals will go to great lengths to preserve their own lives and the lives of their kin; this attests to their ability to experience some connection to the future by virtue of how they express their primal aversion to threat.[7] However, according to many authorities, animals do not treat birth or dying as subjects that require explanation; given the constraints upon their language and cognition, it is doubtful that they can even entertain or express such thoughts. It is my understanding that despite the ability of some primates to learn to communicate through sign language, they only learn to signify *current* desires (e.g., hungry for a banana now). Past desires (was hungry for a banana yesterday) and future desires (will be hungry for a banana tomorrow) are not part of their communicative repertoire. For reasons such as these, Heidegger claims that an "abyss of essence" separates humans from the other animals, making them, thus, along with things, "world poor" (Heidegger 1993). And whereas their primal relation to death allows for animals to "perish," it is the human capacity to organize existence around an understanding of lifespan that, according to Heidegger, allows us, and only us, to experience "death" at the end of our days.

Having just detailed a chain of associations running from chess
to temporality to the unique human relation to death, we can now
turn to the second issue that Bergman's treatment of chess
evokes—namely, the theme of humans as natural beings. This
theme is raised at the margins of the film's examination of cognitive limitations. Here's how.

In addition to temporal considerations, the game of chess also
provides an occasion for players of varied skill to reflect upon their
cognitive limits. This is because learning how to play chess—as
well as learning how to improve upon past chess performance—is
a process that requires players to develop a sophisticated grasp of
how to *think about thinking*. As FIDE Master Amatzia Avni notes,
by raising introspective questions, such as "How should I tackle
this problem?" and "What strategy of problem-solving should I
adopt?" players increase their *meta-knowledge*. They learn, in other
words, how to estimate what they know and how to discern the
extent to which their awareness is limited (Avni 2002, 62–63).

Because such inquiry into the relation between knowledge
and ignorance can allow chess players to appreciate how their
subjectivity is biased, the process evokes the ancient Greek
injunction, "Know thyself!" Although Socrates is said to have
uttered these words to convey that the unexamined human life is
not worth living, a parallel to chess is still warranted. The unexamined chess game is not worth playing because one of the
game's deep allures is its potential to reveal a player's finitude.
Put otherwise, inquiry into meta-knowledge can provide a bene-
ficial antidote to hubris because it has the capacity to remind participants that as finite and embodied beings, all chess players are
subject to distraction and fatigue, capable of misinterpreting overt
and subtle forms of behavior, and prone to under- and over-
preparing for foreseeable conflict. It is the arrogant or naive person, the one who believes that embodiment can be transcended,
that experiences the resistances offered by life and chess as
painful and frustrating instead of as essential limit conditions that
make struggle a fundamentally meaningful human activity. For
reasons such as these, Bergman's embodied depiction of Death is
a masterfully poetic image; it allows him simultaneously to portray Death as a supernatural force and as an embodied presence
who, qua embodied being, is distractible.

What, then, could be a more appropriate cinematic vehicle for
Bergman to have raised questions about the limits of the human

intellect—about whether, in the end, all matters of scheming and planning are expressed through our embodied limitations? In short, Bergman might have focused upon chess playing to convey existential insights because the game can be understood as a *memento mori*—a reminder of fragility and mortality. As with even the best games of chess, the most rousing lifestyles remain imperfect and cannot endure forever. Even if humans experience death differently than animals do, both remain organic beings—and as such, both experience life through the matrix of bodily imperfection and, ultimately, its cessation through bodily dissolution. To return to the first of the memorable scenes highlighted earlier, even priests cannot forestall the inevitably of earthly departure.

Dreyfus—Chess against the Machine

Having provided a symbolic analysis of Bergman's cinematic portrayal of *chess,* we have established an important context. Bergman shows that when human beings play chess, they play a game that challenges both their bodies and their minds. Indeed, Bergman succeeds in conveying deep existential insight by "arguing" that when Death takes human form to play chess, it is inevitable that he comes to place limits upon his supernatural powers.

On the basis of these general considerations, I will now highlight the specific dimensions of embodiment that Hubert Dreyfus's account of chess playing fails to register. To do so, we move from symbolic issues concerning the human condition, temporality, and reflection to the theme of what the human experiences of perception and action entail—particularly with respect to matters of temporality and reflection. The transition to this theme, however, requires preliminary consideration of Dreyfus's views on how computers approach the game of chess. These ruminations have appeared in numerous books and articles, and they form the basis of his interview with Jim Lehrer after Garry Kasparov, World Champion from 1985 until 2000, lost to I.B.M.'s Deep Blue.

According to Dreyfus, the computers that are currently programmed to "play" chess are not designed to understand its nuances. During matches they do not, properly speaking, engage in the human activity of play. This is because they do not "think" about what they or their opponents are doing; neither do they feel anxiety, elation, or any affect at all. Whereas humans find it difficult to avoid taking what the philosopher Daniel Dennett calls the "intentional stance" when they encounter machines that give the appearance of intelligent behavior, "chess-playing" computers do not impute deception to bluffing players or boldness to unorthodox moves. What makes chess-playing computers so successful, then, is that they are brute calculators who simplify the game into a "micro-world," that is, a mathematical problem that can be formalized through extensive and efficacious calculations.[8]

Succinctly put, computers' success at chess lies in their ability to rapidly and consistently assign weighted numerical values to many facets of the game in order to render a quantifiable evaluation of a given position—an evaluation that will determine, algorithmically, which move is best to execute.[9] In this context, the mathematical technique, *alpha-beta pruning*, enables computers to limit the number of alternative moves that require analysis, and *heuristics*, which are basically "rules of thumb," determine which kinds of moves computers will examine and attempt first. Some computers, such as Deep Blue, are even programmed to compare—mostly through programmed input—how Grandmasters have assessed positions with their own computational determinations. In addition to this impressive feature, Deep Blue also uses *selective-search* to identify scenarios where a certain number of moves involve forced responses.

Given the pronounced disparity between the calculative powers that humans and computers display, Dreyfus claims that humans and computers engage with chess in different ways. While Deep Blue could analyze an astonishing sixty billion board positions in the three minutes that players are allotted to select their moves, at best Grandmasters can only evaluate three board positions per second (Litch 2002, 91). And yet, despite being outmatched on a calculative scale, Kasparov somehow proved capable of defeating Deep Blue on more than one occasion!

Before clarifying what accounts for the disparity between how humans and computers engage with chess, one final contextual remark is in order. I have already noted that human experts and digital computers show stark differences in mathematical capacities. Dreyfus and his mathematician brother Stuart agree, and, further, claim that the mathematician's aptitude for problem-solving can actually hinder his or her acquisition of advanced chess skills. While this may seem counterintuitive, it is actually a reasonable proposition. They explain that brute calculation works well, but only so long as it can occur at the speed of a digital computer:

Stuart and his mathematical friends never got beyond the competent level. Students of math may predominate among chess enthusiasts, but a truck driver is as likely as a mathematician to be among the world's best players. Stuart says he is glad that his analytic approach to chess stymied his progress because it helped him to see there is more to skill than reasoning. (Dreyfus and Dreyfus 2004, 400).

Chess Players: Skilled Humans

Given how poor our mathematical capacities are when compared with computers, how, then, do Grandmasters go about playing chess? According to Dreyfus, the fundamental point of contrast between humans and computers is that Grandmasters typically do not deliberate about strategy or tactics. Unlike computers, they simply perceive the patterns that the chess pieces form as meaningful images and respond accordingly. Humans may not be naturally disposed to memorize and execute long lists of rules, including complex heuristics for playing successful chess games, but they do not need to be—not to excel at chess, and not even to engage in long-term planning in general.

Such immediate responsivity to chess patterns is possible, Dreyfus declares, because the human perceptual system can reliably and rapidly associate particular sensory inputs with behavioral responses that are appropriate, given the context and the agent's needs and desires. Our perceptual system may require external structures (e.g., writing instruments and surfaces) and culturally standardized forms of symbolic notation (e.g., numbers and letters) to process complex logical operations, but even when these tools for cognitive scaffolding aren't present, the human perceiver still remains primed for pattern recognition. Dreyfus speculates, for example, that Grandmasters can "directly discriminate perhaps hundreds of thousands of types of whole positions" (2005, 55).

In characterizing the Gestalt experience of Grandmasters as "direct," Dreyfus claims that in the blink of an eye they can visually identify chess patterns as relevant and "compelling." Such instantaneous perception is possible, he insists, because their perceptual acts are not slowed down by processes of conceptual and computational processing. Mediated acts, such as introspecting about each of the opponent's moves in order to mentally translate them into identifiable structures from which explicit inferences would be drawn, are too cognitively expensive. For example, it is inefficient for Grandmasters to perform the following two-part process: first, conceptualize the pattern of an opening sequence as a variation of the "Sicilian Defense," then deliberate about retaliatory options by evaluating from among the possibilities that internal memory stores as a list of potentially useful countersequences. Such formalized behavior may be necessary for players with moderate skills, but Grandmasters can get better and quicker results without performing a decision-tree style of analysis.

In order to ensure that Dreyfus's account does not appear unduly mystical—mostly because it posits such stark cognitive and perceptual differences between experts and novices—a brief comparison between Grandmasters and skilled athletes who compete in physically intense domains is in order. Instead of waiting for their brains to convert their visual fields into symbolic forms, Grandmasters discipline their hands to follow the same reflexive responses exhibited by athletes who enter into a motivational state that sports psychologists term the "zone."[10] In the zone, the primary comportment that players experience the world through is "flow." Flow is a state of focus that is plagued by neither boredom nor anxiety; it allows for such attuned concentration to occur that consciousness can transfix on tasks without being hindered by distracting considerations. Just as flow enables ball players of all stripes to successfully pass their games' sacred object to teammates without experiencing a reflexive moment in which they will their hands to open up from a tight grip to a pulsating release, so too do Grandmasters' hands respond to perceptual "affordances" by "spontaneously" moving chess pieces to their appropriate-looking locations.[11]

Again, such spontaneity is not random. Rather, it is a *normative* perceptual response in which the body is drawn to get a "maximal grip" on its environment (Dreyfus 2005, 57). Dreyfus considers such perception to be normative because it has "satisfaction conditions" that, to quote philosopher Sean Kelly, "say something about how the world *ought to be* for me to see it better" (Dreyfus 2005, 57). The correlative elation that comes from executing this type of direct Gestalt-motivated action is normative as well. Grandmasters and athletes do not typically become elated because arbitrary standards justify their performance as excellent. Instead, they experience positive affect because they excel at tasks that require them to push their skills to the limit, whatever their limitations have evolved to be.

To summarize: From Dreyfus's perspective, Grandmasters do not, ordinarily, deliberate—in any formal and sequentially calculative sense—about what to do. They simply allow "intuition" to motivate their deeply attuned conduct, and by giving in to this disposition enter into a trancelike state—a feeling of harmony in which the chess player becomes impervious to distraction and perceives him- or herself to be united with the objects of engagement.[12] As psychologist Mihaly Csikszentmihalyi, the theorist credited with coining the term and study of flow, notes: "The concentration is like breathing—you never think of it. The roof could fall in and, if it missed you, you would be unaware of it" (Csikszentmihalyi 2000, 39).

To crystallize these points about immediate, direct, and focused responsivity, Dreyfus invites us to consider the case of "lightning chess":

> Grandmasters must make some of their moves as quickly as they can move their arms—less than a second a move—and yet they still play Master-level games. When the Grandmaster is playing lightning chess, as far as he can tell, he is simply responding to the patterns on the board. At this speed he must depend entirely on perception and not at all on analysis and comparison of alternatives (Dreyfus 2005, 53).[13]

As further evidence of the fact that Grandmasters do not play chess by mentally performing intricate mental calculations, Dreyfus and Dreyfus offer up the following experimental "data":

> We've recently performed an experiment in which an international chess master, Julio Kaplan, had to add numbers at the rate of about one per second while playing five-second-a-move chess against a slightly weaker but master-level player. Even with his analytical mind apparently jammed by adding numbers, Kaplan more than held his own against the master in a series of games. Deprived of the time necessary to see problems or construct plans, Kaplan still produced fluid and coordinated play (Dreyfus and Dreyfus 2004, 400).[14]

While I think that, in general, Dreyfus correctly identifies the crucial differences that demarcate how Grandmasters and computers play chess, I also find his analysis of perception and action to be hindered by questionable assumptions. To clarify what these assumptions are and how they can be corrected, we turn now to the issue of perception and embodiment.

Perception and Embodiment

When Dreyfus discusses the Grandmaster's ability to "intuitively" perceive what move to make, he asserts that such a style of interaction is, in actuality, a common form of human engagement. It is a way of "being-in-the-world" that all experts share, and its scope extends from mundane to more rarified interactions: "This holds true for such refined skills as chess, jazz improvisation, sport, martial arts, etc., but equally for everyday skills such as cooking dinner, crossing a busy street, carrying on a conversation, or just getting around in the world" (Dreyfus 2005, 58). What, then, accounts for such a potent perceptual disposition? Dreyfus's answer is *embodiment*—more specifically, "the nonconceptual embodied coping skills that we share with animals and infants" (2005, 47). Accordingly, he writes:

> We need to consider the possibility that embodied beings like us take as input energy from the physical universe and process it in such a way as to open them to a world organized in terms of their needs, interests, desires, and bodily capacities without their *minds* needing to impose a meaning on a meaningless given . . . nor their *brains* converting the stimulus input into reflex responses (Dreyfus 2005, 49).[15]

While it is obvious that in moving her hand, the Grandmaster moves a *body part*, it is less clear from Dreyfus's writing why the perception underlying that physical movement is attributable to a *robust notion of embodiment.* Recognizing this lacuna, Harry Collins, a prominent sociologist, has recently charged that Dreyfus's analysis conflates "embodiment" with "embrainment." Collins's point is that the human brain is the organ responsible for our perceptual activity—even "minimally embodied" beings with human brains could, presumably, still play chess.[16] Indeed, despite the heavy rhetorical emphasis on embodiment, Dreyfus's actual attempts to establish the *scientific plausibility* of his account of perception and action emphasize, of all things, brain and brainlike activity! His main appeals are to Walter Freeman's "idea of the brain as a nonlinear dynamical system" and "the way simulated neural networks can be programmed to produce reliable responses" (Dreyfus 2005, 49, 54). Moreover, in order to bolster his account of chess playing with recent neuroscientific evidence, Dreyfus notes that "recent brain imaging confirms that amateur and expert chess players use different parts of their brain" (2005, 53). In other words,

Dreyfus declares that a shift from "left to right hemisphere processing" occurs during the transition from "detached analytical rule-following" to "an entirely different engaged, holistic mode of experience" (2005, 52). And, in what appears to be the most explicitly contradictory of his remarks, Dreyfus actually depicts Kasparov as a "disembodied mind": "There are cases when the affordance is relative to the *disembodied* mind. To Kasparov, but not to a merely competent player, a specific situation affords a checkmate" (2005, 35).

In one sense, it is understandable that Dreyfus would rely on distinctly brain-oriented rhetoric. From a naturalist perspective, the brain and the body form an inseparable biological system—to talk about embodiment is thus to talk about brain states and functions. Moreover, in putting matters this way, Dreyfus can posit that his phenomenological descriptions are compatible with solid scientific findings, including (although he does not reference it) the discussion of "thin-slicing" made popular by Malcolm Gladwell in his recent *Blink: The Power of Thinking Without Thinking* (2005). For reasons like these, I do not find it at all objectionable to discuss how the brain's capacities relate to our perceptual experiences. What I object to are the conceptual implications that follow from the specific manner in which Dreyfus discursively shifts from emphasizing embodiment to focusing upon brain activity. To clarify this point, I will discuss why I find Dreyfus's depiction of Kasparov to be untenable.

On a superficial level, the notion of a "disembodied mind" is inapplicable because Kasparov might, like other famous chess players, have a strongly embodied pregame regime—a regime that influences what state of mind he's capable of playing in. And even if he doesn't, other obvious bodily states, such as being hungry or tired, can also impact how his "mind" functions. Moreover, because Kasparov's mind is embodied in a being who is historically and culturally embedded, it is likely that, like other chess players, he would find it easier to compete on a black-and-white board equipped with traditionally shaped pieces. Qualitatively different designs—such as the one created by the Bauhaus School in which the pieces are designed to reflect how they move—would probably take some time to get used to. This is particularly the case if Kasparov's current Gestalt perceptions are wedded to specific geometric forms. Given a charitable interpretation, it is likely that Dreyfus would assent to the validity of these claims. However, on a deeper level—one that a charitable interpretation cannot remedy—we can say that Dreyfus's error arises because the account of perception he provides is too insular; it portrays Grandmasters as always focusing exclusively on the patterns made by the chess pieces, as always in the "zone" and unencumbered by other distractions. In a previous essay, Robert Crease and I put the point this way:

> Dreyfus assumes that the body which acquires skill has no relevant biography, gender, race, or age. He does acknowledge that "cultural styles" affect how skills are learned, noting for example that differences exist between how American and Japanese mothers "handle" their babies. However, this notion of "cultural style" is not developed beyond unsubstantiated generalities, and assumes as well the insignificance of any biographic differences existing within individuals sharing a single culture. From Dreyfus's perspective, one develops the affective comportment and intuitive capacity of an expert solely by immersion into a practice; the skill-acquiring body is assumed to be able, in principle at least, to become the locus of intuition without influence by forces external to the practice in which one is apprenticed (Selinger and Crease 2002, 260–61).

To clarify further how Dreyfus's notion of the unmarked body distorts his account of both the nature of human perception and chess playing, we need to remind ourselves that while Dreyfus dissociates his discussion of intuition from stereotypes about how females perceive the world, male supremacy is one of the stereotypical images that chess evokes. In *Chess Bitch: Women in the Ultimate Intellectual Sport*, Jennifer Shahade, the 2004 Women's Chess Champion, notes: "In the United States, fewer than three percent of competitive adult-rated players are women. . . . In the worldwide ranking system of FIDE . . . the situation is more balanced. There, about six percent of active adult players are female" (Shahade 2005, 3). Shahade notes that a variety of biological, psychological, and social theories have been proffered as explanations of this asymmetry. Those views and their sources can be summarized as follows:

- Kasparov himself alleges that women have a lower capacity to concentrate than men because of their "maternal impulses" (4).

- American Grandmaster and Freudian psychologist Reuben Fine contends that women are less inclined to be drawn to chess than men because patricide is the unconscious motive for playing (4).

- German youth champion Elizabeth Paethz insists that due to evolutionary differences dating back to the division of gendered labor in the Stone Age, women have less of a capacity than men to engage in prolonged periods of focused attention (8–9).

- Grandmaster Susan Polgar argues that since the modern division of gendered labor routinely provides women with fewer opportunities than men to engage in abstract reasoning, women are typically less adept at strategizing than men are (9).

In all likelihood, these claims are merely ideological convictions that present conjecture and anecdote in scientific-sounding jargon in order sound objective. But beliefs of all sorts can be self-fulfilling prophecies, and someone who takes them to be true will act accordingly. Thus, insofar as chauvinist explanations prevail and influence how some chess competitors view their rivals (and possibly themselves), and insofar as some chess trainers actually construct their regimen around the idea that menstruation effects how women, including highly ranked ones, are capable of playing, it is preposterous to assume, as Dreyfus does, that Grandmasters necessarily extinguish or repress all game-influencing prejudices about gender—and race as well—before commencing play.[17] Indeed, one of the striking stylistic dimensions of Shahade's account is that it portrays many of the female competitions as experiences of camaraderie; by contrast, she suggests that male competitors tend to develop acrimonious rivalries marked by explicit hostility.

Thus, contrary to how Dreyfus depicts the essentials of playing chess, body language—including sizing up an opponent (taking note of beads of sweat, furrowed brows, clenched hands) to determine strengths, weaknesses, and potential proclivities—plays an important role in face-to-face chess conduct.[18] Deep Blue may not be programmed to care about how long a player takes to make a move or whether the opponent's lip curls in a certain way, but people cannot help but take these behaviors as direct and meaningful

communicative signs. As a consequence, a rigorous phenomenological analysis of chess would not follow Dreyfus's lead and
restrict its focus to the player's visual attention to the chess pieces.
Instead, it would also attend to the concrete environment that chess
play occurs in. With respect to matters of embodiment, that environment is, as Shahade notes, erotically fraught. Players assume a
relatively stationary bodily position, and, within the context of this
rooted comportment, find their gaze alternating between human
and nonhuman focal points: "The sexual symbolism in chess is a
rich topic. Chess is an intellectually intimate game in which two
players sit for hours, both gazing at each other as well as the chess
board" (Shahade 2005, 70).

Shahade also makes the following observations about the
charged context of chess games:

- *Her game play is directly influenced by the type of person she
  is playing against.* "My own motivation spikes when I play
  against men that I admire or find attractive. I find it fun to
  play against someone I like, and therefore I work harder at
  the board. . . . I realized that I could also experience height-
  ened concentration against women I admire" (71).

- *Some men claim to find their concentration limited because
  they are prone to thinking about sex while playing chess.*
  "According to the 2003 American Champion, Alexander
  Shabalov . . . most men, regardless of their strength, are
  thinking about sex for most of the game" (6).[19]

- *Due to the presence and power of the "male gaze," there is an
  "invisible" but potent difference between how men and
  women think and feel.* "At tournaments, women may find it
  more difficult than men to completely lose themselves in the
  game and reach a zen-like state of total focus. That women
  are trained from a very early age to be constantly aware of
  how they appear may explain this. . . . Such an extra layer of
  self-consciousness makes it hard to experience life directly or
  to feel pure freedom" (156).

This type of testimonial evidence surely does not present us with
sufficient reason to believe that culturally embodied features (such
as prejudice) will, of necessity, causally influence all—or, indeed,
any of—the Gestalts that Grandmasters perceive. Indeed, it is

entirely possible that prejudiced (or amorous) people are able to suspend their biases when playing chess. Bigots, in other words, do not need to express bigotry during every moment they are conscious; they can still be remarkable chess players. What I have been trying to show, therefore, is that Dreyfus's account of embodied chess-playing lack sufficient ontological rigor. Dreyfus's philosophy suffers precisely because he pursues a descriptive orientation that is hermetically sealed; a more hermeneutic—which is to say, interpretative—approach would be open, from the start, to considering the question of how eros and prejudice might influence the ways that embodied Grandmasters think, perceive, and act.

Conclusion

What, then, are we to make of Dreyfus's account of Grandmasters in light of observations such as the ones Shahade makes? After all, the concrete details she provides ultimately reinforce the more symbolic and general account of embodied chess playing that Bergmann puts forth. Both Shahade and Bergman agree that as an embodied activity, chess cannot offer complete transcendence—perceptual or otherwise. If computers could play chess like human Grandmasters, they would need to do more than become better at pattern recognition. To play like humans, even the most skilled of us, they would need to be capable of perceiving their opponents in erotically, culturally, and biographically charged ways.

Dreyfus could, of course, retort that because his account of chess playing focuses on Grandmasters, it is immune to the kinds of evidence and concerns that have been articulated thus far. From Dreyfus's perspective, Grandmasters and less-skilled chess players simply relate to the game in wholly different ways.

Before responding to this possible refutation, one final contextual remark is in order. I would emphasize that Dreyfus is not interested in how Grandmasters perceive chess pieces simply because he wants to understand the intricacies of human perception. Rather, his philosophical intervention is oriented towards more explicitly normative concerns. What Dreyfus wants to do is establish criteria that demarcate human judgment from computerized decision-making.

Although Dreyfus does not use the term, he clearly depicts the Grandmaster as a hero. Indeed, he goes so far as to represent the Grandmaster as a symbol of perceptual excellence that the computational conception of mind has "endangered" to the threshold of extinction. He and Stuart thus contend that the pervasive misunderstanding of the type of intuition routinely displayed by Grandmasters has already contributed to several negative states of affairs (Dreyfus and Dreyfus 2004). Here are some examples of this misunderstanding in action:

- Diverse fields, including diagnostic medical domains, are beginning to use so-called expert computer systems. Even though intuitive human experts can generate more accurate results than such systems, zealous advocates still characterize this technology as cutting edge.[20]

- College and high school classrooms are now bringing in computer applications to perform tasks ranging from tutoring to distance learning. Zealous advocates characterize these machines as indispensable even though such devices cannot replicate the quality of face-to-face, intuitive human pedagogical excellence.

- Business schools are now teaching "scientifically sound" methods of business entrepreneurship that fail to prepare business students to respond intuitively to contextual considerations. Despite this deficiency, zealous advocates represent these techniques as thorough.

- Extremely expensive (and taxpayer funded) artificial intelligence projects are sold to the U.S. Department of Defense that cannot possibly yield the results that their advocates promise. Such projects run the additional risk of adversely affecting how the civilian sector adapts to similar technology; automated systems can be slated to replace intuitive contributions.

It is precisely because Dreyfus wants to combat these scenarios philosophically—as well as other cases in which computationally instantiated mathematical algorithms threaten to guide crucial decisions that are "best left to human judgment"—that he offers up his analysis of how Grandmasters play. His narrative, in other words, is constructed in the spirit of consciousness raising. It is intended to produce the inspirational effect of reorienting how his readers treat their core relationships to technology.

Although it is commendable that Dreyfus wants to provide this service, the problem is that he sets the demarcation bar too high. While in some cases Grandmasters probably are able to play chess in the manner that Dreyfus depicts, he goes too far in assuming that every time they play Grandmaster style chess their relation to the game is always immune to the forces of eros and prejudice. If Grandmasters could consistently play in such a pristine and pure way, they would not be human. Instead, they would be relating to other people through the mediation of the chess pieces and board in an affect-inhibited manner that applies more to computerized deliberation than intersubjective human engagement. To admit this point, however, Dreyfus would have to concede that human intuition is subject to greater fallibility than he represents. One promising way to revise this type of inquiry would be to revisit classic matches such as the one between Kasparov and Deep Blue and examine how both competitors were coached in between games. Doing so might reveal that far from merely being a contest of "human versus machine," it was a hybrid competition between human and nonhuman agents—both of which required external input (computer and human generated) to compensate for both human and computational limitations. Such investigation would also focus upon whether Kasparov's losses to Deep Blue are more directly attributable to his perceptions of what it meant to play against a computerized opponent (and from the inability of his support team to adequately deal with these perceptions) than any other failing.

NOTES

I am grateful to many people for their assistance with this chapter, notably: Jesús Aguilar, Tim Engström, Don Ihde, John Mix, Jack Sanders, Noreen Selinger, David Suits, and Patrick Wolff.

1. Of course, humans don't always try to establish self-worth in this way. Nevertheless, the use of equipment for this purpose has been a significant recurring historical motif.

2. My colleague, Jesús Aguilar, objects to my analysis on the grounds that it focuses too intently on the contingencies of chess playing. In doing so, Aguilar contends, I fail to address chess itself. That latter, Aguilar insists, is a formal domain that can be instantiated in many ways—some of which might include far less embodied interaction than the ones I'm

concentrating upon. In other words, to talk about the "game of chess" is to discuss all the possible conditions under which chess can be formalized and played. On this matter, I plead for phenomenological tolerance. I'm confining my interests to ways in which chess has actually been played by humans who happen to play chess in this world with the bodies they happen to have. Thought experiments that conjure additional variations are, therefore, not being entertained.

3. Existential phenomenologists focus on clarifying core dimensions of human experience—not only the conditions under which we perceive, act, feel, and think, but also the sensual quality of such experiences, such as what it is like for human beings to actually undergo experiences of perception, action, feeling, and thinking. While many disciplines ranging from psychology to sociology and neurobiology also explore these features of mentality and embodiment, existential phenomenologists typically contend that alternative perspectives distort essential dimensions of "lived experience": some accounts allow theoretical conjecture of how experience should be organized to trump careful description of experience itself; others wish to reduce the significance of experience to the natural causes that produce such an experience.

4. Clearly, the historical connection between chess and the medieval knight's seven virtues is a relevant background consideration. Nevertheless, it would overstate the case to claim that Bergman is engaged primarily with the presence of chess in knightly literature and practice.

5. While these specific points of demarcation are not explicitly addressed in the manifest content of Bergman's film, the creative license that I'm taking here is justifiable on aesthetic grounds. Despite memorable dialogue and an unyielding thematic focus, the film's logic is not conveyed propositionally; the issues it raises about human hopes and frustrations are disclosed through poetic *combinations of image and sound*—combinations that elicit existential thoughts from many viewers precisely because some of the ideas they call to mind are not themselves displayed didactically, as, for example, clear and distinct lessons put forth for viewers to passively absorb.

6. My discussion of the limits of "things" is meant to convey the essence of Heidegger's position. More contemporary theorists who study digital technologies, cybernetic systems, and "quasi-objects" could, of course, complicate this account of what things can and cannot do.

7. My colleague David Suits claims that only humans can have an aversion to death. Nonhumans might, he suggests, experience a primal aversion to pain in the scenario detailed above. Due to the focus of the chapter, this question will need to be explored in detail elsewhere.

8. David Suits suggests that it is probably incorrect to refer to computers as "solving" chess problems. The formalism involved, Suits claims, probably entails that computers treat chess like a "puzzle," that is, like an

entity for which there is no known solution to the whole thing, but only useful and less useful ways of addressing the well-defined parts.

9. Such calculations include, but are not limited to: computing the value of the pieces found on both sides of the board, determining how much of the board each side manages, measuring how many squares a given piece can move to, and so forth.

10. Dreyfus, appropriating the term from ecological psychologist J. J. Gibson, also refers to the perceptual inputs as the "ambient optic array." Dreyfus 2005, 54; Gibson 1979.

11. "Affordance" is another term that Dreyfus appropriates from Gibson. See Dreyfus 2005, 56, and Gibson 1979.

12. Although Dreyfus claims that the Grandmaster's play is ordinarily bereft of deliberation and rule-following, he does acknowledge that there can be occasions in which "some sort of disturbance occurs"; in such instances, a skilled player may need to deliberate about why a particular move did not call for an immediate response, or why several responses were solicited "with equal pull" (Dreyfus 2005, 57). Even the "rules of the game" (the particular moves each piece can make, the moves that count as cheating, etc.), Dreyfus declares, are not normally internalized as policies that skilled players follow—either consciously or unconsciously. Instead, the rules that novices are typically taught through formal instruction become cognitively transformed; through the acquisition of experience-based skill, the rules come to be "experienced in the background as a limit on what appears as worth doing" (2005, 53). Skilled players, in this sense, display "sensitivity" to the rules of the game simply by virtue of experiencing a constrained perception of how to proceed during a given turn (2005, 53).

13. Ben Hale notes that given how "lightning chess" differs from tournament chess, it is debatable as to whether it deserves to be considered "chess" at all. This is a good question, one whose answer would bring us beyond the scope of this essay. For present purposes, it will be useful to follow the logic of the argument presented by the Dreyfus brothers in order to determine how persuasive their account of intuition is.

14. In order to fully detail Hubert Dreyfus's account of Grandmaster perception, it will be helpful to place that description within the broader context that he intends for it to be understood within. To accomplish this, a review of his famous account of skill acquisition is in order. Dreyfus first developed the basis for his descriptive account of expertise with Stuart during the 1960s, when hired by the RAND Corporation as a consultant to evaluate their work on artificial intelligence. His research culminated in a 1967 paper "Alchemy and Artificial Intelligence," and this, in turn, provided the basis for his famous 1972 book *What Computers Can't Do*. But it was not until their 1986 collaboration *Mind Over Machine: The Power of Human Intuition and Expertise in the Era of the Computer* (1986) that the

two brothers developed a model of skill acquisition whose scope is, they claim, universal. According to the Dreyfuses, they found a way to detail how the typical human learner acquires intellectual as well as practical skills by apprenticing a standardized pedagogical experience that begins with formal instruction and proceeds developmentally. Each educational stage that they identify is cumulative, and each marks a distinct advancement upon what previously transpired. Ultimately, they claim that the sequencing of five distinct phases from "novice" to "expert" is a rite of passage that culminates in the profoundest of cognitive and affective transformations. For more on this, see Selinger and Crease 2002.

15. Evocations of "embodiment" occur throughout Dreyfus's discussion of intuition and expertise. One of the dominant motifs that he appeals to is Merleau-Ponty's notion that our bodies are drawn to obtain a "maximal grip" on the environment (Dreyfus 2005, 57). He also associates the phenomenological notion of "coping" as expressed in both Heidegger and Merleau-Ponty as well as Gibsonian "affordances" as activities that "embodied" agents perform (2005, 53–54).

16. For more on this, see Collins 1992, 1996, 2000, 2004a, and 2004b, Selinger 2003, and Selinger and Mix 2004.

17. Shahade, for example, notes how surprised she was to learn that one of her Russian trainers wanted to know her menstruation cycle in order that she could change her game playing accordingly. He even mentioned a computer program that had been developed to "determine how, on any given day, the menstrual cycle could affect play" (2005, 15).

18. Body language likely also plays an important role in online chess games. If one knows that an opponent is human, then certain moves that are perceived as "retreats" will also be ones that are perceived to be inspired by "fear." While fear is something that, to some degree, can be learned through stories, the most basic connection to it that allows its complexities and proclivities to be understood is, of course, a personally embodied experience.

19. Shabalov actually informs Shahade that during most games, he thinks "about girls for about fifty to seventy-five percent of the time" (Shahade 2005, 6).

20. Timothy Engström suggests that in order to clarify the differences that distinguish medical diagnoses made by computers from ones made by physicians, it would be necessary to distinguish their respective orientations towards temporality.

REFERENCES

Allen, Woody. 1978. "Death Knocks." In *Getting Even*, 26–30. New York: Vintage.

Avni, Amatzia. 2002. *Practical Chess Psychology.* London: Batsford.

Collins, Harry M. 1992. "Dreyfus, Forms of Life, and a Simple Test for Machine Intelligence." *Social Studies of Science* 22.

———. 1996. "Embedded or Embodied? A Review of Hubert Dreyfus' *What Computers Still Can't Do.*" *Artificial Intelligence* 80.

———. 2000. "Four Kinds of Knowledge, Two (or Maybe Three) Kinds of Embodiment, and the Question of Artificial Intelligence." In *Heidegger, Coping and Cognitive Science: Essays in Honor of Hubert L. Dreyfus,* edited by Mark Wrathall and Jeff Malpas, 179–95. Cambridge: MIT Press.

———. 2004a. "Interactional Expertise as a Third Kind of Knowledge." *Phenomenology and Cognitive Science* 3, no. 2.

———. 2004b. "The Trouble with Madeleine." *Phenomenology and Cognitive Science* 3, no. 2.

Csikszentmihalyi, Mihaly. 2002. *Beyond Boredom and Anxiety: Experiencing Flow in Work and Play.* San Francisco: Jossey-Bass.

Dreyfus, Hubert. 2005. "Overcoming the Myth of the Mental: How Philosophers Can Profit from the Phenomenology of Everyday Expertise." *Proceedings and addresses of the American Philosophical Association* 79, no. 2.

Dreyfus, Hubert, and Stuart Dreyfus. 1986. *Mind over Machine: The Power of Human Intuition and Expertise in the Era of the Computer.* New York: Free Press.

———. 2004. "Why Computers May Never Think Like People." In *Readings in the Philosophy of Technology,* edited by David M. Kaplan, 397–419. New York: Roman & Littlefield Publishers.

Gibson, James Jerome. 1979. *The Ecological Approach to Visual Perception.* Boston: Houghton Mifflin.

Gladwell, Malcolm. 2005. *Blink: The Power of Thinking without Thinking.* New York: Little, Brown, and Company.

Heidegger, Martin. 1993 "Letter on Humanism." In *Basic Writing,* edited by David Krell, 217–65. San Francisco: Harper.

Litch, Mary M. 2002. *Philosophy through Film.* New York: Routledge.

Selinger, Evan. 2003. "The Necessity of Embodiment: The Dreyfus-Collins Debate." *Philosophy Today* 57, no. 3.

Selinger, Evan, and Robert Crease. 2002. "Dreyfus on Expertise: The Limits of Phenomenological Analysis." *Continental Philosophy Review* 35.

Selinger, Evan, and John Mix. 2004. "On Interactional Expertise: Pragmatic and Ontological Considerations." *Phenomenology and Cognitive Science* 3, no. 2.

Shahade, Jennifer. 2005. *Chess Bitch: Women in the Ultimate Intellectual Sport.* Los Angeles: Siles Press.

6

The Difficult Ways of God and Caïssa: Chess, Theodicy, and Determinism in Gadamer

BILL MARTIN

There is something of an underground tradition of philosophers who have found chess to be useful in discussing philosophical problems. Foremost among these is Wittgenstein, and among contemporary figures there is Daniel Dennett, but there are other important examples, one of which I take up in this chapter: Hans-Georg Gadamer. Gadamer invokes chess while addressing a theological issue, theodicy. The term "theodicy" comes to us from Leibniz. It is made up of the Greek words for God and justice (*dike*), but rather than meaning something like "God's justice," theodicy is a vindication or justification of God *as* just, in light of the existence of at least *apparent* evil and injustice in the world. While I think the arguments Gadamer put forward are important and interesting, I will actually disagree with his conclusions—on the grounds of chess itself. Caïssa, as most readers will know, is the goddess of chess, whose ways may or may not fall under God's necessitarian scheme.

Does it matter if a philosopher "gets chess right"? The answer is obvious in the case where the fit between the larger argument and the chess analogy that is supposed to support the argument is presumably very tight. But surely there are cases where, even if the chess analogy is not entirely accurate in its portrayal of chess, there still might be some support for the more general philosophical argument. After all, analogies are only supposed to go so far. Still, chess seems particularly well suited to making at least some kinds of arguments in philosophy. When chess is invoked one would hope that the philosopher gets things right. In grappling with what I like to call "the method of chess in philosophy" (playing on Donald Davidson's title, "The Method of Truth in Metaphysics"), we might compare the way philosophers depict chess with how it is depicted in films or novels (and sometimes in paintings).

It is well known to observers on this issue that these media commonly make the most basic mistakes in how they portray chess. A film will show the board set up with a dark square in the lower-right corner; a novel will describe a game with impossible moves. Do these things matter to anyone in the audience other than a few "chess nuts," however? Apparently there are some wonky moves in Walter Tevis's *The Queen's Gambit* (2003), which is widely regarded as one of the very best chess novels (and certainly I hold it in high regard). These moves went right past me, as I was too absorbed in the story to think them through. But then, I am not at a level of chess ability where, hearing or reading a series of moves, I can hold them all in my mind's eye. (For a few moves I can do this, but it makes my head hurt.) Perhaps the person who can do this, however, has a perfect right to be annoyed—especially if chess is the main subject matter of the work.

A well-known philosophical argument from recent years that uses chess is from *A Thousand Plateaus*, by Gilles Deleuze and Felix Guattari (1987). In order to explain their concepts of the "war machine" and the "State apparatus"—in the French way, they capitalize the "s" in "state"— Deleuze and Guattari make a comparison between chess and the game of Go (352–53). Readers of their work know that they argue for the nonlinear, against linearity; linear logic or action is characterized as "arboreal" (treelike) in their scheme, while nonlinearity is "rhyzomatic," more like a tumbleweed or a fungus. Chess is aligned with the linear, the arboreal, and the State apparatus. Now, in my view, Deleuze and Guattari go a little too far in making chess suit their case. For instance, chess is certainly linear when compared with Go, and certainly one could make the case that chess is essentially linear, or even "unidirectional," in that there is one ultimate object in the game: to place the king in checkmate. Be that as it may, there is a sense in which, especially in what is called the "positional game," the more powerful strategy is to avoid being overly linear, to "skirt" linearity. The typical figure of the overly linear player is the beginner who pulls out the queen at the earliest opportunity and makes various attempts to aim directly for the opponent's king. Except in a game against another beginner, this is a losing strategy every time. Of course, the hypermodern movement in chess contributed a great deal to the idea of a less linear style of play. And yet, it does not seem that Deleuze and Guattari, despite this and similar criticisms that might be made about their somewhat overdetermined characterizations of chess, are so wide of the mark. Even the most nonlinear style of chess play, if it aims to be sound, will probably not approach the sorts of nomadic and guerrilla tactics found in Go.

Well, a good deal more can be said about Deleuze and Guattari's argument, but that is another essay. (I wrote about their comparison in terms of the influence they have had on contemporary music in my book *Avant rock* [Martin 2002, 229–36].) My main reason for mentioning their analysis here is to give an example where the characterization of chess may not be exactly right, but the analogy to chess still works well enough for the purpose at hand. It seems to me that something else happens in the case of the chess analogies from Gadamer. The difference, however, is a bit hard to pin down, and so let us turn directly to their chess arguments, each in turn; in conclusion I will return briefly to the problem of argumentative strategies of chess in philosophy.

There is something a little fishy about the passage from Gadamer that I would like to discuss, but allow me first to quote it, and then I will tell you what the fishy thing is.

> This idea recalls what we said about the *atopon*, the strange, for in it we have "seen through" something that appeared old and unintelligible: we have brought it into our linguistic world. To use the analogy of chess, everything is "solved," resembling a difficult chess problem where only the definitive solution makes understandable (and then right down to the last piece) the necessity of a previous absurd position.

My only source for this passage is the epigraph from a book of poems by David Solway, *Chess Pieces* (1999).[1] Now, I am not any kind of scholar or deep reader of Gadamer, but this does sound to me like something that Gadamer could have said. Here the plot thickens, because, in the same year that *Chess Pieces* was published, it came to light that Solway had been the perpetrator of a literary hoax. For some years Solway had championed the work of

a "humble fisherman," a poet from the Isle of Crete. Apparently,
this poet, "Andreas Karavis," has even been considered for the
Nobel Prize in literature.

Of course, it has long been known that all Cretans are liars,
even if this aspersion was first cast by a Cretan. What, however, is
the status of the liar's paradox as stated by a fictional Cretan? For,
it turns out, Andreas Karavis was the invention of Solway, and the
liar's paradox was employed in Solway's own devious chess game.
It is an interesting philosophical problem in chess as to whether
there really can be deviousness, something akin to the poker
player's "bluff." Supposedly, in chess, "nothing is hidden," to borrow Wittgenstein's phrase. To analyze this question fully would
take us down other avenues than the main ones I want to explore
here, but there is something of the "nothing is hidden" problem at
work in the Gadamer passage (or perhaps, that is, the "Gadamer
passage"). Personally, I find Solway's literary hoax hilarious, and it
also has had the amusing result that Karavis's poetry has probably
garnered more appreciation than Solway's.[2] Regarding the
Gadamer quotation, the plot thickens yet again with a more recent
(since the Karavis hoax) set of ruminations from Solway, regarding
his undergraduate study in philosophy, where he writes, "I spent a
weekend filling two examination booklets with my cogitations on
Gadamer and Dilthey, neither of whom I had ever read . . ."
(Solway 2003). Solway goes on to report that his ruminations
earned him the second-highest grade in the course, and one has to
wonder if his success in this endeavor inspired his later efforts at
the intersection of literary fictions and, to coin a phrase, truth and
lies in an extramoral (aesthetic?) sense.

Certainly there are further layers to be peeled away here. The
liar's paradox, which is also known as "performative contradiction,"
is almost the flip side of the prisoner's dilemma, the latter much
beloved of philosophers who apply rational choice theory and
game theory to ethics and political philosophy. And yet these theories, based as they are on decision trees where each nodal point is
formed by strict binary logic, do not come close to capturing the
sense of either a "game" in Wittgenstein's sense, or "play" in
Gadamer's sense (or in that of theorists of play such as Johan
Huizinga, Roger Callois, or Brian Sutton-Smith). Human rationality
is perhaps better modeled on the complexity of chess, and this even
includes what the late Grandmaster (and, some say, KGB informant
in the time of the Soviet Union) Eduard Gufeld called "the search

for the chess Mona Lisa" (2001)—in other words, an irreducible aesthetic element, what is also called "chess beauty."[3] "Chess rationality" may have a certain linearity to it, but the calculation procedure in chess does not appear to be analyzable into a strict hierarchy of "yes/no" decisions. Chess logic is much more synergistic, despite what may be the outward appearance, where chess players calculate at the board by running through possible moves, rejecting them in turn until what appears to be the correct move is found.

And yet Gadamer, or at least Solway's "Gadamer," speaks of a solution to a problem that, retroactively, makes the strange familiar. Let us for now dispense with concerns over the authenticity of the passage. I have to admit that, at a certain stage, I became less interested in finding the passage in Gadamer's work, precisely because of an irreducible aesthetic principle, that of the *comedy* that is provided by Solway's amusing escapades in philosophy. This comic relief is relevant to the case at hand, however, because Gadamer's passage finds a kind of "theodicy" in chess, and what is theodicy for, at least from a human point of view, other than to "explain" the *tragedy* of human existence—to use Heideggerian terms that would have been well familiar to Gadamer, the tragedies of human mortality and human radical finitude?

Something that seems out of place is given a place, and therefore a sense, a meaning, in a larger scheme. The "previously absurd position" is seen to not be absurd after all. What, however, is it to be "absurd," and how might the idea apply to chess? What is it to "go to" or "go toward" the "surd"? ("Ab" is one of those pharmakological—to use Derrida's term—particles of language that can mean two opposite things, "to go toward" and "to go away from.") The etymology of "surd" goes first of all to mathematics and secondarily to linguistics.[4] In math, a surd is an irrational number; in linguistics, a surd is a "voiceless sound." This latter seems especially absurd, unless I interpret the notion to mean that there are "sounds" that have not yet received voice. A further interpretation may render the absurd as simply that which is without voice. What, then, is the "previously absurd position" in chess? Certainly every chess player, at whatever level, has had the experience of seeing an opponent's move and saying to him- or herself, "I don't know what that means," or even, "I cannot for the life of me figure out the meaning of this move." Now, *positions* are not in themselves *moves*, but a position is arrived upon through the making of moves—though of course these are moves of two players, each of whom hopes to defeat the other. We might, then, pin the moment of the absurd position on a particular move, and then we have to ask if the position only *seems* to be absurd. In other words, we may ask if the move that brings about this position only seems to be without a definite place in a rational calculation, or whether it only seems to be the case that the move is truly without a voice in the larger contrapuntal musical work that is a chess game.

To move very quickly again, let us set out three forms of philosophy and their perspectives on the absurd in order to place Gadamer's position in context. One perspective, let us call it "existentialism," is that there is ultimately no way around the basic absurdity of existence itself. "At bottom," reality is not governed by laws that function under the mode of necessity; instead it is the case that lawlike motions are temporary (even if *relatively* long-lasting) forms of order against the background of contingency. Not unrelated to existentialism is pragmatism. In this perspective, the contingent and the "absurd" (in the form of the "irrational" at least as it applies to calculability, and in the form of that which apparently happens "without meaning" or "without reason") may indeed govern "reality, at bottom," reality in its "foundations," or "reality" in some "timeless" sense, but the fact is that we humans are temporal beings, even "temporalizing" beings (to use Heideggerian language), and the things we have to do to live our lives in this world for the much greater part, at least, have little or nothing to do with the timeless or with metaphysical foundations. Pragmatism, at least in the forms practiced by William James, George Herbert Mead, John Dewey, and Richard Rorty, is geared toward the "human scale." If there is any "making sense" of things, it is in terms of this scale; to use language from Donald Davidson, which Rorty finds congenial, meaning and understanding, and even truth as correspondence and objectivity, arise in "triangulations" that are necessarily "local," at least in the sense of not being completely "cosmic" or going to the metaphysical "underpinnings of reality."[5] Of course, neither the pragmatic nor the existential traditions provide enough sense to life, or to "things" (or, to borrow a favorite expression of an "experimental religious thinker" who might be called the "Richard Rorty of theology," Don Cupitt, to "it all") to satisfy some people, and the question is whether this satisfaction can be gained only by turning in a Platonic or classically theological direction, in which there is a "scheme of meaning" in some cosmic or transcendental sense. Arguably, this is the direction in which

Gadamer turns, at least as evidenced by his chess example. Thus we might define a third path in philosophy, hermeneutics, as a theory of understanding that is premised on the notion that understanding is truly and ultimately possible.

There are many affinities and contrasts among these different paths in philosophy that are begging for exploration, even specifically in terms of "chess philosophy." This would be the work of a book or several books, and thus we must set aside many issues (which I find tantalizing and even profound) here. However, there are a few of these issues that are unavoidable, even if they can only be explored superficially in the present context, and it also has to be admitted that a fourth perspective has been introduced into this scheme, that of "Platonism." I place the term in scare-quotes because there is much that goes under this heading in the history of Western philosophy that says little of interest regarding the actual philosophy of the actual philosopher Plato. Be that as it may, as in mathematics, logic, and (significantly) music, there are a number of issues in chess that are helpfully explored in terms of Platonism. The question is whether Gadamer's perspective on the absurd, using chess as his example, partakes of a Platonic formalism, in which every move does ultimately find its place, its rationality, and its voice.

Let us return to the example and discuss its specifically "chessic" elements. The condition that Gadamer sets for the "atopon"— the out of place, or the "strange," or, to use another language, "the other"—to have turned out to not have been out of place after all is that "only the definitive solution makes understandable (and then right down to the last piece) the necessity of a previous absurd position." This is a formulation that in fact contains a great deal of subtlety. To begin with, Gadamer does not speak here of a chess *game*, but instead of a chess *problem*. Chess problems are often set up with positions that are not likely to be found in actual games. Indeed, the chess problem, artifacts of what are called problemists or composers, circumvent the dialogical process by which positions arise in a chess game. In an actual chess game, it is often the player's hope, in making a move, that the "meaning" of the move will be difficult for the opponent to calculate. Dialogically speaking, the analogy might be to the parable or some other bit of language that is heavily figurative. Perhaps we will miss something in Gadamer's argument, then, if we shift the terms to a position that arises in a chess game, and if we make the "meaning" of a particular move our specific "problem." However, let us pursue this simplification of Gadamer's example at least for a moment, as there is a concern with the non-dialogical nature of the way that Gadamer uses the term "chess problem." That is, a "chess problem," again as the specific artifact of a composer, is already "front-loaded" with its own "local theodicy." That is, the composer sets the problem up with a definitive solution, "down to the last piece," to begin with. Of course chess composers are interested in positions that seem strange and even absurd, for it is in such positions that the *art* of the problem is achieved, as opposed to the sorts of problems that might be set up as pedagogical devices for beginning and intermediate players.[6] But the chess composer is also interested in setting up the problem as solvable, and the question might be whether we are even talking about a "problem" if there is not a solution—and, again, in the case of the chess problem, it is a matter of a solution down to the placement of the last piece. Indeed, this can be a model of theodicy fully under the mode of omniscience, in the case where the chess composer has a final position in mind and then achieves the initial position through retrograde analysis. This latter would have to be of a specific kind, one where only one singular line connects the initial position to the *definitive* solution. Thus the definition of the strange is achieved, but my point is simply that the "strange" had to already be understood in this example, at least by the composer, and therefore, in the end (or, as things "come out in the wash," so to speak) there was only ever the *apparently* strange. Is Gadamer's point that, in fact, this is the case both in chess and in life, the universe, and everything; that every strange thing is not in fact truly strange, and that, at least from a certain (omniscient?) perspective, everything is right where it is supposed to be?

However, with the chess problem we are not yet talking about a chess game. Let us ask how Gadamer's argument stands in this latter context. One would hope, of course, that reality is not, in the end, nothing more than an extraordinarily (but not impossibly) complex chess problem, though, in fact, the idea cannot be immediately ruled out from either a theological or a mathematical perspective. Indeed, Gadamer is better known for his dialogical view of interpretation, in which understanding arises from the "fusion of horizons," a process perhaps not so different from Davidson's triangulation. It takes two to play this game, and it also takes a world, or a chessboard. Perhaps the difference between Davidson and

Gadamer on this point, though the issue needs much further exploration, can be seen in the fact that the chessboard (and the pieces and the rules for moving the pieces) presents a definitive coordinate system in which "proper," "meaningful" moves can be made (even if the moves are bad or inaccurate ones), while, at least for Davidson, the world that we hope to understand does not have to come equipped with any such system of universal coordinates. (To put it simply, there is no definitive, built-in "north" or "south" or "up" or "down," and, while temperature can be measured according to scales such as Fahrenheit or Kelvin, there is no "temperature as such," apart from these scales.) Neither does Davidson think that such a system of coordinates exists. But what about Gadamer? Does the chess example depend on the idea of such coordinates in the world (or *of* the world) in order for there to be a "definitive solution" that gives place to the seemingly placeless?[7]

My argument is that Gadamer's chess example, apart from what he may hold in other parts of his philosophy, does indeed depend on such a coordinate system—in the world as much as in chess. As a thought experiment, Davidson posits the idea of an "omniscient interpreter" to further his argument that, in the process of triangulation, coherence yields correspondence. In Gadamer's chess example, it seems as if such an omniscient interpreter must actually exist, so that, indeed, the previous absurd position (whether in chess or in the world) can be understood as having a definitive solution, and therefore as not absurd after all. My argument, however, is that the chess example, when properly understood in the real terms of chess, does not support Gadamer's notion of the "definitive solution." The "strange" *can* occur in chess, and it is not absolutely always the case that the "absurd" (as defined previously) turns out to make complete sense in the end. Let us see how this argument plays out in terms of chess, then we can ask what it might mean for Gadamer's larger point if the chess example goes differently than he thinks it does. The latter inquiry might tell us something about the value of the method of chess in philosophy.

Again, let us consider the chess game rather than the problem, and the move, which results in a particular position. In these terms, what is the "previous absurd position"? Such a position is the result of a move, the meaning of which is at least for a time obscure. Now, many moves in chess are not of this sort—we can see what the player is "up to" with many moves. The better the player, the better he or she is able to see, for the most part, what his or her opponent is attempting to achieve with a particular move. Conversely, the better the player, the better he or she is at coming up with moves that baffle the opponent. The question arises, then: To *whom* does the position appear absurd? Perhaps only in blitz chess does the player make moves that baffle even him or herself, in the attempt to bring confusion to the game and thereby win on a time advantage. As with the problemist, the seemingly absurd position is created for a purpose—what might even be called a "higher purpose"—which then retroactively confers sense upon the position. In the case of the chess composer, the higher purpose is a certain kind of aesthetic value that derives from a definitive solution to what at first appears to make little or no sense. The comparison might be made to a musical composition where an apparently hopelessly polychromatic sequence is resolved, though it is in the form of the resolution—the definitive solution—that the possible aesthetic value is found, not simply in the fact that chromaticism can be pulled out of polychromaticism or even atonality. The comparison breaks down in that there is no completely definitive mathematics or logic of such a resolution in music; however, aesthetic value makes a resurgence in the fact that "elegance" is also considered an important property in mathematics and logic. How do things stand in chess? Is it more like mathematics and logic (leaving aside the differences between these two, which are significant) or more like music? To return to the blitz chess example, the "higher purpose" that is served by a seemingly absurd position is the aim of winning the game, and this aim, as with the solution in math, would seem to place aesthetic value (elegance, beauty, brilliancy, even "coolness") squarely in secondary position.

Sometimes a sports coach is heard to say, "It wasn't a pretty win, but we'll take it." Blitz chess is full of wins that are not only not very pretty, but that are in fact purposely ugly. Furthermore, in blitz the dynamic by which a player determines which move to make might be the very opposite of that in chess composition. In the latter, the composer presents a problem that is vexing to the person who tries to solve it, but the composer him- or herself is already working from the definitive solution. Indeed, this form of working is itself definitive of theodicy, the godlike mastery of time and movement in the context of a predetermined outcome. In composition, there is the sense of working *backwards from* clarity to confusion and even *apparent* absurdity. In blitz there is often the aim of working *forwards to* confusion and perhaps *real* absurdity, and the positions thereby achieved may be absurd to both players—in other words, just as much to the player whose move makes the position absurd. In composition, the absurdity turns out to not be absurd after all, for it is part of the "definitive solution right down to the last piece" (though this latter notion might be examined as well, for there is the curious phenomenon in chess that goes to the old saying, "They also serve who stand and wait"; even the piece or pawn that never moves for the entire game may be doing something very important); in blitz, the absurdity "makes sense" as part of a strategy toward winning, but it also makes sense as part of that strategy *only* if in fact it does not make sense.

In between the extremes of composition and blitz is something more like "real" or "normal" or "standard" chess. Of course, this "normal" chess takes many forms as well, depending on the time controls in a competition, or the circumstances of a "friendly" game that is perhaps less competitive.[8] Let us for the moment quickly move past these distinctions and complications by just saying that "real" chess is a game between two people that is unhurried and allows for reflection. (We will come back to the problem of playing chess with either a calculating machine or God.) In such a game, a player's previous move creates a new position, and that position is a problem for the other player. The solution to this problem that the other player attempts to find is one that aims to advance a winning strategy, and it might be said that the "definitive solution"—*if there ever truly is such a thing,* in chess or elsewhere—is the line that leads from any given previous move to the winning of the game. Even this simple scenario has to admit of complications. For instance, there might be situations where a "positive outcome" means something other than winning the game in the conventional sense; for instance, a situation where a draw is the most appropriate way to advance in a tournament, or even where a loss is the best way to help the overall goals of a team. However, my point here is not to go into all of these complications but instead to give reasons for avoiding the completely contrived situation where there never really is anything that is absurd, irrational, senseless, voiceless, or out of place. How does the absurd stand in a "real" chess game, and what is the upshot for Gadamer's argument?

In a "real" chess game (though certainly also in blitz and composition) there is undoubtedly a coordinate system to the "world" in which triangulation takes place. I side with Davidson in thinking that no such system is needed for the world in order for humans,

through triangulation, to progressively come to understand it (and
to hold global skepticism at bay).[9] Another way to put this is that
a game of chess would not be possible without a coordinate system that the players adhere to, and without which it could not be
said that the players understand anything of chess. It is within
chess's coordinate system that a position might appear "absurd."
The argument about a possible coordinate system to the world cannot help but verge on the theological (even if the argument is conducted in purely Platonistic-mathematical terms), and it might be
said that what Gadamer is doing with his chess analogy is biting
the bullet on this point, and that the outcome is theodicy, a scheme
in which everything has a place and in which nothing is absurd in
the end. Of course this question is pursued in countless philosophical arguments, down through the centuries, regarding the
existence of God and the notions of Providence and a divine plan
(or narrative) of creation. Regarding these arguments, it is worth
saying that Davidson's triangulation argument is significant for
showing that, even if there were a cosmic coordinate system, such
a system is not a *necessary* part of the human intersubjective ability to make sense *in* the world, and, in that way, to make sense *of*
the world. Certainly, this leaves aside the question of a "cosmic"
sense *of* or *to* the world that confers sense upon everything in the
world—through a kind of "placement," as it were. This distinction
between a "cosmic sense" and the "local sense" (and the "maps"
that we make through triangulation—the term is apt because it
could be said that even a global positioning system is not a cosmic
positioning system that somehow locates each of us according to
the coordinates of existence itself; such a system would simply be
theology by another name) simple repeats Heidegger's ontologi-
cal/ontic distinction. That does not mean that the distinction is a
bad one, per se. However, and here is the rub, even with a coordinate system, it is not the case that everything absurd, meaningless, irrational, or tragic comes out in the wash, and this is where
it is important to show that, at least on this point, Gadamer is
wrong about chess.

In my slight, "realistic" reformulation of Gadamer's scenario, a
move that appears to lead to an absurd position can be one of two
things: either the move is an outright (and probably egregious)
blunder, in which case the move will "make sense" in terms of the
gain that the other player may derive from it, or the move may be
part of a deep strategic calculation that only appears on the surface

to have been absurd, irrational, or meaningless. In either case, the meaning of the move is determined, or at least determinable, in terms of a larger scheme. My objection to Gadamer's "problem" version of the example is that the definitive solution is "front-loaded" by the composer from the start, so of course there is no doubt that we will find in the end the rationality of what had at first appeared irrational. But one cannot extrapolate from this example to the idea that there is a "cosmic composer" in whose grand scheme everything makes sense in the end.[10] It is reasonable to assume that Gadamer wanted more from his example (than getting again out the back end, as it were, what was put in at the front end), thus again my "realistic" reformulation.

Whatever the move in the chess game, and barring some intervention into the game from some element external to chess (the board is tipped, fire in the café, and so on), there will be an outcome: win, lose, or draw. In Gadamer's scheme, the meaning of any given move, even the move that appears to lead to an absurd position, is given in the outcome. The case that he specifies comes down to this: winning the game shows that the previous absurd position was not absurd after all.

This itself makes for a nice model of theodicy. As too many in our culture, including many of our undergraduates, like to say, "everything happens for a reason." Of course, if you ask what the reason is, exactly, the point of the statement becomes clear: the "reason" cannot be understood as a reason by finite, mortal minds as such, but only by a mind that grasps the totality of existence, a mind in possession of a cosmic positioning system. In this case, however, there is no difference between saying that "everything happens for a reason" and "nothing happens for a reason" (or "everything happens for no reason"), and this would not be a satisfactory outcome for Gadamer, at least in terms of the chess example. Such an outcome would be the very opposite of the definitive solution right down to the last piece; it would be a completely undefinable "solution" without specifying anything about any piece—which is the superficial theodicy we generally get from folks who say "everything happens for a reason." (Especially when this banal statement is offered as some sort of response to a tragic event, I am tempted to retort, "Yes, the reason is clearly that God hates humanity and will do most anything to cause suffering to humanity.") At least in what appears to be the overwhelmingly rational "world" of the chessboard, there would appear to be a clear connection, even if one that in some cases can only be seen in hindsight and through deep analysis, between any given move and the outcome of the game. Indeed, it is a useful exercise for a beginning player, especially, to analyze a lost game and to find the moves where things took a decided turn for the worse. Often there is one move in particular where the game was already decided. Perhaps the sign of the true beginner is in how early in the game this move occurs. To take a simple example, a player who opens with a rook pawn is almost always giving away his or her status as a rank beginner. The position is already absurd, from the first move! But wait! There is the exceedingly rare, but not never-occurring, case where this player may seem "crazy" (for doing something absurd, irrational, meaningless—which also could be understood in chess terms as what happens when a "tempo" is lost, a completely wasted move, or for making the pawn "atopos," out of place), but the player turns out to be "crazy like a fox."

Let's stay with this pawn move for a moment, a3 or h3. The player (on white) who opens with a3 seems to have committed a blunder with the very first move, indeed an egregious blunder that shows that he or she is not much of a chess player. In *Unorthodox Chess Openings*, Eric Schiller, the renowned opening specialist who worked with Garry Kasparov in the latter's matches with Anatoly Karpov, says of 1. h3, "There really is no point to this move" (Schiller 1998, 94). Of 1. a3 Schiller is slightly more enthusiastic, saying, "The move a3 may be simply irrelevant, but then again it may not" (1998, 48). When are these moves *not* either pointless or irrelevant (leaving aside that point that, for true absurdity we would at least want "pointlessness," irrelevancy is probably not enough—though irrelevancy does have the "virtue," for our purposes, of evoking the "atopos")? The answer is simple enough: when either of these moves is part of a strategy, and when the strategy leads to a won game. Then it turns out that, for instance, 1. h3 was not so "pointless" after all. The reverse applies as well. If 1. h3 was truly made as an egregious opening blunder by a player of very limited ability, then the meaning of this blunder will also become clear in a lost game.

The larger point is that there is no fundamental *undecidability* or *underdetermination* in Gadamer's scheme, at least as regards the chess example—which we then want to project upon something larger, where this scheme becomes theodicy. Again, there are two issues: (1) Whether the chessboard is an adequate analogy for the way the world works; and (2) Whether the workings of the chessboard are as determined and decidable as Gadamer seems to think they are. It seems to me that the analogy may go differently from how Gadamer intends, that if the chessboard (or, more accurately, everything involved in a game of chess: a board, pieces, and two players—though we will have to come back to the question of whether the players have to be human or not) is not indeed a structure in which there is no fundamental underdetermination or undecidability, then it seems hard to imagine that the world could be such a structure either. In other words, if chess actually does have a place for the absurd, a "place" or "moment" that cannot be ruled out by the rationality of the structure, then it seems more than likely that the world does too.

What I have tried to do with raising the issue of the rook's pawn move is to thematize a certain question, which turns out not to be so hard to understand. Yes, of course, this move is almost always played by a beginner who does not know what she or he is doing (so perhaps this person is even a "pre-beginner," and this itself raises a difficult problem, because it could be said that such a person is not yet working within the structure of chess), and this lack of understanding will come out in the wash, in the form of a lost game. Therefore there is not, in the end, anything anomalous about the move—or, to put it in slightly different terms, there is a difference between the foolish and the absurd. At the other end of what might appear to be a "spectrum" (for locating all chess moves, for giving them a place in the game, this spectrum corresponding roughly to the "Elo" rating system), is the exceedingly rare but not absolutely unheard-of case where a Grandmaster plays a rook's pawn opening. Here the seemingly absurd move is *intended* as part of a deep strategy, a strategy that aims for a win. The question of the undecidable and the underdetermined manifests itself in three ways in this context. First, the "spectrum" may not be absolutely "smooth" or linear. The simple demonstration is the case where player A is on the whole better than player B, and player B is on the whole better than player C, but sometimes player C can pull out a win against not only player B but even against Player A. In other words, there is not consistent transitivity. (This sort of thing is a problem for game, decision, and rational-choice theories in general: a preference is expressed for chocolate over vanilla, and vanilla over strawberry, but then the next subject prefers strawberry over chocolate.) This does not

mean that there really is no "spectrum" (which is another name for
a kind of coordinate system), but instead that the existence of a
spectrum does not rule out anomalies.

Second, perhaps there is a point within the upper reaches of
the spectrum where it is undecidable whether the deep strategy
predicated upon a seemingly absurd move really would lead to a
win. Perhaps this is a matter of taking a chance. Chess, however,
is what mathematicians and game theorists call one of the "games
of no chance"—to quote from the front matter of a book with
this title, "Combinatorial games are finite, two-person, full-infor-
mation games such as chess, checkers, go, . . . and many others"
(Nowakowski 1998). Such games, it is argued, can indeed be
"solved," right down to the last piece. (Another way to put this is
to say that there is an algorithm for chess and other finite, full-
information games.) Now, let us assume that this is right—I would
like to be able to disagree with the idea, but I am far from having
the competence to do so. The definition of "chance" for our purposes, then, and in the present case, is the strategic bet that the
player makes that the other player will not be able to figure out
what he is doing. This language of the ability to "figure out" is purposely vague, because it can mean at least two different things. In
chess, figuring out is typically a matter of calculation, in other
words, solving a kind of math problem. Now, even if chess is a
finite game, it still involves an astounding, astronomical number of
possibilities and combinations (or, in more straightforward terms,
possible moves and the positions that result from these moves). So,
a player is often betting that his or her opponent will not be able to
sort out this problem in the time allowed—and, even in a café or
correspondence game, in chess, as in life, we do not have all the
time in the world. However, in chess, a player also has to wonder
what his or her opponent is "up to," and the question is whether, at
whatever counts as the far reaches of calculation for any two players in a particular game, the bet is on an absolutely clear line toward
a win (or the desired outcome, which in some cases may be a draw)
or, instead, on a line that will lead the opponent into insurmount-
able complications and confusions. Is there some way in which the
opponent can be absolutely sure of the difference, in a given move,
between "pure calculation" and something like wiliness?

Third, this process of betting, if it means anything for the opponent who is presented with a problem, is also a process in the mind
of the player who makes the move. In other words, can there not

be moves where even the player who makes them cannot be absolutely sure of the difference between "pure calculation" and wiliness? The bet the player makes against the opponent is also a bet the player makes with him- or herself, and not only because even the player who is the most brilliant at calculation still has calculating ability that is short of infinite, but because the player has to attempt to put the game into a kind of psychological space where not everything is determined by calculating ability. (This need for the "wily" strategy applies only in cases where the players are of roughly the same ability.) In making this attempt, the player has to enter that space as well, where not everything is determined. To return to the earlier terms of the discussion, and to be, I hope, a bit more clear about what is occurring in this psychological space, the player hopes to give his or her opponent cause to reflect over the meaning of a particular move. Certainly the cause for this reflection can be what appears to be, and may very well be, a deep calculation. But another cause for reflection may be the point where it is unclear whether the move is the result of a deep calculation (which, however, may also be a mistaken calculation) or something like an attempt to mess with the opponent's mind. To attempt to cause the opponent to enter this particular psychological space of underdetermination, however, the player has to enter this space him- or herself.

Perhaps this sort of bet is especially likely to happen because of the nonlinear or non-"smooth" aspects of the aforementioned spectrum. Ordinarily, I may not be able to beat a certain opponent, but if I play in a certain way that I know will mess with his mind, perhaps I can win. "Messing with someone's mind" in this context may mean something like disturbing the ability to calculate, but it is not simply the same thing as a deeper calculation. It is more like a disturbance of the rational through the introduction of something that seems irrational—and then the point is that it is not the introduction of this seeming irrationality that is itself irrational (because this introduction occurs in the attempt to achieve something rational, namely a win in the game), but instead in what this introduction does to the calculative process.

In Gadamer's example, this moment—though the term has to be problematized, because there is a question of irreducible temporality here—is assimilated, in the end, to a larger rationality. Even without getting into the problem of temporality, the idea is that what appears to be incalculable "in itself" can always be folded into a larger calculation. Thus we need not have a Pythagorean fear of "irrational" numbers. However, I don't think that Gadamer had in mind (at least in his example) the way that a chess player might toss an "irrational number" into the mix as a factor that has force and significance as much psychological as calculative—and that, for this to really work (which does mean, yes, as part of a larger strategy that aims to win and that is therefore rational in that sense), this "number" (this move) has to be "irrational" for the player who makes the move as well. The positing of an infinite (or, very, very large—big enough) terrain does not cancel a puddle of irrationality; the positing of a potentially infinite sequence does not make the square root of negative one anything other than what it is. Then again, what *is* this "number," this "i"? Perhaps, taking a cue from this "i," there is a distinction to be made between those numbers that are grasped by reason (perhaps even products of reason, or of some universal Reason) and those that are only grasped—and in this case more likely to be inventions—by the imagination. In theodicy, however, the finite is bound by (and invented by) the infinite—everything makes sense by and by, because there are no time constraints, and, besides (here is our chess composer again), everything was set up to make sense in the first place, though of course it is this "setting up" that itself confers sense. But this is again the case where saying "everything happens for a reason" is no different from saying "everything happens for no reason."

Be that as it may, the more difficult problem would be to show that there can be a moment of underdetermination in chess that would stand as such even to God (whether this be the god of classical theology or to "a god" who can handle sufficiently large calculations—there are some interesting reflections on these gods in terms of chess, infinity, and computer science in Donald E. Knuth, *Things a Computer Scientist Rarely Talks About* [2001]), the "omniscient interpreter," among other things; this is perhaps what would have to be shown in order to prove that Gadamer is wrong in his chess example. There are at least two modes of argumentation that apply to this issue. One of these has to do with the fact/value distinction, and how this distinction might appear even to God. Is there, in the determination of the beautiful or the good, a moment where reason, especially in the form of calculation, has to leave off? "Determination" cannot ultimately be the right term here, because the point is that it is in the nature of the good and the beautiful that, if they are simply the results of calculations, then they are not what they are.[11] To narrow the field to the aesthetic, perhaps this means that there is no beauty in mathematical calculation, at least from the standpoint of the infinite calculator. If, however, there is beauty in chess to the finite participants in the game, then, does not even the infinite calculator have to recognize the role that beauty plays in the mind of the finite calculator in order to make a place for the finite within the infinite?

This goes to the other mode of argumentation, namely that, if God does not comprehend what is underdetermined for the players of chess, then God does not comprehend the players themselves, and therefore God does not comprehend chess. Therefore, the infinite calculator must allow a space or moment for the underdetermined, *even if* this moment must in some sense "stand alongside" the infinite calculator's ability to trace the mathematical connection between any given move and the outcome of the game. *Therefore*, it is the frisson generated by this "standing alongside" that is the true moment of "absurdity" in the game; the frission is generated precisely because the form of this "standing alongside" cannot be precisely specified.

Surely a thing is not strange or undecidable or underdetermined or absurd or out of place or incalculable simply because it is one or more of these things *to me*. The notion of incalculability cannot depend on my or anyone else's inabilities with calculation, though the notion may depend on the necessary limitations of finite minds, especially finite minds that are inextricably connected to (or "based in," or even identical with—this is not a question that need worry us here) necessarily finite, material, bodily organs. One thing that it is crucial to understand is that we can imagine a case where bets are made and have to be made, even if these bets are "based in" calculation "up to a point"—and even if very few of us are capable of following these calculations.

I am often mindful of a very instructive (to me, at any rate) scene in the film *Searching for Bobby Fischer*. The Bruce Pandolfini character has come to see the Fred Waitzkin character in the latter's office, to ask about young chess prodigy Josh Waitzkin. There has been a period of estrangement between Bruce and Josh. Bruce asks Fred how Josh is doing, and Fred avers that Josh is playing chess "better than ever." Bruce responds, "How would you know?" Fred has to admit that, in fact, he does not know. I think about that scene a lot. Sometimes, when I am playing my café games with my friends, I or my partner (opponent) will say, "this is a really interesting position." Well, we are not advanced chess players, so we might as well say, "this is a really interesting position to us"—a passing Grandmaster might see the position and quite understandably laugh at it as a representation of chess ineptitude. The passing Grandmaster might even find the position absurd. Compared to me and my chess buddies, the Grandmaster is a great deal closer to the ideal of "perfect calculation" (and among the perfections is completeness). Indeed, we might ask if there are degrees of magnitude of finite differences between chess players, say two- or three-hundred Elo points, or, certainly the difference between someone such as myself, an avid player but who is, in terms of ratings, no more than an advanced beginner (or lower-tier intermediate player perhaps) and, say, a Grandmaster, that render the game not really a game after all. And yet—here is my point—even from the standpoint of "perfect calculation" there is not *absolute knowledge* of the difference between a sacrifice and a blunder. The difference will always depend on what the other player thinks and is willing to bet on, and therefore even the perfect calculator has to make a bet on the other player (and this moment of underdetermination is not overcome even if the perfect calculator is God and has the ability to read the mind of the other player). In other words, this difference and the knowledge of it has a certain structure, and this structure has to do with more than human (or even calculating machine) finitude.

The real Fred Waitzkin wrote not only *Searching for Bobby Fischer*, a book I like very much, but also a very interesting biography of Garry Kasparov, with the significant—especially for my purposes here—title *Mortal Games* (1993). Now, if I were to say, reprising the Fred Waitzkin character in the film, that Garry Kasparov's calculating ability probably exceeds that of any other chess player in history, a Pandolfini character could rightly ask me how I could even imagine that I know what I am talking about. But I will simply take this on authority that Kasparov has extraordinary calculating ability—that seems a safe enough assumption! Given this, one of the most interesting parts of Waitzkin's biography is his depiction of the pressroom during the 1990 world championship match between Kasparov and the former world champion Anatoly Karpov. For instance, in his description of game nineteen, Waitzkin writes:

> By the twenty-ninth move of the game, the position had reached a condition of stasis. Neither player was doing much and either might

have offered a draw. But on the following move, Kasparov sacrificed a pawn in order to gain a strong queenside square for his knight. "This is a typical Kasparov decision," commented Maurice Ashley. "He sacked material for dynamic play. Maybe at this point in the game Kasparov knew that the right match strategy was to draw, but he is not the kind of player that can easily do this. He was wavering between planning to draw and craving to win."

This pawn sacrifice caused havoc in the pressroom. International master Jonathan Tisdall called it a blunder and predicted that Kasparov would lose. But after a few more moves, Tisdall and virtually everyone else had changed their minds. With Kasparov's rook deep into Karpov's queenside, and his queen controlling a key file, the world champion now appeared to be winning. "Kasparov's sacrifices are often more difficult to assess than the sacrifices of other grandmasters," observed Ashley. "He sees more deeply through the jungle of ideas, and therefore the compensation he gets is not as obvious, because it comes further down the road. When he sacrifices material, it appears that his opponent has many viable responses, but then when you analyze closely, you see that most of these are complete losers. In the pressroom, we watch his games and are inclined to say, look, Kasparov sacrificed a pawn, and he has nothing tangible in return, he has no attack, and there are weaknesses in his position, he must be losing. Then four or five moves later, with Kasparov's rook penetrating Karpov's position and another rook poised to deliver the death blow, we can finally see the value of the sacrifice" (1993, 220–21).

The analysis of Kasparov's games over the years is filled with such "live" episodes. At least in the "live" situation, this is what the notations "?!" and "!?" are made for. What Maurice Ashley (at that time an IM, now a GM) is saying, however, is that the undecidability indicated by these notations is resolved upon further analysis. What I want to dispute is whether this undecidability is *always completely* resolved.[12]

The resolution of the undecidability, between blunder and sacrifice, depends in Ashley's analysis, as with Gadamer's, on the outcome of the game. If the game is won, then the move must have been a sacrifice, a well-calculated one; if the game is lost, the move must have been a blunder. Notice how such an analysis is a kind of "structuralism" that presumes to avoid the subjective element—and not only the subjective element, but, what is even deeper, the *inter*subjective element. For instance, a player may indeed make a blunder—and the player may realize this upon making the move. However, if in wondering what the player is up to, the opponent assumes that the player has made a sacrifice, and the opponent responds as such, the player may be able to turn the blunder into a sacrifice. (One could easily imagine this happening in a game with Kasparov, where the opponent is not likely to expect Kasparov to make an outright blunder.) It seems to me that this intersubjective element is irreducible, and the interesting question would be to see if this is the case even when calculating machines are playing each other. Even in this case, apart from the difficult question of whether the machines are actually "playing chess" to begin with, the machines are programmed with certain expectations about what appears to be a sacrifice and what appears to be a blunder. Indeed, in the computer matches against Kasparov, the machines are programmed with Kasparov's games, and therefore are programmed with expectations regarding sacrifices and blunders as played by Kasparov. The secret to beating the machine, then, is in subverting these expectations, and so the point is the same: there is something going on here that is beyond calculation, beyond the solution down to the last piece.

Another way to put this is, could there not be "correct" moves, even brilliant moves (in the chess definition of brilliancy—which, significantly, the *Oxford Companion to Chess* connects to the idea of the "beautiful combination"; that still do not win the game? (See Hooper and Whyld 1992, 59). Could there not be blunders (even Grandmasters, for example, occasionally miss the chance to checkmate) that still do not result in a loss? Of course it is overwhelmingly often the case that we can draw a line from the brilliant move to the win, or from the blunder to the loss—indeed, the players themselves draw these lines in making the subsequent moves. But I would hope that the foregoing discussion has lent credence to the idea that there are chess moves that retain their undecidable character, and therefore there are chess games where there is no absolute destiny at work, and where the outcome remains underdetermined.

In the Jewish and Christian traditions, theodicy takes the form of a narrative or unfolding toward a redemptive end. The things that happen in the world along the way to this end are justified in the end by the victory of the good. The story or unfolding works toward and in accord with this "higher purpose," and nothing is left out of the account. Indeed, each character in the story, as with each chess piece in the definitive solution, is taken into account and called to account in the end. At least retroactively, a meaning is conferred upon the life and actions of each character in the story, and, again, there are no remainders or, to use another language, "innocent bystanders." For the creator of the story, the formulator of the cosmic plan, there is no "retroactive" conferral of meaning, because the plan has been there since "before the foundation of the world," and the cosmic planner is eternal, all-knowing, and all-powerful. My argument with the Gadamer passage has been that, certainly, in the case of the chess composition, there is a direct analogy with this kind of theodicy (which is sometimes called the "final harmony" argument in response to the problem of evil—"everything works out in the end"), but that this sort of theodicy only works if the chess problem is "front-loaded," so that of course the solution that comes out is the one that is set up in the first place. I argue, however, that this example is not that of a real chess game, and that, in a real game and the positions and problems that are found within it, this logic of an account without remainder is not as certain or airtight.

Theodicy of the cosmic, redemptive plan variety, when understood as originating in a god who possesses the classical "omnis"—omnipotence, omniscience, omnibenevolence—would seem to issue in determinism, and theologians and philosophers have grappled with this problem for many centuries. In Leibniz's famous scenario, God looks out upon something like what Wittgenstein in the *Tractatus* called "logical space" (I mention this in part because, though Wittgenstein's chess examples come after the *Tractatus*, the chess set would seem to present an excellent example of logical space), and, because God is omnibenevolent, he brings about the best of all possible worlds. One of the ingredients of this best of all possible worlds is freedom of the will, and it is this human free will that is the cause of at least some of the evil in the world. That which goes against the good is itself the result of a calculation for the sake of the greatest possible good. Significantly, perhaps the guiding vision of Leibniz's intellectual career was the development of a universal calculating machine. As mathematician/computer scientist Martin Davis explains,

> Leibniz had a vision of amazing scope and grandeur. The notation he had developed for the differential and integral calculus, the notation still used today, made it easy to do complicated calculations with little thought. It was as though the notation did the work. In Leibniz's vision, something similar could be done for the whole scope of human

knowledge. He dreamt of an encyclopedic compilation, of a universal artificial mathematical language in which each facet of knowledge could be expressed, of calculational rules which would reveal all the logical interrelationships among these propositions. Finally, he dreamed of machines capable of carrying out calculations, freeing the mind for creative thought. (Davis 2000, 4)

Clearly there is much to meditate upon here, but for my present purposes I want to focus on two questions. First, there is the question that we have already pursued at length, that of whether chess is exhausted by calculation. We see "Leibniz's dream," as Davis puts it, coming to fruition in our time, in terms of computers that seem close to the moment when chess is completely exhausted by calculation because it has been, as a totality, "solved." Second, and relatedly, the idea that creative thought occurs once the mind is freed from calculative thought is fascinating. This freedom has to come in a certain way; namely, not through the setting aside of calculation, but instead through making sure that the necessary calculative work of human life is taken care of by a machine that does this work for us.

There is much in this vision that is insightful, and we might especially wonder where calculation leaves off and creativity begins, or if the line can always be drawn in a sharp or completely determined way—indeed, this is what I have been asking in my discussion of the chess example from Gadamer (or was this a creative extrapolation from Gadamer by David Solway?). With a slightly different twist, this is my question now, in the context of theodicy. For, if everything *about* the cosmos is itself the result of a divine, omnipotent calculation, what room is there *in* the cosmos for creativity? Again, this is an old problem, where the omnipotent creativity of God seems to rule out any *real*—as opposed to apparent, from a finite perspective—human creativity. Leibniz's solution to this problem of determinism is not so different from Augustine's, though perhaps understood more in terms of a complex calculation: the idea that what appears contradictory from a finite perspective would be resolved from the standpoint of infinity. This might be Gadamer's solution, too, except that he is not *directly* concerned, in the chess example that we have, with the problem of determinism. Gadamer is concerned, however, with the problem of meaning, and the problem of meaning is certainly, and deeply, connected to the questions of freedom, responsibility, and determinism (or, to use slightly different language, underdetermination and overdetermination). To use language from William James, what is the *point*, what is the meaning, of this human existence, if this life is not a "real fight"? But how can life be a real fight if the outcome is already known by an omnipotent God? In other words, how could life be a real fight if we finite, mortal humans have no fighting chance to make things other than they are always already known to be by an omnipotent God? God's "omnis" appear to be in contradiction to human freedom, and thus we are stuck in a determinism. This has been called, in the philosophy of religion, the problem of "compatibilism" (that is, how is God's omnipotence and foreknowledge compatible with freedom of the will by finite creatures?); James attempts to show, by use of a chess example, how this compatibility is possible.

In conclusion, let us return to the very idea of the "chess argument." Good, critical arguments in philosophy sometimes succeed through "failure"; these arguments may not show what they intend to show, but they get the critical juices flowing, and, upon reflection, we get somewhere with the argument, just not exactly to the place the author intended. The chess arguments from Gadamer are of this sort, I think. However, these arguments, in not exactly succeeding, lead us into at least three concerns.

The first of these is that, whatever else he is doing (given the slippery "source" of the passage, I can only infer the larger purpose), it appears that he got the chess part wrong. It isn't that he mischaracterizes chess composition, but that instead he chooses the wrong chess example (or "situation") to presumably say something of substance about the "strange" or absurd. In the case of philosophers who make use of chess, it would be useful to know their actual involvement with chess.

The second concern springs from asking, therefore, what difference it makes if a chess example is used as the pivot of an argument, but the chess example is not set up correctly. Stated more directly, what is chess such that it can be part of a philosophical argument? Can chess be such a central part of an argument that, if the "chess part" actually goes to some other conclusion than is presumed, then the whole argument has to go the other way, too?

Third and finally, the question, What is chess such that it could be a part of a philosophical argument? must necessarily lead to the larger question, What *is* chess? Analogies can be made to chess in a philosophical argument, just as analogies could be made to many things, from basketball, tennis, the health of the human body and the "body politic," or what have you. But chess seems in some ways different from and "bigger" than some other things or subjects that are useful in making analogies. Chess is good not only for supplying the content of an analogy, but it is also good, at least in some cases, for modeling the form of an argument, and clearly this is because there is a logic in and of chess. Furthermore, chess may a useful model for philosophical arguments because there are elements in chess, at least when it is played by two mortal, finite, biologically based beings (but perhaps even when it is played by computers or the infinite mind, though the latter, in my view, is a notion that cannot be made to make sense), that exceed logic or that at least are different from logic. In this respect, in its logical and psychological complexity, chess is a powerful microcosm of human life, something on a quite other level than the way that the two-person prisoner's dilemma is used as the basic model of "rationality" in game theory in the social sciences. (The veritable "bible" on this subject, *Game Theory in the Social Sciences* by Martin Shubik, contains some interesting comments on this subject; see esp. pp. 232, 299, 412.) And yet even these characterizations do not capture the full appeal of chess, for chess is not only microcosm, it is, like the work of art, a *cosm*, a world of its own where creativity and craft can give rise to not only beauty, but, some would maintain, the sublime.

NOTES

1. I later discovered that the quote comes from *Philosophical Hermeneutics* (Gadamer 1976, 32).

2. There are numerous accounts of the hoax; see, for example, Yanovsky 2000.

3. On the possible KGB connection, see Genna Sosonko's unfriendly and unflattering obituary for Gufeld (2003).

4. My source for this admittedly quick and superficial investigation is the *American Heritage College Dictionary*, 3rd ed.

5. Taking on this Davidsonian language, and making the problems of language and meaning central to his work, is Rorty's way of working around what had hitherto been the central concept in pragmatism—namely, *experience*. This avoidance and eschewal of the concept of experience places Rorty in an ambiguous relationship to the tradition of American pragmatism, to say the least. Meanwhile, it would have been

interesting, I think, if Davidson had taken up chess as a test case for his notion of triangulation.

6. We might make an interesting comparison between the chess composer and the musical composer around what is perhaps the most important piece of music that was originally written as a set of student exercises, J. S. Bach's *Six Suites for Violincello Solo*.

7. The foregoing represents a gloss on ideas that are much more difficult, complex, and subtle than can be explored here, and it seems silly to give as a "reference" a work as massive as Gadamer's *Truth and Method*, where the notion of "fusion of horizons" is developed. Davidson develops the themes I mentioned in a number of essays, but of course the essential reference for these themes is the well-known essay, "On the Very Idea of a Conceptual Scheme." Significantly, and no doubt unexpectedly for most analytic philosophers, Davidson devoted two essays to Gadamer's work, "Dialectic and Dialogue" and "Gadamer and Plato's *Philebus*"; these can now be found in the fifth volume of Davidson's collected essays, *Truth, Language, and History*.

8. The latter case—"café chess"—has its own complications, such as the difficulty of working out a balance of friendliness and competitiveness in a setting where the stakes are almost entirely bound up with the ego—unfortunately, this is most often the male ego, or where there are not only other things going on at the same time—conversations, other distractions—but where these distractions may be used in the game by one or both players.

9. Again, I am simply glossing on arguments from "On the Very Idea of a Conceptual Scheme" and other essays such as "A Coherence Theory of Truth and Knowledge."

10. Incidentally, one of Charles Hartshorne's arguments for the existence of God runs along similar lines; as Donald Wayne Viney summarizes Hartshorne's "epistemic argument," "[T]he concept of reality is meaningless when divorced from the concept of knowledge or experience. But the only idea of knowledge adequate to clarify the concept of reality is divine knowledge." See Viney 1985, 95, and Hartshorne 1970.

11. Of course, this line of reasoning can also be used to argue that in fact there really are no such things as the good or the beautiful; there is a relationship here to the coincidence of "everything/nothing happens for a reason"—on the infinite stage beyond all finitude, to say that everything is part of a grand scheme, and that this scheme is "good," is no different from saying that the grand scheme is "evil." These issues have a long lineage in Western philosophy, to be sure, going back to Plato's *Euthyphro*, and remaining thoroughly alive in Kant's thinking on reason and judgment.

12. I should add that the part following this passage is fascinating for its own reason, namely the friendly postgame analysis between Kasparov

and Karpov, where these two old enemies had their first civil conversation in many years. As Kasparov told Waitzkin the next day, "No, I haven't changed my mind about Karpov. . . . But you have to realize that he is the only serious opponent for me. I am talking chess with the number two in the world. I wouldn't go to a restaurant with him, but who else can I really talk with about these games? Spassky? Who else can Karpov talk with? Karpov is the man who understands chess at the same level as I do" (Waitzkin 1993, 224).

REFERENCES

Boyd, Gregory A. 2000. *God of the Possible*. Grand Rapids, MI: Baker Books.

Davidson, Donald. 1984. "On the Very Idea of a Conceptual Scheme." In *Inquiries Into Truth and Interpretation*. Oxford: Oxford University Press.

———. 2001. "A Coherence Theory of Truth and Knowledge." In *Subjective, Intersubjective, Objective*. Oxford: Oxford University Press.

———. 2005. *Truth, Language, and History*. Oxford: Oxford University Press.

Davis, Martin. 2000. *Engines of Logic: Mathematicians and the Origins of the Computer*. New York: Norton.

Deleuze, Gilles, and Felix Guattari. 1987. *A Thousand Plateaus*. Translated by Brian Massumi. Minneapolis: University of Minnesota Press.

Dennett, Daniel. 1984. *Elbow Room: The Varieties of Free Will Worth Wanting*. Cambridge: MIT Press.

Derrida, Jacques. 1970. "Structure, Sign, and Play in the Discourse of the Human Sciences." In *The Structuralist Controversy*, edited by Richard Macksey and Eugene Donato. Baltimore: Johns Hopkins University Press.

Gadamer, Hans-Georg. 1976. "On the Scope and Function of Hermeneutic Reflection." In *Philosophical Hermeneutics*, translated and edited by David Linge. Berkeley: University of California Press.

———. 1986. *Truth and Method*. New York: Crossroad.

Gufeld, Eduard. 2001. *Chess: The Search for Mona Lisa*. London: Batsford.

Hartshorne, Charles. 1970. *Creative Synthesis and Philosophic Method*. Chicago: Open Court.

Hooper, David, and Kenneth Whyld. 1992. *The Oxford Companion to Chess*. Oxford: Oxford University Press.

Huizinga, Johan. 1955. *Homo Ludens: A Study of the Play Element in Culture*. Boston: Beacon Press.

James, William. 1956. *The Will to Believe*. New York: Dover.

Knuth, Donald E. 2001. *Things a Computer Scientist Rarely Talks About*. Stanford, CA: CSLI Publications.

Martin, Bill. 2002. *Avant Rock: Experimental Music from the Beatles to Bjork.* Chicago: Open Court.

Nowakowski, Richard J., ed. 1998. *Games of No Chance.* Cambridge: Cambridge University Press.

Schiller, Eric. 1998. *Unorthodox Chess Openings.* New York: Cardoza Publishing.

Shubik, Martin. 1982. *Game Theory in the Social Sciences.* Cambridge, MA: MIT Press.

Solway, David. 1999. *Chess Pieces.* Montreal: McGill-Queen's University Press.

———. 2003. "Recollections of a Pseudo-Philosopher." *Arts & Opinion* 2, no. 2; www.artsandopinions.com.

Sosonko, Genna. 2003. "Death of a Salesman." In *The Reliable Past.* Amsterdam: New In Chess.

Sutton-Smith, Brian. 1997. *The Ambiguity of Play.* Cambridge, MA: Harvard University Press.

Viney, Donald Wayne. 1985. *Charles Hartshorne and the Existence of God.* Albany, NY: State University of New York Press.

Waitzkin, Fred. 1993. *Mortal Games: The Turbulent Genius of Garry Kasparov.* New York: Putnam.

Ware, Bruce A. 2000. *God's Lesser Glory: A Critique of Open Theism.* Leicester, U.K.: Apollos.

Yanofsky, Joel. 2000. "Who is Andreas Karavis?" *Montreal Gazette.* Nov. 20.

7

Who Plays Games in Philosophy?

AHTI-VEIKKO PIETARINEN

Opening

The jingle "the games people play" is without doubt a part of everyone's vernacular. Can we give a reasoned account of the notion "the games *philosophers* play," figuratively speaking? How has the game metaphor been utilized in the recent history of philosophy? What has been achieved by philosophers on the "game" front—a front which reflects both time-honored approaches to practical reasoning, but also the logic and methodology of the contemporary sciences?

The last century was marked by a linguistic turn in philosophy. Because of this, those seeking to understand the expression of natural language sometimes chose to focus on games. That language may be compared with games, and specifically with strategic and rational interactions, is an ancient idea. It may have started as a metaphysical thought in the opposition of *chôra* and *kosmos* in Plato's philosophy, or in the opposition between the feminine and the masculine, the distracted and the ordered, the changing and the permanent.

Aside from cosmological speculations, similar oppositions recur in ideas ranging from Newtonian force to Friedrich Nietzsche's will to power, and from the Cartesian concept of motion to the opposition of action versus passion. Such oppositions have permeated Kant's transcendental philosophy and the Hegelian ego versus non-ego. As a metaphor for argumentation, Aristotle's *Topics* and its later incarnations (such as the scholastic *Ars Obligatoria*) are set up as dialogical duels. Logics exploiting this idea resurface in twentieth-century attempts to clear up the concept of argument and proof. The game metaphor has retained its strength in contemporary theories of computation as well (Pietarinen 2004b; Japaridze 2006). Computation itself has been recast in terms of interaction between the computing system ("myself") and its environment ("nature"). In mathematics, this was noted decades ago by Stanislaw Ulam (1960, 120), who wrote that it was "rather amusing to consider how one can 'gamize' various mathematical situations (or perhaps the verb should be 'paizise' from the Greek word παιçιν, to play)."

As far as language is concerned, dialogic thought recurs throughout the better part of the history of Western philosophy. Space permits only a brief historical overview—from the early modern period on. This chapter seeks to uncover the complex network of thinkers who have given rise to the synergy of games and the philosophy of language.[1] Thoughts on games and language are found in the writings of Charles S. Peirce, Edmund Husserl, Ferdinand de Saussure, Ludwig Wittgenstein, L. E. J. Brouwer, Paul Grice, and Jürgen Habermas. Each has also used chess as an example to make his point. My question for this chapter is this: Is the game metaphor in general, and the chess/language analogy in particular, worthy of serious philosophizing?

C. S. Peirce (1839–1914)

The story begins with the American fin-de-siècle philosopher and scientist Charles S. Peirce:

> Thinking always proceeds in the form of a dialogue,—a dialogue between different phases of the *ego*,—so that, being dialogical, it is essentially composed of signs, as its Matter, in the sense in which a game of chess has the chessmen for its matter. (Peirce 1967, MS 298, 1905)

Peirce expresses here an allegory for thinking, in which thought is always mediated by expression, just as pawns and knights mediate the purposes and intentions of those playing the game of chess.

But who thinks in such ways? Who plays such games? If thought is dialogical, can we identify the components that are supposed to comprise it?

Peirce does not provide a definite answer. He said it was "a sop to Cerberus" to explain the meaning of signs in terms of strategic dialogues that refer to actual persons uttering and interpreting those signs (Peirce 1998, 478; Pietarinen 2005).

This leaves something to be desired from the proposed analogy. What is more, the concept of strategy that is integral to game theories of rational decision was not available to Peirce. In place of a strategy, he used the concept of a *habit* of acting in certain ways in certain kinds of circumstances.

The first mathematical result concerning games was suggested by Zermelo in 1912 on certain finite, strictly competitive two-player games of perfect information, such as chess. He showed that a player can only avoid losing for a finite number of moves (if the opponent plays correctly), if and only if the opponent is able to force a win. The result was published in Zermelo 1913. The modern version of the theorem states that every such game is determined: either player 1 or player 2 has a winning strategy.

The notion of strategy was properly formalized during the 1920s by Borel, von Neumann, and others (see e.g., Borel 1921, Kalmár 1928–29, König 1927, von Neumann 1928). The theory of games was then established in von Neumann and Morgenstern's 1944 locus classicus, *The Theory of Games and Economic Behavior*.

Peirce's motivation for his allegory was to think of the content of thought and reasoning being represented by certain moving and dynamic forms of graphs and diagrams. Such representations may well be similar to what chess players see on the board and what they describe as complex networks of observable forces and processes (Kasparov 1987).

Peirce also admitted to having been deeply impressed by Friedrich Schiller's *Aesthetische Briefe*, a work in which Schiller discusses "World-spirit's *Spiel-trieb*" (*Ger.* "the drive or motivation to play"). Peirce dubbed it "mere amusement" and "the play of musement" but also "play-instinct." He interpreted it to mean "the most energetic part of the cultivation of ideas," and that the name was chosen "because the fine arts exemplify the highest action of this instinct."[2] The creativity of chess seems to lie partly in its being subject to something like the Schillerian *Spiel-trieb*.

Husserl (1859–1938)

Before game theory was born, Edmund Husserl suggested the term *Spielbedeutungen*, or "game-meanings," in vol. 1 of *Logical Investigations* (1900–01).[3] A few years earlier, in 1895, he had noted, "Obviously the meaning now lies in the rules of the game. It is completely like in a game of chess. Bishops, castles, etc." (Husserl 1994, 29). He was referring here to the possibility of defining the meaning of arithmetic in terms of the rules of an axiomatic calculus. Husserl's rules are thus those that define the legitimate moves, not strategic rules. David Hilbert (1862–1943) expressed similar sentiments in his program for axiomatizing the theory of arithmetic.

Husserl's statement resonates with recent theories that conceive of computation as interaction. A striking instance is what French mathematician Jean-Yves Girard has termed *Ludics*. The slogan he coined is this: "The meaning of logical rules is to be found in *the well-hidden geometrical structure of the rules themselves*" (Girard 1998, 1). This clarifies Husserl's idea of meaning being in the rules uncovered as they are applied—earlier meanings beget new meanings. Witness here Wittgenstein's oft-repeated remark, "You can't get behind rules, because there isn't any behind" (Wittgenstein 1978, 244).

Soon after the turn of the century, Husserl's "game-meaning" evolved to describe the use of objects, signs, and expressions in the context of the game:

> The true meaning of the signs in question emerges if we glance at the much favoured comparison of mathematical operations to rule-governed games, e.g. chess. Chessmen are not part of the chess-game as bits of ivory and wood having such and such shapes and colours. Their phenomenal and physical constitution is quite indifferent, and can be varied at will. They become chessmen, counters in the chess-game, through the game's rules which give them their fixed games-meaning. (Husserl 1984, Husserliana XIX/1, I§20)

The game of chess has indeed been a central point of reference in philosophical reflections covering all kinds of contests, plays, and recreations that bear a resemblance to mathematics and logic. What about language?

Saussure (1857–1913)

As a subject of allegory and comparison, chess was not only philosophers' pet metaphor, but was also heavily used by the semioticians of the early twentieth century. Ferdinand de Saussure (1857–1913), a pioneer of structural linguistics, considered chess to be the artificial counterpart of what language provided as a natural process. He was soon accompanied by Louis Hjelmslev, Roman Jakobson, and many others peculiar to the tradition of semasiology.

Saussure went on to offer some close comparisons between language and chess, such as their dynamics, their conventionality of rules, and their positionality (Saussure 1916/1983). The difference that he suggested lies in deliberation: while in chess the player intends various moves, in language moves are spontaneous and fortuitous. Unfortunately, the comparison does not seem to hold water: if we interpret the difference as that between what is strategic and what is nonstrategic, the difference that Saussure advocates ends up erasing practically all he wanted to be chesslike in language.

Wittgenstein (1889–1951)

But the chess allegory resurfaces. Wittgenstein penned the following paragraphs after Husserl and Saussure:

> Again a case where you can learn that the word has meaning by the particular use we make of it. We are like people who think that pieces of wood shaped more or less like chessmen or draughtstones standing on a chessboard constitute a game even if nothing has been said as to how they are to be used (Wittgenstein, 2000–, item 147:39v, *Grosses Notizbuch*).

> I want to play chess, and a man gives the white king a paper crown, leaving the use of the piece unaltered, but telling me that the crown has a meaning to him in the game, which he can't express by rules. I say: "as long as it doesn't alter the use of the piece, it hasn't what I call a meaning" (Wittgenstein 2000–, 309:19, *Blaues Buch*).

> If you show someone the king in a chess game and say, "This is the king of chess", you do not thereby explain to him the use of this piece, — unless he already knows the rules of the game except for this last point: the shape of the king piece. We can imagine that he has learned the rules of the game without ever having been shown a real chessman. (Wittgenstein 2000–, 226:20).

Wittgenstein agrees with Husserl: using language begets meaning.
Yet Wittgenstein seems to have fared better and in fact vindicated
Peirce's original vision. The first pages of Wittgenstein's
Philosophical Investigations (1953) introduce the idea of a language
game in order to show that the words of a text, or even a complete
primitive language, derive their meaning from the role that they
have in certain nonlinguistic activities. These activities are what he
calls "games."[4] For Wittgenstein, the foundational purpose of
games is not something that can be found in logic or language but
is external to them. He considers games conceptually prior to symbolic codes. They are the activities and practices from which logic
and language derived their meaning. "For what we call the meaning of the word lies in the game we play with it," he writes in the
thirties (Wittgenstein 2000–, 149: 18).[5] In a similar vein he states: "In
which case do we say that a sentence has [a] point? That comes
[close] to asking in which case do we call something a language
game. I can only answer. Look at the family of language games that
will show you whatever can be shown about the matter"
(Wittgenstein 2000–, 148:36v).

The purpose of players in Wittgenstein's language games may
be accounted for in terms of the activities of "showing or telling
what one sees" (Pietarinen 2004b). What the players try to achieve
is to bring to the fore what they see to be the case in the context
of an assertion: "It is true that the game of 'showing or telling what
one sees' is one of the most fundamental language games, which
means that what we in ordinary life call using language mostly pre-
supposes this game" (Wittgenstein 2000–, 149:1).

To show or to say that something is the case is to communicate
those findings. In some cases that might involve the naming of
objects, but that would not be the whole story. To name something
is not yet effectual. It does not, Wittgenstein remarks, constitute a
genuine move in a language game:

> Within naming something we haven't yet made a move in the lan-
> guage game,—any more that [sic] you have made a move in chess by
> putting a piece on the board. We may say: by giving a thing a name
> *nothing* [has] yet been done. It *hasn't* a name,—except in the game.
> This is what Frege meant by saying that a word has meaning only in
> its connection with [the context of] a sentence. (Wittgenstein 2000–,
> 226:36)

Seeing and telling what is the case and naming something are not on the same dimension at all. It might suffice to give something a name, and to rest content with that, but that does not reveal anything about the meaning of expressions. Thus language games have to be actively played for a meaning to emerge.

Curiously, thinking of games as theories is not foreign to Wittgenstein: "The theory of the game is not arbitrary, although the game is" (Wittgenstein 2000–, 161:15r). But he did not show any particular interest in advancing the theory. Nothing indicates that he was aware of the works of von Neumann, Borel, or others making seminal contributions in the 1920s. But this is not the end of the story. There is an isolated reference to economic theorizing in his *Nachlass*. It is analogous to the question of what an appropriate description of a narrowly restricted field of application could be, given a system of communication consisting only of words and commands—a narrowly restricted field in describing what a language could be:

> Augustine describes, we might say, a system of communication; not everything, however, that we call language is this system. (And this one must say in so many cases when the question arises: "is this an appropriate description or not?" The answer is, "Yes, it is appropriate; but only for this narrowly restricted field, not everything that you professed to describe by it." Think of the theories of economists.)

This paragraph, which came to be modified and of which the material in parentheses was omitted from the published version of *Investigations*, is immediately followed by: "It is as though someone explained: 'Playing a game consists in moving things about on a surface according to certain rules. . .', and we answered him: You seem to be thinking of games on a board; but these aren't all the games there are. You can put your description right by confining it explicitly to those games" (Wittgenstein 2000–, 226:2).

By the late 1930s, the impact of game theory on economics was not yet fully acknowledged. Even the future developers of this approach were skeptical about such applicability. John von Neumann, in a letter to Abraham Flexner (25 May 1934), confessed: "I have the impression that [economics] is not yet ripe . . . not yet fully enough understood . . . to be reduced to a small number of fundamental postulates—like geometry or physics" (quoted in Leonard

1995, 730). The influence took time, and happened, to a consider-able degree, via Oskar Morgenstern's attention, the coauthor of *The Theory of Games and Economic Behavior*. Wittgenstein's remark above is an indication of his awareness of the possibility of applying games to economic theorizing. He may have omitted the reference to economics from the published version of part 1 of *Investigations*, completed in 1945, because of the improved state of affairs.

Be this as it may, Wittgenstein's remarks in his *Nachlass* bear an interesting relationship to Peirce's concept of the interpretant as a sign of another sign. The affinity between the two thinkers is much more than skin deep. Language games are another way of under-standing Peirce's views on meaning as a dialogue between the utterer and the interpreter. Wittgenstein believed that what is alive in the sentence is what is meant by the thought that is expressed by it (Wittgenstein 1970, 143). For Peirce, this liveliness is the dia-logical relation between successions of signs and their interpre-tants, grounded in the mutually common understanding of what it is to be a sign-carrier, interspersed with rudiments of the grammar and action of language. In the same paragraph of *Zettel* (¶ 143), Wittgenstein asks what a comparable meaning of a configuration of chess pieces on the game board would be, suggesting that it would be something to be found not only in the rules, but also in the experiences that are associated with game positions, and in a com-mon understanding between the players about the usefulness of such a game for some meaningful purpose.

What all this suggests is that Wittgenstein was aware of the eco-nomics-focused atmosphere in 1930s Vienna, was well connected with, although ambivalent about, the philosophical ideas of the Vienna Circle, and took the game idea from his associations with that environment.[6] Essential in Wittgenstein is the idea of language as a rule-governed system or process with variable meaning rela-tions. For him, the language game "is an extension of primitive behaviour. (For our *language-game* is behaviour.) (Instinct)" (Wittgenstein 1970, 545).

Grice (1913–1986)

Game-theoretic approaches to theories of language and communi-cation have recently enjoyed some success. H. Paul Grice's prag-matics (1989) has been devised to provide normative theories of communication that would follow from the postulates of rationality and cooperation. Most attention has been on Grice's maxims of conversation—especially on the maxim of relation in theories of relevance (Sperber and Wilson 1995; Pietarinen 2004a), which he took to be imminent outcomes of these postulates. Much less has been said on the overall ethical project to elicit different maxims from the assumption that dialogue partners are rational and aim to increase the *summum bonum*—the "ultimate good" as scholastics had it—by one kind of cooperative practice or another.

Implementations of the Gricean project suffer from similar difficulties as the overall theory of games. It is not obvious that agents trying to maximize expected utilities in fact increase the potentiality of the *summum bonum*; nor is it clear that language users invariably act according to rational principles. Nevertheless, this does not constitute an argument against using game theory in theories of communication and conversation—or in the "logic of conversation," as Grice calls his project. Rather, what we are given is a preliminary argument to the effect that there is something intrinsically congenial in theories of communication and theories of games.

Some have attempted to spell out this congeniality. For instance, Hintikka (1986) argued that Grice's program ought to be operationalized by assigning payoffs to communicative strategies, not to individual moves that interlocutors make. Only when communication terminates do we have enough evidence and reason to assess the value of the path taken by the speaker or the hearer through a multiplicity of possible conversational situations. Grice's approach is diachronic, while Saussure's synchronic version might be closer to the chess analogy because of its greater positionality.

A further argument in favor of strategic and dialogical outlook on communication is that language use and understanding is reciprocal, and the responsibilities equally and mutually distributed between the speaker and the hearer. Originally, Grice's maxims pertained only to utterances. Even today, the theory of relevance, advocating strategic reasoning in terms of maximization of linguistic information and minimization of the cognitive processing effort required in gleaning relevant information, is one-sided in ignoring that the interpreter may well get to decide what he or she interprets as relevant in the utterance.

Even if attempts to join game-theoretic assets with pragmatic elements of language use were to have their basis in theories of conversation, and even if Grice's cooperative principle were the main principle preserved in conversation, I believe that it is not exactly right to simply equate it with cooperation in the game-the-oretical sense. Grice's technical definition of cooperation (according to which the speaker's contribution ought to be such that is required by the accepted purpose of the exchange) is speaker oriented and says little about the actual and quite complex process of interpretation. In game theory, on the other hand (according to which players' roles are, in normal cases, symmetric in the sense that no one player cooperates less than the others), Grice's definition does not lead to interactive cooperation. And since chess is strictly competitive, it may not be the right analogy for communication or discourse analysis.

In fact, cooperation in the game-theoretic sense is indeed different from cooperation in the sense in which Grice defined it. Cooperative approaches in economics do not attempt to model how agents communicate with each other, because agents are assumed to endorse joint action, and any communication is relegated to preplay situations. Such games are typically "coalitional." From Grice's perspective, agents increase the "idea-potential" of subsets of linguistic communities, not humankind at large.

*   *   *   *   *

At this point we are ready for an intermediate conclusion. Language as a form of life is the common ground of language users. It is a way of experiencing and a way of enjoying common experiences that everyone has and is mutually known and agreed to have by others. This also fits with the previous comment on one of Wittgenstein's most important language games—namely, the game of showing and saying what one sees. What Wittgenstein took "using language" in "ordinary life" to presuppose was exactly these kinds of games (Wittgenstein 2000–, 141:1). Language games are there as roles in our ordinary life. We do not call "using language" a game at all if it is not hooked up with what experiences in human life have been able to provide.

Brouwer (1881–1966)

Grice's program was in line with what the Dutch "significians" were after ever since the late nineteenth century (Pietarinen 2006a). Their goal was to analyze language in terms of its stratification according to function and purpose, spelled out in the ever-increasing connections, conventions, and interrelationships between expressions. The beginning is a primordial state of language, and the most sophisticated level is a scientific, symbolic, and logical layer, arrived at through several intermediate steps.

The term "primordial" is in fact from the Dutch mathematician Luitzen Egbertus Jan Brouwer,[7] who was a central "significist" thinker alongside names such as Victoria Welby, Gerrit Mannoury, and Frederik van Eeden. Of the people previously discussed, Brouwer had met Husserl in Amsterdam and Wittgenstein in Vienna in spring 1928. Brouwer's philosophizing had an effect not only on Wittgenstein's return to philosophy but also on the logicians Evert W. Beth and Paul Lorenzen, who strove to make his intuitionistic thought understood by recourse to games. An understanding was badly needed, because Brouwer had earlier criticized Hilbert in degenerating mathematics into a "meaningless game." Brouwer's comments have to be taken with a grain of salt, however, because at that time, Hilbert was striving to differentiate the interpretation of nonlogical symbols—an extraneous consideration by his own words—from the manipulation of inference relations between formulas. His project was thus actually closer in spirit to the semioticians and significians that symbolic logicians.[8]

Another grain of salt is needed to understand Brouwer's comment on a "meaningless game." For him, games were all-pervasive in mathematics and human communication alike. But they are preceded by "a phenomenon of *play,* occurring when conative activity or causal thinking or acting is performed *playfully,* i.e. without inducement of either desire or apprehension or vocation or inspiration or compulsion" (Brouwer 1949, 1236). Similar playful, cooperative attitude looms large in Schiller's *Spiel-trieb* as well as Peirce's rendering of it as the "Play of Musement."

Thus, in Brouwer's view, there were two kinds of activities: those of games proper that serve calculations and nonsocial instruction in mathematics, and those of "recreations" embedded in linguistic practices and constructions of meaning. The former lack the purpose and life-value of the latter, are more contextual, and involve activity aimed at understanding on all levels of language.

One of the intermediate manifestations between Brouwer's primordial and symbolic strata of language is language as the communicative system of interaction. This point may itself seem obvious to us, but it is remarkable in virtue of coming close to the later dialogic analysis of communicative intentions.

Habermas

Jürgen Habermas (1929–) has sought to drive a wedge between what is communicative and what is strategic in linguistic action. He considers these two modifiers fundamentally different in his own account of communicative practices, and suggests that a similar division ought to apply to Peirce's theory (Habermas 1995). His motivation in drawing this division is not to show that the attitudes of the participants may differ in the two settings—the communicative and the strategic—but because he sees some transparent structural differences in them. In communication, the structure of how language is used is "superimposed" on goal-driven action (Habermas 1998, 205). Communication is replete, Habermas thinks, with notions such as presuppositions, performatives, and other less objective constraints than strategic action. Its essence lies in the idea of interaction, but in Habermas's view, not in interaction that incorporates strategic considerations. On the contrary, he maintains, strategic action is parasitic on communicative interaction.

But is it not misguided to try to draw these distinctions in terms of what is strategic and what is nonstrategic? We know that strategic action may be performed cooperatively or noncooperatively. Notwithstanding the performative contradictions that Habermas thinks ensue from manipulating the listener to give an answer that the speaker desires, communication may well be strategic for the sheer task of understanding and interpreting utterances.[9] We may well play variable-sum games in which the outcomes assigned to total strategies mark the varying degrees of understanding. What Habermas seeks to explain is that, if the crux of the strategic interaction falls within the principle of utility maximization and hence self-interest, then it is incompatible with reciprocal understanding. However, the principle of utility maximization, as operationalized in game theory in terms of strategies (or "plans of action"), well satisfies Habermas's desiderata of reaching understanding and agreement, having coordination, and having cooperation. One just needs to shift the focus to cooperation, negotiation, bargaining, variable sums, and so on. This does not diminish the scope of communication in the least; on the contrary, one inherits more precise tools and methods for tackling the structure of communication and discourse.

The goal of Habermas seems rather to be a reconstruction of the meaning of linguistic competence and awareness of its rules. He assumes that language has an inbuilt notion of validity of which assertions make use. The force that linguistic acts of meaning something (such as "illocutionary" acts) have is based on the assumption that such assertions can be checked for validity. This is similar to Peirce's view of assertions as acts by which utterers accept responsibility for their truth. Moreover, obliging acts convince the hearers. Habermas expresses this as follows:

> With their illocutionary acts, speaker and hearer raise validity claims and demand that they be recognized. But this recognition need not follow irrationally, since the validity claims have a cognitive character and can be tested. I would like, therefore, to defend the following thesis: *In the final analysis, the speaker can illocutionarily influence the hearer, and vice versa, because speech act-typical obligations are connected with cognitively testable validity claims*—that is, because the reciprocal binding and bonding relationship has a rational basis. The speaker who commits herself normally connects the specific sense in which she would like to take up an interpersonal relationship with a thematically stressed validity claim and thereby chooses a specific mode of communication. (Habermas 2001, 85)

The term "formal" is to be taken in the sense of "rational reconstruction." But this does not pardon Habermas for confounding the cooperative and the strategic. Had his investigation moved on a more detailed level of rational reconstruction, the mix-up would have been exposed earlier.

To put the point in simple terms, what Habermas is after is communicative action that aims at reaching understanding, whereas strategic action exerts influence on others. But the former is not devoid of purpose. In explaining what people do, we need goal-driven action structures in both. This has been recognized ever since the early phases of the formation of the theory of games:

> Even if the theory of noncooperative games were in a completely satisfactory state, there appear to be difficulties in connection with the reduction of cooperative games to noncooperative games. It is extremely difficult in practice to introduce into the cooperative games the moves corresponding to negotiations in a way which will reflect all the infinite variety permissible in the cooperative game, and to do this without giving one player an artificial advantage (because of his having the first chance to make an offer, let us say). (McKinsey 1954, 359)

The infinite variety permissible in cooperative games is precisely the kind of problem we encounter in studies of formal pragmatics, which deals not only with conventions but also with interpretations of context and environment. It is difficult to reduce all these to some formal framework of contingent but observable behavior. Even more candidly, Shubik reiterated this point thirty years later, suggesting that

> in much of actual bargaining and negotiation, communication about contingent behaviour is in words or gestures, sometimes with and sometimes without contracts and binding agreements. A major difficulty in applying game theory to the study of bargaining or negotiation is that the theory is not designed to deal with words and gestures—especially when they are deliberately ambiguous—as moves. Verbal sallies pose two unresolved problems in game-theoretic modelling: (1) how to code words, (2) how to describe the degree of commitment. (1985, 293)

Over and above the chess analogy, language use unearths a rich frontier for strategic interaction, which has only recently started to be probed in full generality.

Ending

Games as a comparison with language are no illustration of Vaihingerial philosophy, or something that was termed by Rom Harré "the weakest of all forms of theory—the use of metaphors." Nor is it any resort of theoreticians of science engaged in the process of trying to select the "candidate for reality" from among the multiplicity of models (Harré 1961, 26).[10] Nor should the game paradigm be confined to the loose metaphor of the "finite versus infinite games" we get to choose in social life (Carse 1986).

What the allegory represents is a serious and deep-seated philosophical problem concerning the relationship between thought, language, and reality. All told, we have a concept that marries philosophical thinking with scientific methodology, such as the theory of games and rational decisions, linguistic pragmatics, logic, and countless others. However, those disciplines have positively advanced beyond the mere chess metaphor. After all, from a game-theoretic perspective, chess is trivial. It is a two-player, noncooperative, strictly competitive (save for the draw conventions), and finite-horizon (save for the stop rule) game of combinatorics, having no hidden information and no signaling or screening of moves.

This said, one of the fundamental similarities between chess and language is generalization. Peirce illustrated the idea with respect to mathematical thought:

> Another characteristic of mathematical thought is that it can have no success where it cannot generalize. One cannot, for example, deny that chess is mathematics, after a fashion; but, owing to the exceptions which everywhere confront the mathematician in this field—such as the limits of the board; the single steps of king, knight, and pawn; the finite number of squares; the peculiar mode of capture by pawns; the queening of pawns; castling—there results a mathematics whose wings are effectually clipped, and which can only run along the ground. Hence it is that a mathematician often finds what a chess-player might call a gambit to his advantage; exchanging a smaller problem that involves exceptions for a larger one free from them. Thus, rather than suppose that parallel lines, unlike all other pairs of straight lines in a plane, never meet, he supposes that they intersect at infinity. (Peirce 1931–58, 4.236, c. 1902, *The Simplest Mathematics*).

In a similar vein, to learn and use language effectively calls for masking an immense multitude and intensity of thought behind cost-effective expression, which at the same time permits general, inexact interpretations.

NOTES

1. Pietarinen 2006b compiles studies on the relationships between games and language from semantic and pragmatic points of view. Pietarinen 2003 is an overview of games across the sciences.

2. Peirce 1967, MS 1343, c. 1902, *On the Classification of the Sciences*. Second paper, *Of the Practical Sciences*.

3. *Spielbedeutungen* could also be translated as "play-meanings," but I will stick to the translation of *Spiel* to "game" because Husserl (just as Wittgenstein) uses real games as examples.

4. According to an anecdote recounted by Norman Malcolm (1958, 65)—reporting what he was once told by Freeman Dyson—the word "game" simply sprang into Wittgenstein's mind as he passed a field on which a soccer game was in progress.

5. His *Nachlass*, a work that long remained unpublished, has now seen the light of the day and has turned out to be a very valuable and instructive source on the controversial role of the language game in his philosophy.

6. And so his comment to Dyson was a hoodwink; see note 4.

7. A curiosity: Max Euwe, a chess world champion, was Brouwer's student.

8. Hilbert's attitude was implicit in the significists' stratification of language, especially in the distinction between primordial language (in which the meaning of all words appeals to profound emotions and strikes one's consciousness much like a child learns and understands words and symbols) and logical languages (in which meaning no longer depends on the content of expressions and has no bearing on the hearer, since the symbols already have their application in the preceding levels). Curiously, this resembles Alfred Tarski's famous account of logical consequence, the model-theoretic import of which is that a conclusion follows from the hypotheses just in the case that every situation, case or a model in which hypotheses are true is a situation, case or a model in which the conclusion is true. The problem concerns the underlying logical notions that warrant such an explication. This was what dialogic constructivism endeavored to tackle soon after.

9. My thanks to the reviewer for pointing out how easily strategic language use gives rise to performative contradictions.

10. Harré was attacking the idea of mathematical and formal models as such candidates.

REFERENCES

Borel, Emil. 1921. "La théorie du jeu et les equations intégrales à noyau symétrique." *Comptes Rendus Hebdomadaires des Séances de l'Académie des Sciences* 173:1304–8. Translated by L. J. Savage as "The Theory of Play and Integral Equations with Skew Symmetric Kernels," *Econometrica* 21 (1953): 97–100.

Brouwer, L. E. J. 1949. "Consciousness, Philosophy, and Mathematics." In *Proceedings of the Tenth International Congress of Philosophy*, edited by E. W. Beth, H. J. Pos and J. H. A. Hollak, 1235–49. Amsterdam: North-Holland.

Carse, James P. 1986. *Finite and Infinite Games: A Vision of Life as Play and Possibility.* New York: Ballantine Books.

Girard, Jean-Yves. 1998. "On the Meaning of Logical Rules I: Syntax vs. Semantics." In *Computational Logic*, edited by Ulrich Berger and Helmut Schwichtenberg, 215–72. Heidelberg: Springer.

Grice, H. Paul. 1989. *Studies in the Way of Words.* Cambridge, MA: Harvard University Press.

Habermas, Jürgen. 1995. "Peirce and Communication." In *Peirce and Contemporary Thought*, edited by K. Laine Ketner, 243–66. New York: Fordham University Press.

———. 1998. *On the Pragmatics of Communication.* Edited by Maeve Cooke. Cambridge, MA: MIT Press.

———. 2001. *On the Pragmatics of Social Interaction: Preliminary Studies in the Theory of Communicative Action.* Translated by Barbara Fultner. Cambridge, MA: MIT Press.

Harré, Romano. 1961. *Theories and Things: A Brief Study in Prescriptive Metaphysics.* London: Sheed and Ward.

Hintikka, Jaakko. 1986. "Logic of Conversation as a Logic of Dialogue." In *Philosophical Grounds of Rationality,* edited by E. Grandy and R. Warner, 259–76. Oxford: Clarendon.

Husserl, Edmund. 1984. Husserliana XIX: *Logische Untersuchungen.* Ergänzungsband. The Hague: Nijhoff.

———. 1994. *Early Writings in the Philosophy of Logic and Mathematics.* Translated by Dallas Willard. Dordrecht: Kluwer.

Japaridze, Giorgi. 2006. "In the Beginning was Game Semantics." In *Logic and Games: Foundational Perspectives,* edited by O. Majer, A.-V. Pietarinen, and T. Tulenheimo. Dordrecht: Springer.

Kalmár, László. 1928–29. "Zur Theorie der abstrakten Spiele." *Acta Scientiarum Mathematicarum (Szeged)* 4:65–85. Translated as "On the Theory of Abstract Games," in *The Foundations of Game Theory I,* edited by M. A. Dimand and R. W. Dimand, 247–62 (Cheltenham: Edward Elgar, 1997).

Kasparov, Garry, and Donald Trelford. 1987. *Child of Change: The Autobiography of Garry Kasparov.* London: Hutchinson.

König, Dénes. 1927. "Über eine Schlußweise aus dem Endlichen ins Unendliche" [On a Consequence of Passing from the Finite to the Infinite]. *Acta Scientiarum Mathematicarum (Szeged)* 3:121–30.

Leonard, Robert J. 1995. "From Parlor Games to Social Science: von Neumann, Morgenstern, and the Creation of Game Theory 1928–1944." *Journal of Economic Literature* 23:730–61.

Malcolm, Norman. 1958. *Ludwig Wittgenstein: A Memoir.* London: Oxford University Press.

McKinsey, J. C. C. 1954. *Introduction to the Theory of Games.* New York: McGraw-Hill.

Peirce, Charles S. 1931–58. *Collected Papers of Charles Sanders Peirce.* 8 vols. Edited by Charles Hartshorne, Paul Weiss, and A. W. Burks. Cambridge, MA: Harvard University Press.

———. 1967. Manuscripts in the Houghton Library of Harvard University. Identified by Richard Robin in *Annotated Catalogue of the Papers of Charles S. Peirce* (Amherst: University of Massachusetts Press, 1967) and in "The Peirce Papers: A Supplementary Catalogue," *Transactions of the Charles S. Peirce Society* 7 (1971): 37–57.

———. 1998. *The Essential Peirce: Selected Philosophical Writings.* Vol. 2, 1893–1913. The Peirce Edition Project. Bloomington: Indiana University Press.

Pietarinen, Ahti-Veikko. 2003. "Games as Formal Tools versus Games as Explanations in Logic and Science." *Foundations of Science* 8:317–64.

———. 2004a. "Grice in the Wake of Peirce." *Pragmatics & Cognition* 12:395–415.

———. 2004b. "Logic, Language Games and Ludics." *Acta Analytica* 18:89–123.

———. 2005. *Signs of Logic: Peircean Themes on the Philosophy of Language, Games, and Communication.* Synthese Library 329. Dordrecht: Springer.

———. 2006a. "Significs and the Origins of Analytic Philosophy." *Journal of the History of Ideas.*

———, ed. 2006b. *Game Theory and Linguistic Meaning.* Oxford: Elsevier.

Saussure, Ferdinand de. 1916/1983. *Course in General Linguistics.* Translated by Roy Harris. London: Duckworth.

Shubik, Martin. 1985. *Game Theory in the Social Sciences.* Cambridge, MA: MIT Press.

Sperber, Dan, and Deidre Wilson. 1995. *Relevance: Communication and Cognition.* Oxford: Blackwell.

Ulam, Stanislaw M. 1960. *A Collection of Mathematical Problems.* Groningen: Interscience Publishers.

von Neumann, John. 1928. "Zur Theorie der Gesellschaftsspiele." *Mathematische Annalen* 100:295–320. Translated by S. Bargmann as "On the Theory of Games of Strategy," in *Contributions to the Theory of Games 4*, edited by A. W. Tucker and R. D. Luce, 13–42 (Princeton: Princeton University Press, 1959).

von Neumann, John, and Oskar Morgenstern. 1944. *Theory of Games and Economic Behavior.* New York: John Wiley.

Wittgenstein, Ludwig. 1953. *Philosophical Investigations.* Oxford: Blackwell.

———. 1970. *Zettel.* Berkeley and Los Angeles: University of California Press.

———. 1978. *Philosophical Grammar.* Columbia: University of California Press.

———. 2000–. *Wittgenstein's Nachlass: The Bergen Electronic Edition.* University of Bergen / Oxford University Press.

Zermelo, Ernst. 1913. "Über eine Anwendung der Mengenlehre auf die Theorie des Schachspiels." In *Proceedings of the Fifth International Congress of Mathematicians 2*, edited by E. W. Hobson and A. E. H. Love, 501–4. Cambridge: Cambridge University Press. Translated as "On an Application of Set Theory to the Theory of the Game of Chess," in U. Schwalbe and P. Walker, "Zermelo and the Early History of Game Theory," *Games and Economic Behaviour* 34 (2001): 123–37.

8

Hip-Hop Tactics: A Culturalogic Expression of the African Aesthetic's Role in Determining the Basis of Creativity on the Sixty-Four Squares of Warfare

TOMMY J. CURRY

If U Don't Know—Now U Know?

What you gon' do now Bobby? This was a phrase commonly recited in the halls of Java Café (a Black chess club on the south side of Chicago). It was the beginning of the end for a question / a lesson taught over the board / where a Black man waz lord / and challenged the great white American hope / as a joke / —saying that even the possession of knowledge in Bobby Fisher couldn't save yah from this lesson. In other words, I'm the teacher / you just an extra in this feature / on sixty-four squares of warfare / I'll beat that azz bare.

The Black players on the south side of Chicago taught me a lesson that day that fundamentally challenged the basis of all chess knowledge from the ground up. They showed me that regardless of the theoretical knowledge one possesses at the chessboard, the chess player plays the man—not the book. In other words, whatever games I may have studied would not help me in dealing with the personality and strategies of the person on the other side of the board.

From my own experiences, I know that Black chess players take chess to a whole new level. The game is not only about the battle over the board, but the psychological war waged between the freestyle battles that follow every move and the witty comebacks from the victim of the tactic. Regardless of how many lines I

137

dropped at the feet of an Isaac M. Braswell or William Aramil—at their expense mind you—the battle continued: one pawn, one sac, one victory or loss after the other; in a play of hip-hop tactics.

In a recent interview, Grandmaster Maurice Ashley said,

> Chess and Hip Hop definitely have elements that intertwined. One of those things is creativity. The greatest chess players are creative. Of course there are some calculations that have to be made. There is skill involved. Much like there is skill involved in Hip Hop. But it is not the mathematics that separates the greatest players it's the creativity. It's the ability to change with the environment. Having the ability to deal with any situation that confronts you no matter what the danger. To be able to overcome. To stay cool under all pressure. That's the real mark of a champion in chess. (Banjoko 2006)

The discussion of chess and hip hop extends beyond the realm of mere analogy. While many philosophical commentaries on chess in this volume speak to the role of truth or the impact of technology on chess, this analysis focuses on the psychological and sociocultural elements exposed in the moments of human interaction over the board, especially when that interaction is illuminated in Black. This analysis is part of a modern movement in chess. "The movement in modern chess is away from abstract theoretical thinking and towards a more open and realistic view of the board."[1] This realistic approach necessarily involves the study of both psychology and the tendencies manifested by experience. "Referring to a study by the University of Constance that Grandmasters have access to something like 100,000 stored patterns on the basis of experience, Grandmaster Jonathan Rowson says: 'In my view it's the brain that makes the patterns on the basis of experience, so all the Grandmaster does is expose himself to chess information and lets the brain rack it up in its own mysterious way,' which form the basis for intuitive judgment, which are informed by experience and verified by calculation" (Watson 2003, 12).

Hip hop is the most recent African/a aesthetic movement in America. As an expression of black culture, it is fundamentally saturated with the personal, cultural, and political consciousness of African people in America. For better or for worse, hip hop is the cultural aesthetic articulating Black experience and consciousness of the world at large. It is in this vein that I wish to explore the way through which hip hop—as an African aesthetic (African personality)—structures the way in which people of African descent frame chess.[2]

It's Pretty It's So Pretty. . . .

Have you ever heard a conversation about the role of hip hop in chess? What about culture and its relationship to chess moves? What I think you'll find is that the questions are synonymous when speaking of an African/a culture. What we see on the board is for a large part already determined by the understanding we have not only of chess, but also of the world at large. Many chess lovers hold a commonsense view that our minds are empty spaces awaiting the fulfillment of new chess positions and knowledge; but the realness of the situation is that "new information does not follow a seamless path to a comfortable destination. Chess ideas do not just slot into unfurnished apartments ready to unpack. On the contrary, they are smothered by the assistance of related ideas and arrive in a heavily furnished place" (Rowson 2005, 17). In other words, "we construct our understanding of positions, which means using what we have, however imperfect, to make sense of what we are given. We con (with) struct (structure) our understanding. We learn with structure. Which structure? This varies person to person, but it includes the bio-chemical one we are born with, and the vast psycho-socio-cultural one we have . . . built over the course of our whole lives."[3] Hip hop is life—and this life—this rhythmic style structures the dynamic flair African people display at the game of chess.

Some hip-hop artists like Jay-Z[4] and GZA[5] have taken this view of chess to the streets and made chess a demonstrable aesthetic that maps itself onto the Black experience of the racist American society. This translatability of chess into hip hop is a trademark of the African/a aesthetic. The adaptability and creativity that defines hip hop is itself aesthetic in the sense that it is the life of the African displayed. "Every African person is an artist," who directs her consciousness as will and intends to effect reality; to change what one can see, and to animate the "inanimate" (Richards 1993). The African consciousness, when directed towards life, produces hip hop, and when directed to chess brings the improvisational void of hip-hop tactics to the board. The chess board is animated by the force of understanding; otherwise it would merely be pieces without purpose. In understanding the role of the pieces and directing them through the landscape of sixty-four squares "we" play chess. In other words, the African is bringing hip hop to the board.

Hip hop is the context of creativity for the African. It is life and is carried with the African in both person and consciousness. It seeks objects and a material reality to form and creatively mold. Hip hop is the medium chosen by Africans in America to both express and represent the flux of African/a culture. With this said, chess then is both partner and victim to the African's aesthetic. The game of chess could be understood as a raw matter that lends itself to be formed in a partnership with the African, but on the flipside chess is a victim to the cultural and psychological dynamisms the Africans enact in their intimate touch. Under this light, chess does not produce art itself—rather chess is the reflection of art's capacity in the consciousness of the culturalogical player. The African creates art on the board only as "possibilities" that can arise from the thinking of the African mind when it meets the board. Hip-hop tactics emerge in the meeting of the board and the African's active construction of his understanding of chess itself.

In this context, creativity is not the selection of the unexpected in the range of possibilities but the creation of possibilities from the conditions that give rise to the un/expected. The African improvises not only the move, but arranges the context through which the aim of one's movement can constitute "this" move. In that moment, the moment through which an African consciousness understands the "chess" before him, chess becomes art.

The Culturalogic Moment: Reassessing the Logic of Chess

Most notable International Masters and Grandmasters hold to the fundamental principles of chess and only deviate from established theory under the most calculated and dire situations. Many see chess as bound by a set of formal rules and structures that dictate and guide sound and correct play. Chess is played with the right moves at this level and it is assumed that the "right move" is the move that holds material while not overextending or underprotecting. This is the opinion of International Master Rashid Ziyatdinov and can be seen as he argues:

> Chess is much like a language. It has a very logical structure wherein fundamental rules and structure combine and connect to create and

explain ever more complicated positions. Like a language, chess has a basic alphabet and sentence structure. From these, all chess knowledge can be built, and to these all possibilities in a game of chess can be traced. (Ziyatdinov 2000, 11–12)

For Ziyatdinov and many other high-level players, this seems to be the case. Even spectacular combinations and sacrifices that seem to bend the formal rules of chess and static advantages seem to fall victim to an analysis of positions and logic. These theoreticians believe that all chess moves and knowledge are fixed. It is only a question of recognizing the position and the truth in any given game. Even Jeremy Silman, who appears to believe in dynamic play free from such constraints, argues that combinations arise from three general factors: (1) an open or weakened king—or a stalemated king, (2) undefended pieces—excluding pawns and (3) inadequately defended pieces (Silman 1997, 47). Ziyatdinov agrees:

> In chess, there often occur the most amazing and beautiful combinations. It may seem that these arise as if by magic. The great former World Champion Mikhail Tal was sometimes referred to as the Wizard of Riga, due to his ability to conjure combinations out of the most innocent looking positions. Yet, in each case, later analysis has shown that the seeds of the combination were present in the position. . . . (2000, 11–12)

With very few exceptions this view of chess has solidified a tendency to only evaluate the most "sound lines" and focus on static advantages such as pawn structure, minor piece coordination, and material superiority. While these can change during the playing of a game, the view used to evaluate a position or opening line is based on the accepted theory that assumes that material advantage is sound and correct. Even roughly equal positions are evaluated in this logical and linear perspective, because it is generally thought that static advantages grow as one has and holds material (Silman 1997, 245). For these theorists, the material advantage defines and dictates the realm of the dynamic and spontaneous.

The idea that dynamic advantage is temporary and fleeting seems to undercut GM Maurice Ashley's view, in which he privileges an understanding of chess pieces not individually but in weight of their role as part of the Black or White sides' arsenal.

> GM Ashley once mentioned that after attaining a certain level of skill, one no longer sees chess figurines moving about the board. The pieces become forces of energy that are to be employed in an efficient manner. In yet another interview, he mentioned the attributes of time, space and force as key interlocking principles in chess. Of course, these attributes can be understood in both the physical (e.g., time on clock, positional space on the 8X8 matrix, attacking initiative) as well as metaphysical realm (e.g., elevating to a higher plane during deep concentration). (Shabazz, "Metaphysics of the Chess Mind")

In his view, chess is about two counteracting forces that assert themselves on each other in balance and imbalance. Competition is seen as the waging of forces as a whole, not the superior acting of individual pieces under the command of the king. This is a paradigmatic argument against traditional ideas of chess theory and is similar to the ideas of an African worldview that understand the world in terms of forces and "ashe" (creativity).

Being is force.[6] "Every great Africanist—and the African informers and researchers in the first place—have confirmed this fundamental principle of African ontology. The latter could very well be formulated in this way: 'the stuff of matter is energy'" (Senghor 2001, 146). The sensibilities in people of African descent are then directed to the feeling of the dynamics in a position rather focus on the objective value of pieces and position. What the position "means" then is determined by a radically different criterion.

Many psychologists want to stay away from the role "meaning-making" plays in chess, but the reality of the situation, especially the chess situation, is that what we see, feel, and believe to exist on the board is what we base our moves on. Our ability to calculate or sacrifice a piece for an attack is largely determined by our assessment of initiative and game on the board. So words like "compensation," "calculation," or even the claim that one has the "initiative" or "advantage" are relative and will be based on whether or not the chess player believes she has an attack or combination despite being down a pawn or an exchange. Despite this growing view of chess involving the psychological preconceptions of chess, many chess players still view chess as a primarily intellectual game, which is art, to quote Mikhail Botvinnik, only insofar as it is "the art that expresses the science of logic" (McDonald 2004, 1). According to Rowson, "Chess is a logical game in the sense that it is concerned with a kind of reasoning, but the most salient logic is not the digital logic of mathematics or the emotionless logic of Star Trek's Mr. Spock. It is a logic that swims around in the sticky undercurrents of our thoughts, the logic of our psyches; or our psychologics" (2005, 30). This psychological analysis has largely been absent from traditional articulations of chess. For the most part, traditional chess theory has vacillated between accounts of chess as an art (a creative process) or a science (a logical process). Rowson, however, sees that chess is not more or less one or the other, but rather a personal journey—a psychological tension—emerged in an individual's temperament that pulls a player towards a specific personal logics of creativity. So instead of thinking about chess as game with a fixed truth, Rowson challenges the reader to think of chess as an aspect of one's personality.

While Rowson's perspective is novel in its use of psychoanalysis to bring individuality into chess reasoning, what Rowson's Freudian perspective overlooks is the inability of a subjective logics to describe the social and cultural drives that exist as the motivating agendas of individuals' psyches. A game of chess, rather than being the deliberate creation of a philosophical treatise or work of art solely dependent on the individual genius of the player, is instead a narrative through which a series of purposive chess maneuvers create what the players take to be their truth and what can be seen over the board as beautiful. In short, Rowson's theory overlooks the potential of chess moves having a normative significance. Because the unconscious is a storehouse of drives and biases in need of regulation for Rowson, he forgets that these drives and biases also entitle the player to various creative myths that serve as the foundations of the realities they propose over the board.

The moves chess players make during chess games are in large part determined by the threats they see to the aspects of the game they choose to value most. For example, chess players who place the highest value on their queen would be less likely to sacrifice that piece for attacking chances or mating possibilities. Just as players who value their pawn structure would be less likely to accept an open file as a compensatory justification for double pawns. These dispositions are in large part related to narratives we play by in a game, or the myths we believe in to determine the "right moves." We formulate a story of a kingside attack that will mate our opponent in seven moves, and then we enact the myths, double the rooks in front of the king, and sacrifice the light squared bishop on h3 for the mate. These formulas are based either in the static truths of this position or the dynamic potential we see through the attack, but in both cases they are our motivations—the plots—used to construct our narration of truth. These aspects guide our determinations of positions because they disclose to us what meanings will emerge from our moves. What I am proposing to the reader is that chess is not true in any objective sense over the board, but rather the confrontation of two competing myths for the temporal space of trueness in a game.

Tommy J. Curry vs. D: An "A" player from Chicago [B90]

1. e4 c5 2. Nf3 d6 3. d4 cxd4 4. Nxd4 Nf6 5. Nc3 a6 6. f3 e6 7. g4 Nfd7 8. Be3 b5 9. Qd2 Nb6 10. a4 Nc4 11. Bxc4 bxc4 12. 0-0 Be7

This is your typical Najdorf Sicilian. Black is behind in development, but ironically he never really has any problems because of it. In this position, theory would probably advocate 13. a5 as an attempt to really lock down Black's queen side. After 13. a5 I could envision White continuing with Na4, with the idea of Nb6 with the dark-squared bishop supporting the Knight. This is all very logical, but I was actually concerned with Black playing Bb7 and d5.

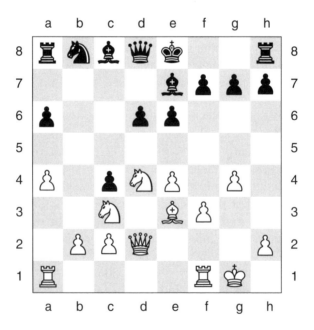

The paranoia then of not letting Black get in d5 was my justification for my next move.

13. Nf5

I cannot really explain the justification of picking this move over say 13. a5 or even 13. Qe2 attacking the weak pawn on c4, except to say it seems to give me the d5 square or cost Black his dark-squared bishop. In my mind, the dynamic compensation of 13. . . . exf5 14. Qd5 justified the sacrifice of the knight, and would pose the most problems for Black.

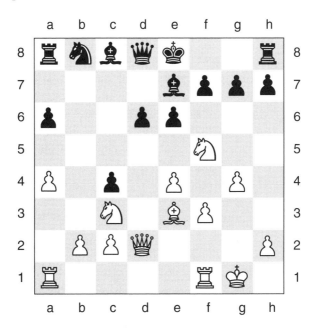

13. . . . exf5
14. Qd5

This was the whole point at least in my mind. I did not see how Black could salvage himself after this. **Qc7 15. Qxa8 Bb7 16. Nd5 Bxd5 17. Qxd5 fxg4 18. fxg4 0-0 19. Rf5 Nd7 20. g5 Ne5 21. Raf1 g6 22. R5f2** And White wins easily. **1–0.**

There is not any overarching logical principle that allowed me to see 13. Nf5. My selection of the move was made based on my personal assessment of the position (I don't want to deal with losing the d5 square) and I started calculating the variations from the position that was already determined by my contextual (psychocultural) determinations of what is called for. The move then is not an expression of the "best move," but an expression of the necessary determinations from the context through which it is created. In other words, I thought "I should stop d5; is that the most threatening assault for Black?" Probably not, but it is the basis of my inquiry and the single most important determining factor in the context of choosing a move.

Psycho-logics, then, not only involves the narratives and myths that justify our play but the fundamental tools we have in our psyches to construct our stories and implement our myths. A story based on positional chess and static advantages, like pawn structure and piece value, would formulate stories that preserve those valued advantages, just as a dynamic story would tell tales of noble sacrifices and fanciful combinations. To account then for the sociocultural templates producing the stories and myths, the philosopher should embrace the "culturalogic" expressions of ontology through psychology. In philosophical terms, the subject can only think about objects that exist, and that existence of objects and how the subject "thinks about the objects" or "knows of the objects" are fundamentally determined by culture—their culturalogic.

Perhaps this could be better demonstrated by a "lightning chess" game I played on the Playchess.com server where the time controls are only one minute. In lightning chess, players work from instinct, an instinct that is not given to the player from birth or a transcendental connection to truth, but an instinct that is formed through the relationship that the player takes up through experience in their social and cultural context. In this sense, chess becomes a performance that links the individual not only to his success or fear of failure in a game, but a context through which that success or failure is displayed as a possible narration of truth, where the board represents the contestation of alternate realities. The game, then, played between two players is not simply a series of the most correct moves, but a narrative conflict seeking to debunk the personal novella of the chess player to an anecdotal myth and raise the tale of one author to the most compelling story that captures not only one's opponent, but the audience, the community, and the social group that makes the performance possible.

Zukertort (2444) vs. Tommy J. Curry: 1m+0

1. d4 Nf6 2. c4 g6 3. Nc3 d6 4. e4 Bg7 5. f3 0-0 6. Be3 c5 7. d5 Qa5 8. Qd2 b5 9. cxb5 a6 10. bxa6 Bxa6

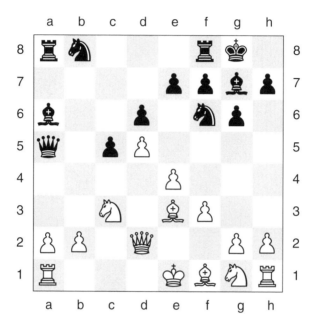

This looks to be a standard King's Indian defense, but what we will see as the game unfolds is that the position itself is dictated not by the correct theory of the King's Indian defense, but by the dynamic momentum that I believed existed on the board. What is most interesting for our philosophical outlook on chess and the relationship chess shares with psychology, culture, and logic is that in the moment of performing the act of the chess move, these traditional philosophical categories are fundamentally indistinguishable, since they are collapsed into a single move. Whether or not the belief in the dynamics of the position actually exist, I still act as if it is real, and furthermore, I take my belief, my *feeling*, of the position at that moment to be the most determining frame through which I understand not only the game in front of me, but also the activity of chess itself.

11. Bxa6 Nxa6 12. Qe2 Nb4 13. a3 This move was unexpected **Na6 14. Qd2 Nc7 15. Nge2 Rfb8 16. 0-0 Nd7 17. Rab1 Ne5**

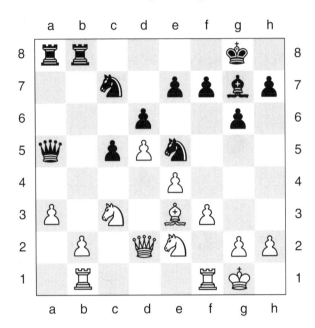

18. Na2 Qa6 I suppose I could have traded queens, perhaps **(18. . . . Qxd2 19. Bxd2 Nc4 20.Bc3 Nxb2)** would have been fine, maybe even winning, but I *felt* as if I needed my queen in such a position—I was still focused on the attack **19. f4 Nc4 20. Qc1 Nxe3** At this point, all I knew is that I wanted a knight on d4 **21. Qxe3 Nb5 22. Nac3 Nd4 23. Qd2 Nxe2+ 24. Qxe2 Bxc3 25. Qxa6** This clearly was a mistake for a 2444-rated blitz player, nonetheless such a blunder results from the triumph of one narrative over the other **Bd4+** (see p. 149).

   26. Kh1 Rxa6 And White resigns because of rook takes pawn on b2. **0–1.** For some this game might demonstrate that I played more correct moves, and as such I won the game. This may be true, but what is of even greater consequence is the realization that the seemingly "correct" moves I made are only "correct" insofar as they directly challenge the attempts of my opponent to impose moves which he/she takes to be just as correct. Thus, chess reasoning, instead of being the recognition of positional truths, is a reasoning through touch, a reason that molds the game in the player's participation. The correct chess move could never be considered as such outside of the moves, motifs, and competing agendas of the opposing player, hence chess reason-

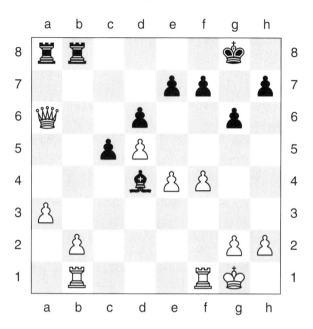

ing is necessarily bound by the endless confrontations of "truths" over the board.

You Feel Me . . . ?

Leopold Sedar Senghor (1906–2001) was one of the founding philosophers of an Africana movement known as Negritude. Negritude was a not only an attitude that responded to the reactions to French colonialism through the early part of the twentieth century, but also an essence—a content—that sought to rediscover the African's past, the African's culture, and the African's ancestors as the determination of African descended peoples' reality. The Senghorian explanation of culture is a sociocultural development that exalts African culture in that it finds in the past the dispositions that make the possibilities of the future realizable, while pointing to the constants in the African soul that inspire modern techniques of action in the political economic and artistic realms of the African consciousness,[7] or as Senghor would say "the ensemble of cultural values of the Black world" (Senghor 1967b, 51).

This sociocultural development is rooted in the use of specific African psychological dispositions toward the reality.[8] It focuses on the culturalogical moment between the consciousness of the African and the meeting of the world with that consciousness:

> The African Negro is by his colour as in the primordial night. He does not see the object; he feels it. It is the pure sensorial field of the third day development of a worm. It is in his subjectivity, at the end of his sensory organs that he discovers the Other. There he is, stimulated, going centrifugally from subject to object on the waves of the Other. And this is simply not metaphorical, since contemporary physics has discovered energy under matter: waves and radiations. Thus, one sees the African Negro who sympathizes and identifies himself, who dies himself in order to be reborn to the Other. He lives with the Other in symbiosis; he is born again (con-nait) to the Other. . . . Here subject and object face each other dialectically in the very instrument of knowledge, which is the instrument of love. 'I think, therefore I exist,' wrote Descartes. The African Negro could say: "I feel the Other; I dance the Other, therefore I exist". Then dancing, especially when it is the dance of love. In any case, it is the best means of knowledge. (Senghor 1967b, 50–51)

Chess is felt by the African; chess is a participation of the African self, where this self is culturally imported to the board. Chess is known as the symbiosis of the activity and the cultural ensemble of the Black world. As an African, we know through touching the extent of an object's utility. We move in conversation with the intent of the game itself; we move with a care not only for ourselves on the board, but an affective attention to the development and esteem of this particular game's character.

Playing chess for the African is the "dance of love" Senghor refers to. The African improvises because only creativity can arise out of the possibilities that emerge from the African "who dies himself to be reborn in the Other." The self is sacrificed in its temporality to be reconstructed as a product of the participation, the playing of the game. It is the "love" of the game that draws out its potential. Playing the game is the play of forces, a construction of reality from the affectation of the chess pieces on the board.

"For the Black African, being is not a substance that has force as an attribute; it is force itself that is the substance of being. Being-force is energy, that is to say a spirit, an ever moving-life, capable of growing and diminishing, of being enriched and altered. It is a vital force, which subtends everything that is identifiable" (Senghor 2001, 146). The African touches not only the pieces on the board but the force of the board itself as if the two were in communication with each other as to the formation of a new narrative. The African literally puts his azz on the line in each move, because the chess game is not him (as a chess player separate from and directing the pieces) but him (as the symbiosis of the pieces and consciousness creating through survival) on sixty-four squares of warfare.

Culturalogics: I'ma Make It Do What It Do!!

No one can deny the preponderance of psychological evidence that indicates that experts are made not born,[9] and pointing out the existence of hip-hop tactics does not refute or lay challenge to this claim. In an Africana worldview, chess becomes a transformative canvas by its nature and in practice redefines the logical binds of traditional theory. Logic is colored by it culturalogical underpinnings, and exposed as a system of thought intimately connected with one's culture, identity, and experiential condition. Culturalogics then posits an explanation of how one in an African/a culture can create in the process of understanding the world through participation. The culturalogical analysis exposes the cultural structures that underpin the seemingly objective and neutral rules of logical laws that have had a long standing with theorist theorizing about chess, because of the alleged intellectualized nature of the activity.

To accept, then, the African, as an African, rewrites the very concept and utility of logic in the game of chess. The African's participation with the object is the knowing of the world as "objects of the African's affections." Culture is imported then onto the perceptions we have of the chess board and plays not only a phenomenological role but a determining function in how we select the moves and aim for the positions we desire over the board. Our identities then formulate how we approach the game and how the game will be determined.

There is an intimate connection / through the reflection of what we consider best. A test of rumination / and contemplation on a text of / sixty-four squares. We become aware / if we dare to question the lessons of the participating self / the wealth of active dance / an intellectual trance / a fusion of the game with manz handz / itz me on the board / where the Black man is lord / and the game is of one of participating / not awaiting the forms of truth / but the root of the self / in creating the means / for the schemes / that give birth to the destruction / of the other man / my brotha man and

myself / in a capoeira / that reveals the aura / of an Africanz passing away in the birth of an-other / the meta-physical self of the
under cover brotha.

This is the point of brotha Senghor. The African is intimately
connected to the use of hip-hop tactics because it is the African that
"is" in the potentiality of creating "creative creations" from the participating self.

NOTES

1. Watson 2003, 11. This is also a perspective taken up by John Nunn
in the introduction to Watson 2001.

2. For the purposes of this project, it is imperative that we clarify what
is meant by the African aesthetic. The African aesthetic is a term used to
express the spiritual basis of the African life. It is not concerned with the
traditional understanding European understanding of "aesthetic" as being
equivalent to "beauty." Rather, the African aesthetic is best expressed by
the Kiswahili words Kugusa Mtima (to touch the heart). African experience
is that of being "touched," "moved," "affected" by a self-consciously created form/phenomenon (Richards 1993, 65). In this way, the African aesthetic is equivalent to the African personality described by Leopold
Senghor in that both terms express the participation of the African—the
African's affective relationship—in the world.

3. Rowson is seeking to explain chess as a psychological and cultural
manifestation. Our personality and our habits determine what moves,
openings, and agendas we form over the board. This is particularly interesting when we look at African/Black psychology and analyze the psychology of African people and the various styles they present in chess.
Rowson places a lot of stock in traditional psychology and attributes the
organization of chess knowledge and skill to what he calls the "intelligent
unconscious." As he says on page 26 of his book, *Chess for Zebras*, "any
comprehensive theory of chess psychology needs to take a stand on non-
conscious aspects of cognition, because recent evidence from cognitive
psychology strongly suggests that the thoughts and perception we are conscious of are dwarfed by the amount of information we are taking in at a
non-conscious level." When looking at African people throughout the
Diaspora, recent research has found strong and consistent evidence that
suggests a presence of what has historically been called an "African personality." I believe that Rowson is correct in assessing the impact psychology has in chess; however, when seeking to determine the particular
psycho-socio-cultural disposition of Africans in America and throughout
the Diaspora, we must utilize different psychological models developed by
Black psychologists and theorists that address people of African descent

on basis of their particular worldview. The African is a different type of subject altogether and any discussion of how one thinks about chess must be articulated as to how "Africans" think about chess.

4. In Jay-Z's song, "This Life Forever" he dropped these lines: "Niggas tryna subtract my life / my mathematics is precise / I carry the nine, so fucking with me just ain't the answer / I cant lose when I was young I was like Fresh / Poppa raised me to chess moves / And though your gone I'm not bitter you left me prepared / We got divided by the years, but I got it from here / Don't sweat that, sounds bump from Marcy to Lefrak / To that pocket in DC where my man caught his death at / Over my years I've seen Rooks get tooken by the Knight / Lose they Crown by tryna defend a Queen / Checkmate, in 4 moves the Bobby Fischer of rap."

5. The GZA has used hip hop as his medium of choice. In his album *Grandmasters*, GZA explores the use of rap as a way to analyze life and the experiences of Black people in America.

6. This is the dominate view of traditional African ethno-philosophy presented both by Jahnheiz Jahn, *Muntu* (1961), and Placide Temples, *Bantu Philosophy* (1953).

7. This is a summarization of the arguments presented by I. V. Thomas in his essay "The Principle Themes of Negritude" (Senghor 1967a).

8. Many white philosophers get a little squeamish when entering conversations that deal with cultural particularity. However, in African and African American philosophy (Africana thought), cultural particularity was the dominate strategy of philosophical reflection, especially in the realm of psychology and sociology. Theorists of this intellectual tradition generally held that "because African people existed, in fact preexisted Europeans as a distinct and independent cultural entity apart form European people, it follows that a distinctive African (Black) psychology existed, irrespective of when and how Black social scientists actually formalized the concept in Western society. African (Black) psychology from this perspective thus derives naturally from the "worldview" or philosophical premises underlying African culture itself (as does Western psychology relative to the worldview of European culture). Clearly then, the justification for African (Black) psychology's existence as well as its independence from Western psychology inheres in the fundamental distinctiveness between and independence of African and European cosmologies" (Baldwin 1991, 126). Today, however, with the uncritical acceptance of humanism and antiessentialism in philosophy, most African-American philosophy rejects the ideas of cultural particularity in favor of participation in the Western philosophical tradition.

9. Ross 2006. Ross's discussion is relevant to my project because it debunks the fiction of innate talent in chess: "this belief in the importance of innate talent, strongest perhaps among experts themselves and their trainers, is strangely lacking in hard evidence." This is especially

interesting given the reasons that Ross chose chess as his area of study. According to Ross "skill at chess can be measured" and chess itself is "the touchstone of the intellect." Ross concludes then that the task for the production of more chess experts and eventually Grandmasters is to be found in child motivation and teaching. I find this information interesting and particularly useful in this project because it points to the ability of any "race" of people to produce chess geniuses given the opportunity and resources. As such, my chapter is not to be seen as an essentialist piece claiming innate chess ability, but rather a discussion of learning styles and worldview analyses that are becoming the centerpiece of multicultural education and African centered psychology discourses. Hopefully, this discussion will spill over into the realms of philosophy as a challenge to the dominant Eurocentric paradigm that only gives credence to white thought.

REFERENCES

Baldwin, James A. 1991. "African (Black) Psychology: Issues and Synthesis." In *Black Psychology*, edited by Reginald L. Jones. Berkeley: Cobb and Henry.

Banjoko, Adisa. 2006. "Controlled Chaos: Chessmaster Maurice Ashley." Chessbase.com. Chess News. www.chessbase.com/newsdetail.asp? newsid=3223. August 7.

Jahn, Jahnheiz. 1961. *Muntu*. New York: Grove Press.

McDonald, Neil. 2004. *Chess: The Art of Logical Thinking*. London: Batsford.

Richards, Dona. 1993. "The African Aesthetic and National Consciousness." In *The African Aesthetic: Keeper of the Traditions*, edited by Kariamu Welsh Asante. Westport, CT: Greenwood.

Ross, Philip E. 2006. "The Expert Mind." *Scientific American*. August.

Rowson, Jonathon. 2005. *Chess for Zebras: Thinking Differently About Black and White*. London: Gambit Publications Ltd.

Senghor, Leopold. 1967a. "The Principle Themes of Negritude." In *Negritude: Essays and Studies*, edited by Albert H. Berrian and Richard A. Long. Hampton: Hampton University Press.

———. 1967b. "The Psychology of the African Negro." In *Negritude: Essays and Studies*, edited by Albert H. Berrian and Richard A. Long. Hampton: Hampton University Press.

———. 2001. "Negritude and Modernity." In *Race*, edited by Robert Bernasconi. Malden, MA: Blackwell Publishers.

Shabazz, Daaim. "Metaphysics of the Chess Mind." The Chess Drum website. The 65th Square. http://www.thechessdrum.net/65thSquare/65_janfeb03.html.

Silman, Jeremy. 1997. *Reassess Your Chess: The Complete Chess Mastery Course.* Exp. 3rd ed. Los Angeles: Siles Press.

Temples, Placide. 1953. *Bantu Philosophy.* Presence Africaine.

Watson, John. 2001. *Understanding Chess Move by Move.* London: Gambit Publications Ltd.

———. 2003. *Chess Strategy in Action.* London: Gambit Publications Ltd.

Ziyatdinov, Rashid. 2000. *GM-RAM: Essential Grandmaster Chess Knowledge.* Davenport, IA: Thinkers' Press.

9

Quiet, Please! There's a Game Here: Discourse and Silence in the Formal Pragmatics of a Chess Match

BENJAMIN HALE

TAL–HJARTARSON
Reykjavik 1987

Sometimes your opponent's pawns or pieces are not controlling key squares but are blocking up important avenues of attack. The key ranks, diagonals, or files must be cleared.

One of the loudest thinkers of our time was world champion Mikhail Tal 1936–1995. His daring sacrifices lit the imagination of many a chess player. In the accompanying diagram, White decides on a barrier removing campaign.

1) Rc5!

The Pawn on d6 is overloaded with its defensive duty of guarding the c5 square and providing support for the rest of the Black pawn chain. If Black responds with

1) . . . dxc5

White will follow with

2) Nfxe5 Kg8
3) Nxd7 Qa6
4) bxc5!

White will have made the good trade of a rook for two pawns and a bishop and will have three connected passed pawns in the center!

—FEALY 1994–2002

In the field of ethics, one question that quickly arises is whether some being or entity can be said to have moral status. An entity's "capacity to reason" has long been an accepted criterion for saying that that entity deserves moral standing, or in the terminology of some, for saying that that entity is morally *considerable*. "Entities that can reason," goes the thought, "ought to be paid the same respect in kind." Entities that cannot reason, it continues authoritatively, ought to enjoy only derivative respect. Not surprisingly, many philosophers find this criterion troublesome. Those who work in ethics find themselves repeatedly arguing against this stubbornly common presupposition to establish the moral equivalence of reasoning creatures. Women, slaves, Jews, Muslims, Christians, and many other marginalized groups have all had to plead their case for moral standing first by demonstrating that they too share the attribute of reason. This task has shown itself to be much more difficult than one might imagine, and the history of modern philosophy charts a long, slow course of liberation. Recently, many philosophers have been arguing the considerability case for extremely marginalized groups—animals, human embryos, and the environment—entities which, according to most accounts, clearly lack the capacity to reason.

One prominent ethical theory—"Discourse Theory," pioneered in part by Jürgen Habermas and Karl-Otto Apel—proposes that moral standing can be established via an entity's ability to communicate its intent, and that moral agents are bound to respect the positions of other Speakers by virtue of their understanding of this intent. The idea draws its strength from the Kantian view that we are obligated to act in concordance with the presuppositions of our reasoning. In the case of discourse ethics, the fundamental presupposition is that in order to be successful participants to discourse, we necessarily always already employ the rule that we must consider another's claims. In turn, this is what qualifies discursive agents (humans) as "morally considerable": it is a presupposition of discourse that their claims must be considered. This chapter draws on that work. It relies on Habermas's discourse theory and the game of chess to demonstrate that understanding what the other intends is more than simply a matter of understanding the words he uses; it is also a matter of anticipating the moves he makes. The grand import of such a thesis is that discourse also necessarily involves considerations of movements and actions in the world. Insofar as this is the case, there is an equivalent rule of discourse that even the actions and responses of nonspeaking entities must be taken into consideration.

The strategy that I employ in this essay turns on our use of the term "consideration." "Moral considerability" is sometimes used synonymously with terms like "moral status" or "moral worth" to suggest that an entity bears status by virtue of some capacity or attribute unique to it. However, this chapter uses "consideration" to suggest that consideration is a fundamental activity in which all rational agents must engage. I will therefore explore only the formal arrangement between a rational chess player and a nonrational opponent—whether computer, human infant, or animal—to argue that acting for a reason means responding to the moves made by the opponent *as though* the moves were rational, and does not depend, as is often assumed, on the opponent *actually being rational.*

That chess is the game under consideration here is important. For one thing, many philosophers cite chess in discussions of rules, rationality, behaviors, actions, and norms.[1] As well, chess is a strategic zero-sum game, which gives it the ostensibly unique feature of being solely purposive; and it is important to see that even strategic arrangements share a formal presupposition with nonstrategic arrangements. Finally, and perhaps most importantly, one of the rules of tournament chess is that there be no verbal communication between the two players. Chess is thus a superb example for cases in which there is no possibility of reliable cooperation between interactants.

Two final and quick distinctions: first, the game of chess differs from many nonzero sum games common to game theory (like the prisoner's dilemma) in several important ways. On one hand, in chess the rules govern the movement of pieces, and not the specific decisions that players make. In other words, the rules of chess dictate the movement of rooks, knights, bishops, pawns, and so on. The rules of game-theory games dictate the moves that *players* can make: in the case of the prisoner's dilemma, either to defect or to cooperate. Thus, the rules of chess leave room for players to choose between any multiplicity of moves, to consider strategy as well as tactics, whereas the prisoner's dilemma leaves room only for a single decision, and reduces "strategy" to a technical term that only the most entrenched game theorist could find plausible.

Second, the games of game theory are understood by way of payoffs. This is intentional, of course, and provides a clear schematic to analyze strategy in its purest context. The stipulations of the game are *strict* constraints on behavior, and disregard any and all nonstrategic elements. The prisoner's dilemma, for instance, is not a *game* that one can play. To put this in terms common to this volume: there is no lusory attitude in view (Suits 2005). The prisoners in prisoner's dilemmas have limited strategic capacities. Games like the prisoner's dilemma, battle of the sexes, chicken, and so on, may therefore be "games" in the "game theory" sense, but they are not games that people *play*, and thus do not involve in any critically accessible sense *interaction*. If we are to investigate practical rationality with regard to behaviors and practices, we must assess the *playing* of the game, and not the *outcome* of the game itself.

To make my case, I will use dichotomous terms interchangeably throughout this paper: in the following section I use the terms "Speaker" and "Hearer" to refer to participants in a binary communicative exchange; in the section on chess I use the terms "White" and "Black." As should be clear, the terms Speaker and White refer to the primary autonomous actors in the examples, while the terms Hearer and Black refer to the coactors. First, however, a bit of background on discourse theory.

Discourse: How Things are Said

Perhaps one of the best places to start thinking about discourse theory is with its founding suppositions. One of these suppositions is that which Jürgen Habermas takes to be a rudimentary distinction between types of action orientations. He proposes, along with other theorists of the Frankfurt School, that humans are capable of acting in at least one of two ways: they may take actions oriented toward achieving their own ends, or they may take actions oriented toward achieving understanding with others. Habermas dubs the first variety "strategic action" and the second "communicative *inter*action." "Whereas in strategic action one actor seeks to *influence* the behavior of another by means of the threat of sanctions or the prospect of gratification in order to *cause* the interaction to continue as the first actor desires, in communicative action one actor seeks *rationally* to *motivate* another by relying on the illocutionary binding/bonding effect (*Bindungseffekt*) of the offer contained in the speech act" (Habermas 1995, 58). In chess, one employs strategic reason; in discourse, Habermas believes, one employs communicative reason.

This distinction gives rise to his analysis of the "pragmatics" of communicative interaction. In many ways, it is one of the central distinctions around which Habermas bases most of his writings. His opus, the two-volume *Theory of Communicative Action*, testifies to the theoretical mileage that he gets from his analysis of the universal pragmatics of communication. Meaning emerges, he argues, through a series of exchanges in which Speaker and Hearer not only understand the words used, but in order to understand, must place themselves in each others' shoes (Habermas 1987a, 1987b).

Imagine that you walk into a bar and utter to the bartender, "Nice weather today." The bartender can offer any number of responses to you. He may respond by concurring with the objective validity of your statement. He may say, "Sure is. Haven't had sunshine like this since September." Alternatively, he may wonder aloud what you want. He may question your subjective intentions by raising a skeptical counterquestion, "How may I help you?" Or, he may even engage your judgment by pointing to broader social norms and values, "This? Nice weather? You haven't seen *nice weather* until you've spent some time in Tucson, Arizona." The point here is that however the bartender responds to you, he will always be responding to *you* in some manner. He will be doing so by calling attention to one of three validity claims on your part: a claim to objective validity (that what you say is true), a claim to subjective validity (that you truthfully believe what you say), or a claim to social validity (that what you say coincides with the norms of a larger social group). In turn, if the two of you begin the process of communication, you can raise responses to him.

This exchange functions in a reciprocal manner. When you raise a claim to the bartender, you act as the Speaker of the utterance "Nice weather today." And the bartender—at that point the Hearer—wonders to himself "What could this person mean by that?" and modifies his behavior to accommodate what he takes your meaning to be. If he thinks that you are being sincere and that you want to talk about the sunny weather, he may respond with a claim about the objective state of the world. If he thinks that you are being insincere and that you are just raising this claim for the sake of getting something from him, he may respond by questioning your sincerity. If he thinks that you are misusing the term "nice," he may offer a counterexample of what "nice" really is. Whatever he thinks you are doing, it is up to him, as your interlocutor, to judge your meaning. If he is truly having a discussion with you, he must give your utterances a charitable read, working with you, rather than against you, to come to an understanding of the claims that you make. He does this by placing himself in your shoes for a moment, wondering not, "What does *this person* mean?" but "What, if I were this person, would *I* mean?" He works with you by assuming your role to understand what you are saying. This is what Habermas calls "taking the role of the Other." However, by "taking the role of the Other," Habermas means nothing so problematic as that participants to communication maintain psychic access to the full psychosocial situation of the Other. This is unnecessary and impossible under most circumstances. Instead interlocutors can only ever *try* to understand what the other interlocutor means when she utters a statement X, given certain circumstances C. This entails leaping *into* (not out of) the contextual fabric of the Other's localized linguistic meaning.

To return to our case, the upshot of this is that both you and the bartender, Speaker and Hearer, engage in a mutual back-and-forth volley of validity-claim raising and yes/no stance-taking. Once you, as Speaker, have made a claim, the bartender, as Hearer, then holds the option of affirming or denying your claim. He himself then becomes a Speaker and you become a Hearer, the two of you switching your roles as Speaker and Hearer throughout the conversation. You each take turns, toggling between the roles of Speaker and Hearer in an attempt to come to an understanding with one another. This hermeneutic continues down the line of discourse, so that language demonstrates itself to be teleological: oriented toward a convergence of positions. What is important here is not that discourse simply happens in this way, but that the way in which it happens necessitates that Speaker and Hearer not only minutely adapt their understanding of each other's position, but that they also adapt their own positions so as to be better understood. They *must*, in other words, take each other into consideration. They must, in still other words, *respect* one another.

Much of the thrust of discourse ethics therefore rests on the presupposition that two interlocutors can make interpersonally valid claims as to how to treat one another. A Speaker, for instance, can claim some privilege over a Hearer, and the Hearer can either accept or reject the Speaker's claim based on his understanding of his own position. The big idea here is that speech-capable creatures can make claims that influence and have meaning within the overall ethical framework. It is clear, given this rendering of intersubjective interaction, that discourse theory is anthropocentric, since those who cannot make counterclaims are not morally considerable on the same grounds that language users are. Nonlanguage users are left to suffer (or benefit) from the decisions of a communicative group. Discourse theory thus leaves the question of how to treat severely handicapped humans, young children, animals, plants, and rocks open to the determinations of the humans who notice that these others might need some ethical attention.

Discourse theorists arrive at this solution because they propose that ethical obligations rest in the capacity of discursive subjects to make claims for their own interests, desires, and rights. Certainly, of course, the fact that Speakers can make claims for themselves makes the task of determining what is right in a given situation easier (though by no means simple), since the two interlocutors can both set to reasoning the issue out together. I take it that this is not, however, the right way to think about discourse. It is not in the *claims* of the interlocutors that one finds norms of behavior, but rather in the *comportment* of the Speaker toward the Hearer. Specifically then, in linguistically mediated intersubjective relationships we find not moral consideration, but the cashing out of *substantive* claims as to how Speakers and Hearers are to be understood and treated. On the other hand, in the *interaction* itself, we find moral consideration. We find, to put it bluntly, that *Speakers* are the ones who take up positions with regard to the world, and insofar as they take up positions regarding the world, they are the ones who bear the onus of responsibility toward their interactants. This is to say only that the actions of the Speaker do not count as moral because the Hearer agrees to them, but because they appeal to norms of interaction that stand apart from the Hearer.

Chess: How Things are Done

Chess is life. —Bobby Fischer
Chess is like life. —Boris Spassky

When I play chess, I play with the intention of winning.[2] To win requires considerable skill on my part. It requires knowledge of the rules of chess, of strategies of play, of tactics for capturing, and so on. But to play chess, above all, requires that I assume that my partner can beat me. After every move, I must work to try to understand the position of my partner *no matter whether I play a novice, a Grandmaster, or a computer.* In fact, if I am playing chess, my actions are actions that demand not a position of assuming that my partner has a "mind" equivalent with my own, but only that my partner can make moves better than, or at least as well as, I can. If I am playing White, I must ask myself "What would I_{Black} do, if I had all the information that I have about where I_{White} am going to move next?" Playing the game of chess does not necessarily require a fully developed sense of strategy or tactics (after all, even novices "play" chess). Nor does playing chess require assuming that my partner will not be psychologically sophisticated enough to parry my moves. Playing chess, rather, requires acting in a way that takes the past moves and the *possible* moves of the other into consideration.

In part, this is much of what makes chess fascinating: not who beats whom, but *why* players move where they move. After a game, commentators scour moves and rank them on a scale of "??" to "!!" (where "??" signifies a possibly bad move and "!!" signifies a brilliant move). It is not uncommon to hear questions like: "Why did White move his rook to c1? What was White trying to do?" If White cannot answer this question when pressed, White has probably made a bad move (or, at least, a move that will get him in trouble later in the game). If Black cannot answer this question, there is a high likelihood that Black will not respond appropriately. Importantly, during the chess game between two participants, much of the answering of this question takes place in a formulation similar to this: "Since I cannot know, without asking, what White is thinking, What would I_{White} be trying to do by moving my piece to that square?" Moves are downright difficult to understand, and understanding each requires considerable analysis. What kind of analysis? Bernd Graefrath argues in this volume that the analysis could involve retrograde reasoning: "How did we get here?" But this clearly is not the only kind of analysis. It also involves assessing the possible future moves of an opponent. Thus, it appears that even in strategic games there is some taking of a position towards the Other. This position taking is not that of thematized speech, since the position taken toward the Other is based only on one action at a time. The position is always a guess as to the Other's intent. It is, in effect, an attempt at understanding and anticipating the actions of the Other. In fact, it is almost imperative, in these sorts of situations, that we, as players, make attempts to understand the Other. *Not* understanding the Other, and the Other's intent, will lose us the game.

Playing chess is a form of interacting. While playing chess is, in fact, interaction in its most strategic form, and the intentions of both players are to win, there are some crucial elements of action that bind the two players together in spite of their inability to communicate. The first is that to play chess, the player must take the role of the other. We can see this rather pointedly by referring to the commentary at the beginning of this chapter. Here, Mikhail Tal is in dire need of opening one of his files. He must devise a strategy to combat the moves of his opponent. His strategy, we see, is to move the rook into a dangerous position so that it will be taken by Black. Doing so loses him the rook, but gains him three other pieces with a total point value higher than that of his rook. The wrong way to think about the pragmatics of this situation is to look at the results of the exchange. For sure, Tal makes a very clever move that ultimately wins the game for him. What Tal also does, however, is put himself in the position of his opponent. To do this, he needs to anticipate which squares are the most important squares to cover, which pieces are the most central to the board, and which pieces are the most valuable to Black's position. Knowing this, in many ways, is an impossibility, so Tal does the next best thing: he makes an educated guess. He assumes that Hjartarson is sufficiently proficient in chess to see the very best moves on the board, and Tal parries with moves that respond to these possibilities. Tal, presumably, would act in exactly the same way if he were playing Garry Kasparov, Deep Blue, or a five-year-old.

In part, my argument here works in accordance with Daniel Dennett, who reasons that there are times when we might be better off taking an "intentional" stance toward other things. Dennett defines the intentional stance as "the strategy of interpreting the behavior of an entity (person, animal, artifact, whatever) by treating it *as if* it were a rational agent who governed its 'choice' of 'action' by a 'consideration' of its 'beliefs' and 'desires'" (Dennett 1996, 27). Dennett does not argue that we must *necessarily* take the intentional stance toward things, only that sometimes it makes sense to explain behaviors (or actions) by appeal to intentions. Whether or not actors actually possess these intentions is beside the point. What is instead to the point is whether we can give some reasonable explanation of the behavior that will help us understand it.

Chess-playing computers are a prime example of such situations in which it makes sense to take the intentional stance. Tal, were he playing Deep Blue or an even less sophisticated computer, would indeed assume that the computer had some sort of plan. He may even do this though he knows that, at another level, he is only playing a hunk of silicon and plastic. For Tal, of course, the intentional stance is not a stance that he must take because he thinks it the "right" or "true" (ontological) stance to take; nor does he make a conscious decision to take this stance. He takes the intentional stance because the pragmatics of the situation require that he assume chess-playing computers have intentions, that they behave *as though* they have intentions—much in the way that the pragmatics of language use demand that we take the intentional stance with regard to our interlocutors.

Animal Interaction: Kings and the Jungle?

> "If you see a bear at close range . . . most important, don't panic or run wildly or scream. Running or other sudden movements may cause the bear to charge. The first thing to do is nothing—make no sudden moves or sounds. Stand still. Be quiet. . . . Then, take a few seconds to carefully assess the situation. . . . Try to identify the bear as a black bear or a grizzly bear. Both are dangerous, but grizzlies are usually more ill-tempered. . . . Keep your backpack on. Look around for cubs. Scout around for climbable trees. And then plot your next move."
>
> —hiker's manual *Bear Aware* (Schneider 1996)

Let it be acknowledged from the outset that animals cannot play chess.[3] Nor can they discuss Middle East politics over a glass of wine. Animals can, and often do, however, take action. Insofar as they sometimes take actions that respond to human actions, I think it safe to say that humans periodically *inter*act with animals. On this reasoning, interacting with, say, a bear, is like playing chess with a computer. Sometimes my actions in dealing with the bear may be oriented toward beating it (if I am a bear poacher); other times my actions may be oriented toward making it out of the forest alive. Whatever my intentions, whatever the bear's intentions, I must grapple with the responses of the bear, as an imposing animal, to my actions. In many cases, it does me no good to assume that the bear is unaware of my intent. In fact, I cannot conceivably parry with the bear if I believe the bear to be unaware of my presence.

I can, of course, ignore its existence, and hope that it does nothing to come at me. (This, I daresay, is the position that Habermas takes with regard to the natural world and its animals: as though creatures are captured zoo critters, display objects for observation and examination only; as though the natural environment is one in which an individual makes passive observations.) No hiker's manual recommends this, however. Hiker's manuals, almost universally, recommend quickly and smartly coming to terms with the fact that you—small, pink, fleshy, and unfamiliar—are staring down the muzzle of a tremendous, unpredictable[4] brute. What really helps in dealing with bears, they imply, is taking an intentional stance with regard to the bear, treating it as though it has some conception of your presence, and responding accordingly: "Although bears use trails, they don't often use them during midday when hikers commonly use them. Through generations of associating trails with people, bears probably expect to find hikers on trails, especially during midday" (Schneider 1996). Ah, there it is: "bears probably *expect* . . ."—that darling, sentimental descriptor used by nature writers, hikers, pet owners, and farmers. "Want," "Desire," "Intend," "Hope." . . . All of these terms are used throughout accounts of relations with animals as a way of making sense of their actions. This is because, whether we like to think that animals actually have intentions or not, we often behave as if they do. In an article on philosophy and psychology, Donald Davidson proposes that behavior consists of the things we do. He reasons, "where there is behaviour, intention is relevant" (Davidson 1990, 229). Now, as far as Davidson is concerned, animals do not have thoughts, and thus cannot be autonomous intentional subjects. In the same article, Davidson reasons that what constitutes a mind is not whatever it *is*, but what it can *do*. I take him seriously in this claim. His claim is deeply pragmatic, reasoning that since we cannot know what constitutes a mind, we might as well concern ourselves with the playing out of behaviors.

The point here is that animals, whether or not they actually have minds, act in surprisingly minded-like ways. Which is to say, animals *behave*. They attack. They retreat. They play with their children. They investigate curiously. They protect their families. They sing. They court one another. And most of all, they respond to us as though we are a part of their environment. Of course, not all animals do all of these things—barnacles, for instance—but many do. And whether or not the actions of attacking, retreating, playing, investigating, protecting, courting, and responding actually are *behaviors* in the strict sense that Davidson may mean it, it makes much more sense for us to think about them as though they *are* intentional behaviors than if we do not. We might as well be placing ourselves in the roles of the animals and taking the intentional stance with them. The intentional stance, however, is not a stance that we must take because we think it "right" ontologically. Nor is it a stance that we take because we make a decision to take this stance. We take the intentional stance because the pragmatics of the situation require that we assume that animals have intentions—much in the way that the pragmatics of language use, and the pragmatics of playing chess with a computer, demand that we take the intentional stance with regard to our interactants.

There is one crucial way in which animals differ from chess playing computers, and perhaps the singularly most important way: we can turn computers on and off. We have almost complete control over their actions. When we want them to print, they print. When we want them to sit silently, they sit silently. When we want them to play chess, they play chess. By contrast, animals we cannot turn off. Animals act of their own accord. We cannot tell them where to go, how to move their heads, or when to make a noise. We may be able to forcibly coerce them to do what we want, but always, somehow, there is an element of uncertainty about how they will behave at any given moment. To get them to do what we want, even if we are the most coercive laboratory scientist, we must interact with them. We must *respond* to their flailing by strapping their arms and their legs into constraining devices, *respond* to their blinking by holding their eyes open, and *respond* to their crying by anaesthetizing them. To do this requires guessing what we would do, were we in their bodies, if someone tried to restrain our arms, open our eyes, or injure us.[5]

Conclusion

The point of this argument should here make itself known. The obligation to consider the position of another under discourse ethics is rooted not in an agent's taking up of substantive claims by another Speaker, but rather in the interaction between the Actor and the Interactant. Where the agent interacts with some Other, she takes a stance and attributes intentionality to that Other. In the case of playing chess with another human or with a computer, there are important ways in which we actually play the game. We wait our turn, we ask ourselves what the Other is going to do, we respond to the actions of our opponent. We do not, by contrast, spit in the face of our opponent, smash our opponent over the head, strap our opponent down, or turn off the CPU. To do this would fly in the face of playing chess. There are no metaphysical restrictions on us doing any of these things, to be sure; and so we are not restricted from doing them in this sense. But we cannot do them and still be *playing* chess. That is the point.

In the case of interaction between human and nonhuman animals, taking the role of the Other is the norm. When we encounter bears in the wilderness, we must assess our situation as though we are in the role of the bear. We assume the role of the bear, for a few frantic moments, in an attempt to understand how the bear will respond to our presence. Have we the means, we can do almost anything to the bear. We can hit it with a stick, we can pelt it with rocks, or we can run like hell. But whatever we *do* with the bear, we can be sure that our action will provoke a response (unless we kill it outright). And here is the crux of this matter: whereas with computers we can end chess games and still be using our computers, we cannot with animals end interactions and still be interacting with them. Put another way, we cannot both end chess games and still be playing chess games. This comprises a flat, logical contradiction. Insofar as we always *are* interacting with animals, always taking the role of the animal in order to understand it, we are always caught up in considering its desires, needs, wants, and intentions. And this, one might argue, lays firm ground for understanding how we *ought* to act.

NOTES

1. See Pietarinen, Vossen, Morriss, and Martin in this volume.
2. For sure, there are many times that I play chess without intending to win. If I play against a young child, for instance, I could intend my chess playing to be more instructive than success-oriented. I will not be considering these examples here.
3. I realize the potential disagreement over such an issue. For sure, humans are animals, and we play chess. As well, there is no good evidence to suggest that there is not an alien colony of Grandmasters travelling the cosmos in search of human opponents. For the sake of argument, however, I will be using the term "animals" to refer to nonhuman animals.

4. By "unpredictable" here I mean "unpredictable to a satisfactory degree of certainty." Our interactions with other humans are, to a certain degree, also "unpredictable," but less so. The Habermasian reconstruction of interaction depends on this unpredictability of action to explain why we must always modify our position and understanding of the other.

5. Put another way, and perhaps more technically, we build computers with our hands and our ingenuity. Insofar as we build them with our hands and our ingenuity, we create them, in essence, as instrumental extensions of ourselves. As instrumental extensions of ourselves, they are stripped of any independent relation to the so-called natural world. The material resources out of which they are made, then, become subordinated to the form of the object qua implement. As an implement, the reason governing these tools is *purely* instrumental, and not in the least discursive/interactive. This to say only that we do not really *interact* with computers (or other technological devices) in the same way that we might interact with something that has not been created strictly for our use. When we interact with chess software, we effectively put the software to our own prespecified use. Computers are tools, made by us for specific purposes. Animals are more than tools, and are not made by us.

REFERENCES

Davidson, Donald. 1990. *Actions and Events*. Oxford: Oxford University Press.

Dennett, Daniel C. 1996. *Kinds of Minds*. New York: Basic Books.

Fealy, Manus P. 1994–2002. *The Great Pawn Hunter: Chess Tutorial*. Accessed July 23, 2006. Available from http://members.aol.com/manusfealy2/ch27.htm.

Habermas, Jürgen. 1987a. *The Theory of Communicative Action*. Vol. 2, *Lifeworld and System*. Translated by Thomas McCarthy. Boston: Beacon Press.

———. 1987b. *The Theory of Communicative Action*. Vol. 1, *Reason and the Rationalization of Society*. Translated by Thomas McCarthy. Boston: Beacon Press.

———. 1995. *Moral Consciousness and Communicative Action*. Translated by Christian Lenhardt and Shierry Weber Nicholson. Cambridge, MA: MIT Press.

Schneider, Bill. 1996. *Bear Aware*. Montana: Falcon Press.

Suits, Bernard. 2005. *The Grasshopper: Games, Life and Utopia*. Ontario: Broadview Press. Orig. pub. 1978.

10

Casuistry and Chess: Some Methodological Lessons for Ethics

PETER MORRISS

How can we tell right from wrong? More exactly, how can we tell how some action (either proposed or already performed) is right or wrong?

In the history of philosophy, there is a way of going about answering this question. It claims that we have certain *principles*, and by using these principles we can decide on the rightness of the action. Examples of such principles are the Ten Commandments, or the Golden Rule ("Act towards others as you would have them act towards you"),[1] or Kant's prohibition on treating anybody merely as a means to one's own ends,[2] or the injunction that we must never violate another person's rights, or the utilitarian demand that we always act so as to bring about the greatest happiness of the greatest number. Although these principles are different from each other, they all work in a similar way. They claim that we know *in general* how to determine whether an action is right or wrong: it is right if it fits with the principle, it is wrong if it violates the principle.[3] Ethics, then, is *deductive* in form: we know the general principles, and we then apply them to a problematic situation by seeing what they say about the specific facts of the case.

That is pretty much how ethics tends to work. But there is an obvious problem: this "solution" simply reproduces the same problem with which we started, but at a deeper level. For how can we tell which *principles* we should adopt? As I have indicated in the previous paragraph, there are several different candidates, and unfortunately they can often give us different answers to the question of what we should do in a given instance.

So how *do* we decide which principles to adopt? I wish I could tell you. Philosophers have labored long and hard to come up with reasons why some set of principles are the best—but nobody has managed to convince even the majority of other philosophers that *their* set of principles must be considered to be the *correct* set. So maybe there is some other approach that stands a better chance of success?

An alternative approach goes as follows: it doesn't matter that we can't decide which principles to adopt—we don't need principles in the first place. Instead we can gain knowledge of what we should do in certain typical cases, and then infer from this knowledge what we should do in more problematic cases. Since we decide on a case-by-case basis, we do not need any general principles. This is the method of casuistry.

The authors of the best recent book on casuistry, *The Abuse of Casuistry*, start their book by telling a story of how they were both appointed to an American bioethics commission set up by the U.S. Congress (Jonsen and Toulmin 1988, vii, 16–19). The members of this commission had widely different backgrounds, and held to different religious and philosophical views. Everybody expected, therefore, that they would find it very difficult to reach agreement on anything. However, as it turned out, they agreed on most things without difficulty.

> Members of the commission were largely in agreement about their specific practical recommendations; they agreed what it was they agreed about; but one thing they could not agree on was why they agreed about it. So long as the debate stayed on the level of particular judgments, the eleven commissioners saw things in much the same way. The moment it soared to the level of "principles," they went their separate ways. Instead of securely established universal principles, in which they had unqualified confidence, giving them intellectual grounding for particular judgments about specific kinds of cases, it was the other way around. (Jonsen and Toulmin 1988, 18)

Casuistry, then, seems to work; and it avoids the difficult and probably irresolvable foundational problems in ethics. Partly for these reasons, the method of casuistry has recently become once more quite popular.

In this chapter I will proceed as follows. I will first sketch how casuistry works. I will then suggest that the process involved is very similar to how a strong chess player decides what move to play in a game. Finally, I will argue that this surprising comparison allows us to gain a deeper insight into the strengths and weaknesses of casuistry as a method in ethics.

Casuistry

Casuistry means, literally, the discussion of cases. It has long been associated with the Catholic Church, and in particular the Jesuits, although now it seems to be gaining a wider following. In this section, I will first briefly trace the history of casuistry; I will then look at its logic; I will lastly look at its contemporary appeal.

Casuistry—like most philosophical ideas—can be traced back to Aristotle, and perhaps beyond. But it became important in its adoption by the Catholic Church. As the Church developed in its first millennium, increasing importance was given to the institution of confession. In confession, a priest hears an account of the activities of the penitent, and has to decide—amongst other things—whether these activities were sinful. If they were, the priest must then determine how serious that sin was and what an appropriate penance would be. Such a determination requires a detailed and nuanced appreciation of when actions are indeed wrong. This appreciation was developed slowly, and reached its peak around the middle of the sixteenth century.

Unfortunately, casuistry at its height became increasingly subtle, in the bad sense of that word. One school—called the "probabilists"—argued that it is acceptable to perform any action that is probably permissible ("possibly permissible" might be a better reading), even if it is "more probable" that the action is wrong. This came to be read as stating that no action is wrong if one can provide *any* reason—however implausible—why the action might not be wrong. Anybody with a sufficiently ingenious mind could come up with such a reason. One *cause célèbre* was the opinion that killing might often be acceptable; for instance, if a gentleman is faced with someone who intends to attack his honor by slapping him, he could kill that person if there is no other way to avoid the insult.[4] This was because honor, to a gentleman, might be more important than life itself. It had earlier been established that one could kill an attacker in defense of one's life; therefore it was acceptable to kill in defense of something possibly more important than life—namely, honor. Although this conclusion seemed to run quite counter to Christ's well-known teaching that one should turn the other cheek, there were some, including some Jesuits, who accepted this argument. Such casuists seemed to some critics to be quite lacking in morals.

One such critic was Blaise Pascal, who in 1656 wrote his *Provincial Letters*: a withering satire on casuistry in general, and the Jesuits in particular.[5] This seems one of the few occasions in the history of thought where one work had the effect of demolishing a school of thought: casuistry was fatally wounded, to the extent that the word gained its modern sense of "a quibbling or evasive way of dealing with difficult cases of duty."[6]

But it has recently been argued that the conclusion drawn from Pascal's critique was too sweeping: the casuistry which he destroyed was bad because it was *bad* casuistry, not because the casuistic method *itself* is bad. Maybe casuistry can be rescued, refined, and restored to a significant place within ethics. That is the task set to those who want to bring about the modern revival of casuistry. Easily the best such account is Jonsen and Toulmin's, which I will here summarize.[7]

Casuistry follows a case-based, not a principle-based, method.[8] We start with simple *paradigm* cases, which are exemplars of right or wrong actions. We then move out from these paradigm cases, by deciding cases that are in some important way *analogous* to them. (In practice, of course, we start with a complicated case presented to us, and we use the method of analogy to establish which features it shares with which of the paradigm cases.) This reliance on analogy is crucial to the casuistic method. Casuistry relies on the logic of analogy, not the inductive-deductive approach of science.[9]

Casuistry does use general statements, but not as principles which are to be held absolutely. Instead, the general statements are *maxims*: rules of thumb, as it were. They enshrine the wisdom of experience, but are not to be employed rigidly. All maxims will have exceptions, and this requires that we be alert to the importance of the circumstances of the case: the maxims are to be applied sensitively to the prevailing circumstances. "The casuists incessantly called the circumstances to attention; they insisted that 'circumstances *make* the case' and inevitably modified moral judgment about it" (Jonsen and Toulmin 1988, 254). Further, it is recognized that very few judgments are certain; instead, the best we can do is to reach conclusions that are *probable*—or that have some degree of probability. This has definite advantages:

> The movement from paradigm through analogies, marked by slightly varying interpretations of accepted maxims, as applied to differing circumstances, gave the casuists a refined sensitivity to the manifold ways in which cases differed from one another. When advice was to be given to particular persons in particular situations, this sensitivity was a virtue. (Jonsen and Toulmin 1988, 255)

By contrast, reliance on principle produces dogmatism.

What we have here is an attractive approach. It is practical, and it is sensitive; it takes due account of the rich texture of moral life. It therefore fits in with some recent trends of thought, which are hostile to the dry rigor of acting on principle (which is nowadays often derided as Enlightenment thought). It appeals to postmodernism, and to the emphasis on *narrative* in understanding the human condition. It also appeals to that strand of feminist thinking known as "care ethics." Care ethicists advocate sensitivity to the richness of cases, and a willingness to understand sympathetically how people can be faced with conflicting claims, particularly those emerging from their relations with others. Like casuists, they reject reliance on abstract principles, but would presumably be appalled to be thought to be following any sort of Catholic thinking.[10]

Casuistry is thus in accordance with several strands in recent thought. Further, its advocates usually support its use in ethics by claiming that the method is one with which we have long been very familiar. Usually comparisons are drawn with the practice of law or medicine—not coincidentally, both are prestigious (and hitherto male-dominated) professions.[11] But what must jump out at any chess player is the similarity between this account and that of how people play chess. I shall now turn to examine the literature on how good chess players think.

Chess

Serious research into chess players' thinking commenced with a path-breaking study by Adriaan de Groot in 1946. He selected a number of positions from actual games . . . and presented [them] to a group of subjects, consisting of grandmasters, masters, experts and less skilled class players. They were not familiar with the positions presented. Each subject was requested to make a move only after proper deliberation, as if he were engaged in his own game, and, in addition, to think out loud as fully as possible so that the protocol would contain a picture of the way by which he had reached his choice of move. This means that the object of the present investigation is not the analysis of the way in which a chess game is built up in its entirety, but rather the analysis of how the chess player (subject) solves the *choice-of-move* problem. (de Groot 1946, 15)

De Groot's Grandmasters were very strong indeed: they included the then-current world champion (Alekhine—universally acknowledged to be the best player at the time), a previous world champion (Euwe), and a player often called the strongest player never to be world champion (Keres); the others were Flohr, Fine, and Tartakower, all top-rate players. No subsequent researcher has been blessed with such a distinguished panel.

What de Groot found was that—as we would expect—the stronger players came up with stronger moves in the test positions. But what is interesting is *how* they managed to do that. The non–chess player might expect the stronger players to spend more time thinking, but they did not: they thought for less time.[12] They also—more surprisingly—did not analyze any more deeply.[13] Where the difference lay was in *what* the Grandmasters looked at: they invariably considered the best moves. Most of the less strong players, however, did not consider the best move at all: they simply did not think it was worth investigating. It can be said that Grandmasters do not necessarily *think* better than weaker players; but they *do* have a much better "feel" for the position. This "feel" is apparent to any chess player of lower rank who has watched a Grandmaster play a blitz game: even though the Grandmaster might play all their moves in only a minute—and therefore has very little time to think, and no time for deep calculations—the standard of play is usually astonishingly high. So the secret of success in chess, as in so much else, is knowing what to look for.

How do Grandmasters manage this? According to de Groot,

The theory of chess strategy is generally formulated in 'rules,' rules that connect typical positions with corresponding strategic schemes.

Although these rules are of great didactic importance in substantially abbreviating the learning process of younger generation players, they have the drawback—not very surprisingly—of never being rules without exceptions. Pawn grabbing in the opening is not always fatal; the Rook need not always stand behind the passed Pawn; the pair of Bishops or a Queen side Pawn majority or a protected passed Pawn or a massive Pawn center is not always an advantage. (de Groot 1946, 303)

One can call these rules "maxims."[14] The secret of success in chess is not only knowing the maxims, but knowing when to apply them. The thought process here proceeds by analogy. Grandmasters are familiar with a large range of positions, and have learned what they should do in them. When presented with a new position, they see that it is "like" a position they know, and look to see if what worked then would work now. This might be called "intuition," providing it is understood as an intuition that is based on a vast amount of experience. It is important that often strong players cannot explain *why* they have arrived at the correct answer; they often seem to the player little more than a hunch.

Characteristically, the implied judgments are by definition supposed to be *generally correct* or at least to be better than chance, while at the same time *the subject cannot (completely) explain his motives.* . . . Most conspicuous are those riveting cases where intuition points in a direction different from the other arguments: the 'feeling that . . .' may at times be stronger than substantial evidence to the contrary. (de Groot 1946, 309–10)[15]

What seems to be clear is that Grandmasters use a method very similar to casuistry: they reason analogically from (known) paradigm cases; they use maxims that need to be followed or rejected depending on circumstances; the judgments they reach are probable and usually not certain. And what is also clear is that this way of thinking *works*. The great advantage that chess has over ethics, law, and medicine is that there is a clear and impartial test as to whether one is any good. There is, in chess, little leeway for gaining success through nepotism, pulling rank, or abusing one's power. If one wants to be good at chess, one has to learn to think in this way. Hence we have established that, in at least one practical test, an approach like casuistry is the one to adopt. That might suggest that it may also be the best approach in some other practical contexts, such as ethics.

It might at this point be worth looking at a different approach to playing chess: that followed by computers. The task of programming a computer to play chess has an obvious appeal to programmers, precisely because the result provides a sure assessment of one's achievement. The first clear account of how to do this was made in 1950 (Shannon 1950), and serious programs were developed soon after. Initially it was thought that the best approach was to try to mimic the human approach to chess, and the winner of the first World Computer Chess Championship in 1974—the Russian KAISSA—did attempt to think analogically.[16] However, these early computer programs were very weak; by human standards, they were little more than a joke. It was then realized that it was too complicated to program computers to think analogically; to be more accurate, the calculations required took up too much memory. Computer programs were better if they approached the matter deductively: not as humans do, but by means of an algorithm, by which a computer can calculate mechanically what it thinks the best move to be. Computers are good at calculating mechanically: they are machines, after all. But computers remained weak chess players throughout the 1980s. All this changed in 1997, with the famous (or infamous) victory by Deep Blue over Garry Kasparov—who was acknowledged to be the strongest player in the world by some distance, and thought by many to be the strongest player ever.[17]

But the fact that modern computers can now play chess to a very high level does not show that the approach adopted by computers is better than that adopted by humans. The main reason that computers have improved so much is that they are now much more powerful. The disparity in power between modern computers and the human brain is astonishing: "Deep Blue can examine and evaluate up to 200,000,000 chess positions per second. Garry Kasparov can examine and evaluate up to three chess positions per second" (IBM Research Department).[18] Given that, the fact that Kasparov only lost the match by 2.5 to 3.5 (and even then only because he virtually threw away the last game of the match) would seem to demonstrate that—other things being equal—the approach adopted by Kasparov was much superior to that adopted by Deep

Blue. So adopting the casuistical method is indeed the best way of performing well at chess.

Conclusions: Some Lessons for Ethics

We have seen that the method of casuistry works very well in a practical test. That suggests that we do have to take the method seriously, and we cannot dismiss it just because it is different from the standard scientific model. Nevertheless, I want to suggest that there are differences between chess and casuistry that should make us wary of casuistry's claims. If I am right, then the casuistical method works in chess *only* because certain features are present in chess; and these features are absent in ethics. If these features are necessary for the casuistical method to work, then this undermines casuistry's claims.

The first difference follows on from the point I was making towards the end of the last section (before the subsection on computer chess). Chess is unlike ethics in that there is a clear and indisputable way of resolving whether people are practicing the activity well. This, I suggested, is a reason for taking the claims of casuistry seriously. But it also makes the activity very different. Not only do we have a fairly accurate way of distinguishing between strong and weak players, but also each player is continuously gaining feedback about what works and what does not. Without even knowing it (and certainly without knowing *how*), the talented player is gaining a sense of what works in what sort of position, and what does not. That is not the case in most other fields of endeavor. As de Groot pointed out:

> the irrefutable argument of victory . . . continually provides the learner with reliable, objective information on the standing of his achievements and shortcomings. In [this] respect, professional skills like those of the family doctor or practising psychologist are much less transparent. . . . In many other fields as well, it is hard to distinguish clearly between real masters and phony masters . . . in which subjectivity, prejudices, and faulty generalizations occur. (de Groot 1946, 352)

The casuistical method seems to work, then, if (and, I suggest, *only* if) there is this continuous feedback, allowing the practitioner to acquire expertise effortlessly. When this is not the case, it is all too easy to simply follow authority (or be *forced* to follow authority); to think that one is right because that is what orthodoxy tells one. Chess is not like that; there is a sense in which it is very democratic. In chess, authority can always be challenged, and is constantly having to defend itself against rivals, in a way that would have appealed greatly to someone like J. S. Mill.

Chess is, in this sense, more democratic than ethics. However, there is another sense in which it is much less so, and here it seems to me that the original practice of casuistry got it right. It is well known that chess players differ widely in strength, and the judgment of a Grandmaster should be taken far more seriously than that of a beginner. Indeed, the use of the word "master" is instructive. De Groot pointed out that the word was used "as an epithet for someone who has attained a high, generally recognized, degree of competence in a special trade or field" (1946, 316). (He says that this use has largely disappeared, except in music.) Such a person is "at home" in this area: "where one feels at home, one may go [one's] own way and bank on *the system of typical operations and thought habits* that were formed through experience" (317). To attain such mastery—to feel so "at home" in an area that one can trust one's judgment—takes time and effort; it has been calculated that to attain Grandmaster level takes a minimum of ten years of concentrated work (Simon and Chase 1973).

Thinking analogically is thus a skill that requires considerable effort and training: not anyone's intuitions will do. We do not trust the ordinary person-in-the-street's chess-playing intuitions; there is as little reason to trust his or her ethical intuitions. This has often been overlooked in the recent resurrection of casuistry, as it sounds too elitist for current sensibilities. Thus one recent advocate of casuistry has asserted that philosophy

> confers no special prestige. The middle-level principles or thick ethical concepts are notions that reasonable people know. Reasonable people should be able to triangulate [i.e., do casuistry] quite as well as philosophers provided they also gain the requisite experience with the appropriate range of cases.[19]

Now it is, of course, just possible that ordinary, and reasonable, people acquire their knowledge of casuistry through their ordinary daily dealings with people. However, consider how little time most people spend thinking about ethics, when compared with the efforts put in by a trainee Grandmaster. For instance, how many ordinary people have ever read a book on ethics? By contrast, to become a Grandmaster one has to work hard studying chess books for thousands of hours, as well as put a great deal of effort into practical play. When one adds in the absence of the automatic feedback effect in ethics, it seems unlikely that untrained people can have any grasp of casuistry. Thus it seems that the Jesuits were right: to acquire ethical knowledge in this way requires rigorous training. And, in ethics, we should *only* listen to people who have had this training. Anybody who finds that too elitist should not embrace casuistry.

There is a further lesson for ethics, which applies more generally than just to casuistry. Recently in philosophy there has been much use of "thought experiments" using fictional stories. Often we are asked to consider what our "intuitions" are about the rightness of the actions described in these stories—or, rather, the author gives his or her intuitions and tries to browbeat readers into accepting these intuitions as their own. I have already suggested that ethical "intuitions" are likely to be worthless: they are often either untrained assertions, or a recitation of the ethical principles in which we have been (consciously or unconsciously) trained. Often "intuitions" about the rightness or wrongness of certain conduct is just another word for prejudices, and therefore should have no part in ethical argument.

But consideration of the casuistical method in chess allows us to be more specific. I have already said that, as we would expect, Grandmasters perform much better than experts when faced with the choice-of-move problem in test positions. But one of the more interesting empirical findings is that this expertise usually disappears if the pieces are placed on the board at random, rather than the position arising from a game in the usual way. Grandmasters have a large stock of paradigm positions in their long-term memory, with which they can compare the new position; by using analogy, they can then grasp the essential points of a new position. But if the position is unlike one they have experienced before, they are as lost as the rest of us. Thus, in one experiment, players of different strengths were shown two positions, one a "natural" position and the other "unnatural," with pieces placed at random. In both positions there was a move available that gave immediate mate, and the subjects were asked to find it; the time taken to find the move was noted. (To make it slightly more informative, in each position there were four other moves giving check.) In the "natural" position, all the players quite quickly found the mate, although the weaker players took more than twice as long to do so than the stronger ones. In the "unnatural" position, players took much longer to find the mating move, and—crucially—there was no significant difference in the times taken by the different groups.[20] So, faced with "unnatural" positions, strong players perform no better than weak players.

This finding carries over to other intellectual areas (see, for instance, Kawamura, Suzuki, and Morikawa 2007). People who have developed an expertise at casuistry have done so by examining a large number of real-life cases. Their expertise is, therefore, limited to such "natural" sorts of cases. Faced with an "unnatural" case, their intuitions would be worthless. Many philosophers have liked producing such "unnatural" cases, sometimes in an attempt to avoid the prejudices that we might have about actual cases. Thus we might be asked how we should react to a group of visiting Martians, rather than visiting Nigerians. But insofar as our ethical experience has not been concerned with Martians, any reactions we might have to them would be beside the point. Therefore, thought experiments that require us to use our ethical intuitions must concern situations of which we have some ethical expertise.[21] Far-fetched scenarios will not do.

I have tried to suggest that we can perhaps grasp the strength and weaknesses of the method of casuistry in ethics, by looking at how the same method works in a very different area in which it is clearly successful. I have suggested that the success of the method in chess gives us some reason to believe that the method is a viable one. (Looking at chess provides stronger support, I think, than the areas to which casuists like to draw attention—medicine and the law.) However, a closer look at the advantages that chess has for this method over ethics makes the case for casuistry less compelling. In chess there is a sure test of validity, and constant feedback to practitioners that naturally leads them to improve their performance; both are lacking in ethics. In their absence, there is less reason to believe that the method of casuistry would be successful. So it may be that the abuse of casuistry, to which Jonsen and Toulmin refer in the title of their book, is not an unfortunate accident, but an inevitable feature.[22] *Without* a sure test of validity, the method can be contorted to produce any conclusion that is desired—or that is allowed by the authorities. We should not, therefore, draw simplistic analogies between chess and ethics. A closer look tells us that it is implausible to suggest that "just as the master chess player can play 5–10 second/move games without significant degradation in her performance—so, too, might the morally mature person simply *see* the moral relevance of particular situations and evaluate accordingly" (Bartsch and Wright 2005, 547). When we look at *why* grandmasters can play very successfully thinking casuistically, we then see that it is unlikely to be a good way of thinking in ethics.

I want to close by suggesting a further reason why that might be the case. This consists of casuistry's vulnerability to slippery-slope arguments. These are arguments of the form that it is dangerous to allow some proposal that deviates from orthodoxy, because—even though the proposal may be acceptable in itself—it will inevitably lead to *un*acceptable claims being allowed.[23] Now, philosophers have typically made short shrift of slippery-slope arguments. They have pointed out that, if this new proposal is indeed acceptable, there must be a *reason* why it is acceptable. By establishing what that reason is, and adding it to our list of moral principles, we can ensure that we do not slide down the slippery slope into the unacceptable abyss. The reason will provide us with a morally adequate cut-off point.

This rejection of slippery-slope arguments works within the principled approach to ethics. But it does not work within casuistry. The approach of casuistry *is* vulnerable to slippery-slope disasters. This is because, in casuistry, we start with a paradigm of what is acceptable (or, of course, unacceptable). We then argue by analogy that the new case is much the same as the paradigm, and so is therefore also acceptable. But we have *not* established a reason, or principle, *why* it is acceptable. So when we find another case, further away from the paradigm but near to our new acceptable case, we tend to find that case acceptable as well. And so— wheee—it's down the slippery slope with us, with no fixed point to cling on to, to stop our descent.

A compelling example of such a fate—given by Bernard Williams—is the art world's acceptance of van Meegeren's forgeries of Vermeer. (See Williams 1985. For a fuller account of van Meergeren's activities, see Kreuger 2007.) Thirty-five paintings were known for sure to be by Vermeer: they were the paradigm cases.

When van Meegeren's first forgery, *Christ and the Disciples,* was "authenticated" by Vermeer experts, it was then added to the canon: although slightly different from the others, it served to show—the experts now thought—that Vermeer produced a wider range of paintings than had been hitherto suspected. From there it was easy for Van Meegeren: he could produce paintings that showed some resemblance to his false Vermeers, but less and less to the original paradigms. The slippery slope had corrupted the judgment of the experts, so that they no longer knew what was quintessentially Vermeer-like.

That casuistry is open to this possibility was one of the arguments Pascal used, in his *Provincial Letters,* to explain how casuists reached the astounding conclusion that it was acceptable to kill to avoid being hit in the face.[24] Others have considered that they have personally been corrupted by failing to avoid some slippery slope: "Charles Lamb complained that by gradual changes, not on his part, but in the spirit of refinement, he found himself growing insensibly into 'an indecent character'" (De Quincey 1839, 357–58).[25]

Casuistry is, then, open to the drawback that a slippery slope may lead us to perdition. But chess is not. When we stray too far from the path of righteousness, we start losing games. That gives us a warning that we have extended too far the analogical likeness to the paradigm. The existence of a clear criterion of validity provides a brake that prevents us from hurtling down the slippery slope. In ethics there is no such brake.

So for both casuistry-in-chess and the principled approach to ethics we need not fear slippery-slope arguments. But for casuistry-in-ethics we do need to fear them. And this, of course, works both ways: there is always the possibility that we will inadvertently step onto a slippery slope and end up in ruin; but there is also the fear—whenever an argument for change is proposed—that *it* is the first step on to the slope. I am not aware of any way of diagnosing in advance which slopes are really slippery; so there is a reason to fear them all. That motivation can make casuistry very conservative. On the one hand, we slide to ruin; on the other, we fear to make any change at all; and there is no test to prevent these twin—presumably both unacceptable—fates.

So it may be that in ethics we cannot give up arguing on the basis of principles.

NOTES

1. "Therefore all things whatsoever ye would that men should do to you, do ye even so to them: for this is the law and the prophets" (Matthew 7:12).

2. "Act in such a way that you always treat humanity, whether in your own person or in the person of any other, never simply as a means, but always at the same time as an end" (Kant 1785, 91).

3. There are also other categories: for instance an action is permissible if it is neither required nor forbidden. I will not consider such complexities here.

4. See Jonsen and Toulmin 1988, chap. 11, for a discussion of this example.

5. Pascal's *Provincial Letters* (1656), which was originally published anonymously.

6. *Oxford English Dictionary*. See also the illustrative quotations, for instance, that from Bolingbroke: "Casuistry . . . destroys, by distinctions and exceptions, all morality, and effaces the essential difference between right and wrong, good and evil" (Bolingbroke 1736, 170).

7. See *The Abuse of Casuistry* (Jonsen and Toulmin 1988), particularly chapters 1 and 13. An excellent historical account of how casuistry worked itself out in the Catholic Church on a single issue is Noonan 1965.

8. I should add that Jonsen and Toulmin seem to prevaricate on this point. While they do argue for the position I here attribute to them, they also sometimes write as if the casuistical move is that of deciding which *specific* cases fall under the agreed general principles. That would seem to make casuistry a principle-based methodology. They do not seem to me to resolve—or even address—this quite important difference. The position I discuss is the more interesting one, and also seems to me to be the position they would opt for if they were forced to make the choice.

9. The inductive-deductive method uses induction to move from an agreed case to a general principle which the case supports, and then uses deduction to move from the (now established) general principle to new cases that fall under it. The standard method of induction-deduction is the one we use when we observe that objects fall to the ground; we then induce to the general law that *all* objects (including those we have not observed) fall to the ground; and we then deduce that this rare Ming vase, being an object, would fall to the ground if it were not supported. The method of analogy involves only one move, not two: we infer *directly* from a known case to an unknown one, without going via a general rule. It is perhaps not a coincidence that Pascal's most important work was in mathematics and physics—both disciplines that reject arguments from analogy.

10. I am not aware of any discussion of casuistry by the main proponents of care ethics. Care ethicists consider that principle-based thinking
is not only wrong, but is a peculiarly male distortion. Yet since every
thinker in the development of casuistry was male—and was usually both
celibate and a member of a supremely male-dominated organization—the
existence of casuistry would seem to be a refutation of the claim that acting on principle is a manifestation of a peculiarly male logic.

11. It seems to me that the recent literature on casuistry adopts an
extraordinarily uncritical approach to law and medicine. It is perhaps note-
worthy that, of the recent works on casuistry which I have read and which
point to this parallel, not one refers to any empirical work on legal and
medical practice. Yet many think that in these fields malpractice occurs too
often to be a coincidence. Advocates of casuistry may, then, not be wise
to rely on these parallels without more detailed investigations.

12. See the summary statistics in de Groot 1946, 317–19. In the main
test position, Grandmasters thought for 9.6 minutes on average; the
much weaker "expert" sample—who would be strong club players—
thought for 12.8 minutes. Four of the five Grandmasters came up with
the best move; none of the experts did. (The fifth Grandmaster's move
was also stronger than any of the experts' moves.) The Grandmasters
did, however, think more efficiently: they considered more different
alternatives per minute.

13. The averages are 6.8 half-moves for Grandmasters and 6.6 for
experts, which is not a statistically significant difference. However, it has
been suggested that the test position was not typical, in that a very strong
player could see that deep calculation was not necessary. It is now
accepted that Grandmasters can calculate more deeply than lesser mortals
when required; but, in the vast majority of positions, a Grandmaster will
come up with a better move than an expert without calculating more
deeply.

Some support for these conclusions comes from a "longitudinal study"
of one chess player (DH), who was tested in 1978 (aged 16) when his
grading was 1570, and again in 1987, when it was 2423 (which is near
Grandmaster strength). When he was given choice-of-move tasks, the
older and stronger DH took slightly less time (506 sec. to 612), had the
same maximum depth of search (7), but a *narrower* breadth (3 to 4.75)
(Charness 1989, 187).

But, for some tentative divergent findings, see Campitelli and Gobet
2004.

14. As everyone knows, the beginner is taught certain maxims, precepts (or
technically, *heuristics*) of positional play which enables him to cope with
apparent disorder, e.g. 'seize open files', 'occupy the 7th rank with a rook',
'avoid isolated pawns', 'put your pawns on opposite coloured squares to those
of your bishop' etc etc. However, skill is marked, not by the application of such

precepts, but by the correct assessment of their competing claims, or by knowing when to violate them. . . . It is cases like this, perhaps, which make the Soviet school lay such stress on 'concrete analysis of the position' rather than on 'dogma'.

When a higher degree of skill is reached a conscious (verbal) assessment of a position in terms of potential rules is transcended. The master tends to 'zero in' on a position rather than use specific heuristics. (Hartston and Wason 1983, 10–11)

15. Thus, "A conversation between players of different strengths sometimes goes like this, when the stronger player rejects a move suggested by a weaker one in a post mortem.

Weaker Player: What's wrong with it?

Stronger Player : It's not good.

Weaker Player: Why not?

Stronger Player: It's not the sort of move you play in this sort of position. (*End of Conversation*)" (Hartston and Wason 1983, 59).

16. Newborn 1997, 43, and Frey 1977, 67–68. As late as 1977, most of the contributors to Frey's collection thought that chess-playing computers should be modeled on human ways of thinking. Thus, "Most workers in the field of computer chess agree that one should strive for a program that selects its moves in ways as similar as possible to the manner in which a human being makes such decisions. . . . Of course, it is conceivable that a machine could be programmed to play good chess even though it operates in a way radically different from its human counterpart, but there is no evidence today indicating that such an approach is feasible or preferable" (Hearst 1977, 186–87). By contrast, Slate and Atkin 1977, in Frey's collection, is a very clear account of an early chess-playing program that did not try to imitate human approaches. Modern programs all follow the basic ideas explained in this article.

17. For an account of the development of Deep Blue, see Hsu 2002.

18. Hsu gives the "theoretical maximum search speed" of Deep Blue as about one billion positions per second, while the "actual maximum speed" was around 200 million (Hsu 2002, 214).

19. Kuczewski 1997, 6. That is to say, ordinary people would be as good at philosophy as philosophers if they were philosophers, which is hardly to the point. And shortly afterwards, Kuczewski admits that, as casuistry uses analogy, "The ability to recognize the most pertinent factors of a situation in prescribing an action is important. It is the nature of this kind of practical reasoning that some persons can do it better than others" (12). That seems to undermine his claim that all "reasonable" people, without any special training, are able to do casuistry.

20. The article was published in *Chess* in 1984; I take this account of it from Przewoznik and Pein 1991, 13–14. The average times (in seconds) for the three groups were as follows:

	Group		
	Strong	**Medium**	**Weak**
Natural Position	8.5	14.25	18.11
Unnatural Position	36.3	35.0	33.4

I should perhaps point out that all of these were weaker players than de Groot's: the "strong" group had an average rating of 2022 (which is scarcely as strong as de Groot's "experts"); the "weak" group's rating was 1316, which would make them weak club players.

For a contrary view, which I do not find persuasive, see Holding 1985, 132–34. His "random positions" seem to me to be recognizable chess positions, albeit unusual ones. For a recent study that supports my argument against Holding, see Cowley and Byrne forthcoming, p. 26 of typescript.

21. Some thought experiments in ethics are designed to tease out the logic of a proposed argument. These are immune from my criticism here, which is concerned only with thought experiments that require ethical intuitions about some far-fetched scenario.

22. Jonsen and Toulmin credit their title to a passage in Kirk 1927, 125: "The *abuse* of casuistry is properly directed, not against all casuistry, but only against its *abuse*." (See Jonsen and Toulmin 1988, 16, 356n13.) The same phrase was used to make the same point, some hundred years earlier, by Thomas De Quincey: "In England, there is an aversion to the mere name ['casuistry'], founded partly on this, that casuistry has been most cultivated by Roman Catholic divines, and too much with a view to an indulgent and dispensing morality; and partly on the excessive subdivision and hair-splitting of cases; which tends to the infinite injury of morals, by perplexing and tampering with the conscience, and by presuming morality to be above the powers of any but the subtlest minds. All this, however, is but the abuse of casuistry; and without casuistry of some sort or other, no practical decision could be made in the accidents of daily life. Of this, on a fitter occasion, I could give a cumulative proof" (De Quincey 1823, 56n). For "the fitter occasion," see De Quincey 1839–40. De Quincey in these works argues for the "casuistry in the minor premise" view that I put aside in note 8.

23. There are many different forms of slippery slope argument. For a good analysis, see Govier 1982.

24. "Verily, fathers, your friend Escobar reasons uncommonly well sometimes; and, in point of fact, there is such a close connection between speculation and practice, that when the former has once taken root, you have no difficulty in permitting the latter, without any disguise. A good illustration of this we have in the permission 'to kill for a buffet,' which, from being a point of simple speculation, was boldly raised by Lessius into a practice 'which ought not easily to be allowed'; from that promoted by Escobar to the character of 'an easy practice'; and from thence elevated by

your fathers of Caen, as we have seen, without any distinction between theory and practice, into a full permission. Thus you bring your opinions to their full growth very gradually. Were they presented all at once in their finished extravagance, they would beget horror; but this slow imperceptible progress gradually habituates men to the sight of them and hides their offensiveness. And in this way the permission to murder, in itself so odious both to Church and State, creeps first into the Church, and then from the Church into the State" (Pascal 1656, letter XIII).

25. The editor of De Quincey's works admits to having been unable to trace the source of the quotation attributed to Lamb. But De Quincey also gives an example of what he considered a benign slippery slope; the attitude to usury had, he thought, changed for the better: "beginning in utter infamy, [it] has traveled upwards into considerable esteem" (1839, 357).

REFERENCES

Bartsch, Karen, and J. C. Wright. 2005. "Towards an Intuitionist Account of Moral Development." *Behavioral and Brain Sciences* 28:546–47.

Bolingbroke, H. St. J. 1736. *Letters, on the Spirit of Patriotism: On the Idea of a Patriot King: And on the State of Parties, at the Accession of King George the First.* London: A. Millar, 1749.

Campitelli, G., and F. Gobet. 2004. "Adaptive Expert Decision Making: Skilled Chess Players Search More and Deeper." *International Computer Games Association Journal* 27, no. 4: 209–17.

Charness, N. 1989. "Expertise in Chess and Bridge." In *Complex Information Processing: The Impact of Herbert A. Simon*, edited by D. Klahr and K. Kotovsky. Hillsdale, NJ: Lawrence Erlbaum Associates.

Cowley, Michelle, and R. M. J. Byrne. Forthcoming. "Chess Masters' Evaluative Expertise." *Cognitive Psychology.*

de Groot, A. D. 1946. *Thought and Choice in Chess.* The Hague: Mouton, 1978.

De Quincey, T. 1823. "Letters to a Young Man Whose Education Has Been Neglected: Outline of the Work." *London Magazine* 7. Reprinted in *The Works of Thomas De Quincey*, vol. 3, edited by F. Burwick, 50–58. London: Pickering and Chatto, 2000.

———. 1839–40. "Casuistry." *Blackwood's* XLVI (October 1839): 455–66 and XLVII (February 1840): 260–72. Reprinted in *The Works of Thomas De Quincey*, vol. 2, edited by J. North, 347–63, 364–82. London: Pickering and Chatto, 2003.

Frey, P. W. 1977. "An Introduction to Computer Chess." In *Chess Skill in Man and Machine*, edited by P. W. Frey. New York: Springer-Verlag.

Govier, T. 1982. "What's Wrong with Slippery Slope Arguments?" *Canadian Journal of Philosophy* 12:303–16.

Hartston, W. R., and P. C. Wason. 1983. *The Psychology of Chess.* London: Batsford.

Hearst, E. 1977. "Man and Machine: Chess Achievements and Chess Thinking." In *Chess Skill in Man and Machine*, edited by P. W. Frey. New York: Springer-Verlag.

Holding, D. H. 1985. *The Psychology of Chess Skill.* Hillsdale, NJ: Lawrence Erlbaum Associates.

Hsu, Feng-Hsiung. 2002. *Behind Deep Blue: Building the Computer That Defeated the World Chess Champion.* Princeton: Princeton University Press.

IBM Research Department. *Kasparov vs Deep Blue: A Contrast in Styles.* Accessed 27 July 2005. www.research.ibm.com/deepblue/meet/html/d.2.shtml.

Jonsen, A. R., and Stephen Toulmin. 1988. *The Abuse of Casuistry.* Berkeley: University of California Press.

Kant, Immanuel. 1785. *Groundwork of the Metaphysics of Morals*, translated by H. J. Paton as *The Moral Law.* London: Hutchinson, 1948.

Kawamura, Satoru, S. Suzuki, and K. Morikawa. 2007. "The Effect of Expertise in Hiking on Recognition Memory for Mountain Scenes." *Memory* 15:768–75.

Kirk, Kenneth. 1927. *Conscience and Its Problems, an Introduction to Casuistry.* London: Longmans, Green & Co.

Kreuger, Frederick H. 2007. *A New Vermeer: Han van Meegeren.* Rijswijk, Holland: Quantes.

Kuczewski, M. G. 1997. *Fragmentation & Consensus: Communitarian and Casuist Bioethics.* Washington: Georgetown University Press.

Newborn, M. 1997. *Kasparov Versus Deep Blue: Computer Chess Comes of Age.* New York: Springer-Verlag.

Noonan, J. T. 1965. *Contraception: A History of Its Treatment by the Catholic Theologians and Canonists.* Cambridge, MA: Harvard University Press.

Pascal, Blaise. 1656. *The Provincial Letters.* Harmondsworth: Penguin, 1967.

Przewoznik, J., and M. Pein. 1991. *The Blumenfeld Gambit.* Oxford: Pergamon Press.

Shannon, C. E. 1950. "Programming a Computer for Playing Chess." *Philosophical Magazine,* series 7, no. 41. Available at http://www.computerhistory.org/.

Simon, H. A., and W. G. Chase. 1973. "Skill in Chess." *American Scientist* 61:394–403.

Slate, D. J., and L. R. Atkin. 1977. "CHESS 4.5—The Northwestern University Chess Program." In *Chess Skill in Man and Machine*, edited by P. W. Frey. New York: Springer-Verlag.

Williams, Bernard. 1985. "Which Slopes Are Slippery?" In *Moral Dilemmas in Modern Medicine*, edited by Michael Lockwood. Oxford: Oxford University Press.

11

Chess Is Not a Game

DEBORAH P. VOSSEN

I have never played a game of chess. I have, however, studied chess by watching others play as well as reviewing a rulebook. As a result, I am confident that I understand how to and that I could actually play chess (although I'm not sure I could win!). This scenario parallels my experience with the Sorcerer's game of Quidditch. I have studied Quidditch[1] from J. K. Rowling's Harry Potter series (Rowling 1998) on the internet and in the movies and, if I happened to gain the ability to fly on a broomstick, I am sure I could participate in a game of Quidditch. Regardless, due to the fact that the actual ability to participate is reserved for Sorcerers, it remains true that I (as a mere Muggle) have never participated and will likely never participate in a real game of Quidditch. This illustration allows for one to make sense of the term "armchair athlete."

So, is chess a *game*? The answer lies somewhere in between my understanding of chess and the fact that I have never actually played it. Is the existence of chess as a game grounded in the understanding of chess or in the participatory experience itself? Of course, the same might be asked of Quidditch. This chapter will explore these questions and takes it point of departure from a theory presented in Bernard Suits's book *The Grasshopper: Games, Life and Utopia* (1978). Suits presents his theory on game playing in and through the mischievous guise of a Grasshopper. For the Grasshopper, "to play a game is to attempt to achieve a specific state of affairs [prelusory goal], using only means permitted by rules [lusory means], where the rules prohibit use of more efficient in favor of less efficient means [constitutive rules], and where such rules are accepted just because they make possible such activity [lusory attitude]" (Suits 1978, 41). Thus, the Grasshopper's necessary and jointly sufficient conditions for game are that any activity must possess *all* of the following four characteristics to qualify:

1) it must be a goal-directed activity (prelusory goal),
2) the rules must limit the permissible means of goal attainment (lusory means),
3) the rules must prohibit the more efficient in favor of less efficient means (constitutive rules), and
4) the rules must be accepted just so as to make the activity possible (lusory attitude).

The first condition requires that the activity be goal directed with the goal understood to be "the end of the activity that all participants aim to bring about in action therein" (Vossen 2004, 78). Essentially, this *prelusory goal* is characterized as a specific and achievable state of affairs describing no more and no less than is required.

The second and third conditions of the Grasshopper's definition refer to *rules* which provide a descriptive, defining framework for the activity at the same time as limit the permissible means of prelusory goal realization. Because these rules (taken jointly with the prelusory goal) identify all circumstances to be satisfied when participating in a game, they are referred to as *constitutive rules*. In my understanding, there are two kinds of constitutive rules; those that require and permit means of goal attainment and those that prohibit means of goal attainment. The means that are required and permitted by the constitutive rules are referred to as the *lusory means* (that is, the Grasshopper's second necessary condition). On the other hand, means that are prohibited by the constitutive rules are characterized as tactics considered more efficient with respect to prelusory goal attainment than those allowed as lusory means. The Grasshopper's third condition specifically requires that the easiest, simplest, most useful, and direct approach to prelusory goal attainment is prohibited by the constitutive rules always in favor of the lusory means which are recognized to be less efficient than the means ruled out by the constitutive rules.

The fourth essential condition is that the constitutive rules must be accepted just so as to make the game possible. This participatory stance is referred to as the *lusory attitude* and is highly unusual insofar as it dictates the acceptance of limitations that require the use of *less* efficient means toward an end simply for the reason that such acceptance makes the activity possible as a game. "In anything but a game, the gratuitous introduction of unnecessary obstacles to the achievement of an end is regarded as a decidedly irrational thing to do, whereas in games it appears to be an absolutely essential thing to do" (Suits 1978, 39). The point is simply that "no rational individual would ever voluntarily choose to set up unnecessary obstacles to make goal attainment more difficult unless that individual is participating in a game" (Vossen 2004, 79). Consider this: An alien from a world of productive and purposeful action (wherein the concept of a game does not at all exist in its experience) arrives to study the behavior of students at the Hogwarts School of Witchcraft. Observing the Quidditch occurrence, the alien would most likely be entirely bewildered as it questioned the logic of this particular scenario: If it is important to have possession of the little moving ball (the Golden Snitch), then why would these creatures release it from its prison only to try to recapture it? Of course, the answer is because they are participating in a game.

Now, although the Grasshopper's theory is entirely capable of addressing the question of whether or not chess is a game, there's one critique contained within the literature that confuses the issue by raising doubt about its coherency. This critique is offered by Angela Schneider and Robert Butcher in the essay entitled "Prelusory Goals for Games: A Gambit Declined" (1997). Accordingly, rather than simply answering the question via a direct application of the theory, this chapter will take a slight detour so as to confront Schneider and Butcher's critique of it. More specifically, I will defend the Grasshopper's theory against the criticism raised so as to justify my faith in its ability to address the question.

Prelusory Goals for Games: A Gambit Declined

So, going directly to the heart of the matter, I turn to the critique itself. Of the four necessary and sufficient conditions forwarded by the Grasshopper, Schneider and Butcher assault one. Essentially, the critics argue that the Grasshopperian notion of a *prelusory goal* is incoherent and unsalvageable and ought therefore to be abandoned within the philosophy-of-sport literature. Of course, since the four conditions work together to provide the Grasshopper's definition, the suggestion is that the theory itself is flawed.

Schneider and Butcher begin with the concept of a *prelusory goal* and clarify its nature as a specifically achievable state of affairs that can be "described before, or independently of, any game of which it may come to be, a part" (1997, 39).[2] With regard to chess, the authors entertain four prelusory goal options including checkmate spatiotemporally defined, arranging tokens in a pattern, checkmate conceptually defined, and immobilizing the king. Basically, *checkmate spatiotemporally defined* involves a list of all potential combinations of chess figures constituting *checkmate*. Except for its reference to concepts unique to chess, this first option is similar to the second, *arranging tokens in a pattern*, which involves the display of chess figures in an array recognized to signify the end of the game. *Checkmate conceptually defined* is similar to *immobilizing the king* insofar as the conceptual definition of checkmate is understood as the capture of the opponent's king with both represented by a scenario wherein the opponent's king is unable to escape inevitable capture.[3]

Using their derived test of independence, the authors disqualify checkmate spatiotemporally defined, checkmate conceptually defined, and immobilizing the king because all three represent ideas that cannot be conceptualized without, at a minimum, an introduction to a chessboard and/or king figure. Since a chessboard and king figure are concepts requiring knowledge of the game of chess, all three options are arguably dependent upon the objects, rules, and procedures of chess and cannot therefore be described before, or independently of, the game of chess. For this reason, all three represent inappropriate options for the prelusory goal of chess. In addition to failing the test of independence, checkmate spatiotemporally defined is flawed insofar as it can be represented by an infinitely large list of patterns that cannot possibly meet the requirements of distinctness or specificity (that is, it also fails the test of specificity). Similarly, the final option of arranging tokens in a pattern is deemed inappropriate as the prelusory goal of the game of chess due to the fact that it fails the test of specificity.

In a nutshell, Schneider's and Butcher's position is that the game of chess has no identifiable object that can be jointly characterized as "specific" and "independently describable of that game." Analysis of each logical possibility reveals that it is inappropriate as the prelusory goal of chess because it is either too indistinct to be

deemed specific (that is, it fails the test of specificity) and/or it is
unable to be comprehended without reference to concepts special
and unique to the game of chess (that is, it fails the test of independence). Essentially, since there is no identifiable goal for the
game of chess that is simultaneously capable of passing both the
test of specificity and the test of independence, Schneider and
Butcher conclude that chess fails to possess a prelusory goal as
defined by the Grasshopper. "This either means that chess is not a
game or that the account of games that requires that they have prelusory goals is false" (1997, 41). Yet they feel it is clear that chess
is a game. Accordingly, they reject the Grasshopper's notion of a
prelusory goal as defined.

Chess is a game. This statement appears commonsensical and,
as noted, fundamental to Schneider and Butcher's (1997) position
against the Grasshopper.[4] Although apparently a rational assumption, it is my position that it is mistaken and that it places the merits of their argument in severe jeopardy. I will demonstrate that
chess, as characterized by Schneider and Butcher, is not a *game* at
all. If this demonstration proves convincing, then we must concede
that Schneider and Butcher's argument is unsound, and since an
unsound argument is incapable of grounding its conclusion, we
can discard as false the assertion that the notion of a prelusory goal
is incoherent and ought to be deserted. Accordingly, we can conclude that the Grasshopper's theory, inclusive of the notion of a
prelusory goal, ought to continue to be embraced as a coherent
theory of games.

A Grasshopperian Critique of Schneider and Butcher's Characterization of Chess

In my opinion, not only are Schneider and Butcher wrong in their
characterization of chess, but also guilty of misinterpreting, mis-
applying, and perhaps even corrupting the Grasshopper's theory
of games. Off to a bad start, Schneider and Butcher begin their
paper with the assertion that a game is defined by a prelusory
goal taken together with a set of constitutive rules that are responsible for denoting the lusory means for achieving the prelusory
goal (1997, 38). They assure the reader that this represents an *elucidation* of the Grasshopper's account, but I will demonstrate that
Schneider and Butcher's position is more accurately described as
a *transformation*.

The Idea of Chess versus a Game of Chess

The difference between the Grasshopper's position on games and
Schneider and Butcher's elucidation of it is as slight as it should be
obvious: The Grasshopper's account includes a *lusory attitude*
while Schneider and Butcher's version completely omits this participatory stance! For the Grasshopper, a *game* does not actually
exist as a tangible *activity* unless *all four* of the earlier mentioned
features are present, whereas for Schneider and Butcher only the
first three appear relevant in classifying games.

The importance of the Grasshopper's lusory attitude cannot be
understated as it represents the *unifying* element of his definition.
This stems from the fact that a *participatory stance* is required that
incorporates the participant's knowledge of as well as commitment to the other three defining features: "The attitude of the
game player must be an element in game playing because there
has to be an explanation of that curious state of affairs wherein
one adopts *rules* which require one to employ worse rather than
better *means* for reaching an *end*" (Suits 1978, 38; italics added).
That is, in order to claim that a game participant has adopted the
lusory attitude, it is essential that he or she comprehend and seek
the prelusory goal, understand and remain confined to the lusory
means required and allowed by the constitutive rules, and avoid
all means specifically prohibited by the constitutive rules. This
means that the game participant willingly accepts the limitations
imposed by the rules and thereby avoids *efficient* means for
reaching the goal.

Again, the participatory stance projected by the lusory attitude
is absolutely essential in qualifying an activity as a *game* for the
Grasshopper and this fact is demonstrated in two specific examples
relevant to his theory. The first can be found in the Grasshopper's
example of Smith and Jones traveling from A to C, which clearly
demonstrates that the lusory attitude makes games different from
all other ordinary life activities. Paralleling the scenario of the alien
attempting to make sense of Quidditch, this illustration demonstrates that traveling from A to C is not a game for Smith, who fails
to possess the lusory attitude associated with the race, whereas
Jones has the lusory attitude and sees the trip as a game:

> Smith knows nothing of games, but he does know that he wants to
> travel from A to C, and he also knows that making the trip by way of

B is the most efficient means for getting to his destination. He is then told authoritatively that he may *not* go by way of B. 'Why not?' he asks. 'Are there dragons at B?' 'No', is the reply. 'B is perfectly safe in every respect. It is just that there is a rule against going to B as you are on your way to C'. 'Very well', grumbles Smith, 'if you insist. But if I have to go from A to C very often I shall certainly try very hard to get that rule revoked'. True to his word, Smith approaches Jones, who is also setting out for C from A. He asks Jones to sign a petition requesting the revocation of the rule which forbids travellers from A to C to go through B. Jones replies that he is very much opposed to revoking the rule, which very much puzzles Smith.

Smith: But if you want to get to C, why on earth do you support a rule which prevents you from taking the fastest and most convenient route?

Jones: Ah, but you see I have no particular interest in being at C. *That* is not my goal, except in a subordinate way. My overriding goal is more complex. It is 'to get from A to C without going through B'. And I can't very well achieve that goal if I can go through B, can I?

S: But why do you want to do that?

J: I want to do it before Robinson does, you see?

S: No I don't. That explains nothing. Why should Robinson, whoever he may be, want to do it? I presume you will tell me that he, like you, has only a subordinate interest in being at C at all.

J: That is so.

S: Well, if neither of you really want to be at C, then what possible difference can it make which of you gets there first? And why, for God's sake, should you avoid B?

J: Let me ask you a question. Why do you want to get to C?

S: Because there is a good concert at C, and I want to hear it.

J: Why?

S: Because I like concerts, of course. Isn't that a good reason?

J: It's one of the best there is. And I like, among other things, trying to get from A to C without going through B before Robinson does.

S: Well, *I* don't. So why should they tell me I can't go through B?

J: Oh, I see. They must have thought you were in the race.

S: The what? (Suits 1978, 39–40).

The second example involves the response to Frank McBride's criticism that the Grasshopper's definition is too broad insofar as it inappropriately includes marathoning which "is not even, for the vast majority, a race . . . [but rather] a festive occasion to meet old friends and to enjoy the countryside and the townsfolk along the route" (McBride 1979, 63). Suits's rejoinder is, "if for some entrants the event is not even a race, then I would hardly want to claim that it was, for those entrants, a game either" (Suits 1988, 56). Essentially, if the lusory attitude fails to be adopted by a marathon entrant interested only in socializing with onlookers, then the marathon event represents neither a *race* nor a *game* to that participant.

From my perspective, Schneider and Butcher's neglect[5] of the lusory attitude proves fatal to their argument insofar as it allows them to incorrectly grant *chess per se* the status of an *activity* and a *game* rather than particular instances or *instantiations of chess* (characterized by lusory attitude adoption) which is what the Grasshopper specifically and clearly requires. Interestingly, a recent article by the Grasshopper's creator, confirms this interpretation. In "Venn and the Art of Category Maintenance" (Suits 2004, 5), Suits submits that it is entirely clear that his use of Venn diagrams to depict the relationship between sport, game, and play is intended to refer to *instances of games* rather than to what Schneider (2001) refers to as *games per se.*

Intuitively, this makes perfect sense. A specifically achievable state of affairs, coupled with a set of means-limiting rules and regulations favoring inefficiency, is unintelligible as any activity whatsoever, let alone a game. An activity is something that is done. It involves action or conduct. A goal taken together with a set of rules is best described as an assembly or collection of concepts and ideas that, in and of itself, is not an actuality let alone an activity or a game. The Grasshopper's theory is one specifically intended to discern the nature of games as activities, not as concepts or ideas. What this means is that chess is a game only as an actualized activity. In order to make the transition from the idea of chess to an actual activity characterized as a game of chess, participation in accordance with the lusory attitude is required.

Since the prelusory goal, lusory means, constitutive rules, and lusory attitude are proposed by the Grasshopper as necessary and *jointly* sufficient conditions, it follows that an activity is a game for a given participant if and only if the lusory attitude (definitionally compounded upon the prelusory goal, lusory means, and constitutive rules) is actually adopted and maintained. Contrarily, the activity fails or ceases to be a game if the lusory attitude is not adopted, is absent, or is abandoned. The Grasshopper's (and later Suits's) discussion of triflers, cheats, and spoilsports supports this statement: "In summary it may be said that triflers recognize rules but not goals, cheats recognize goals but not rules, players recognize both goals and rules, and spoilsports recognize neither rules nor goals" (Suits 1978, 47; Suits 2006, 4). Stated alternatively, players maintain the lusory attitude while triflers, cheats, and spoilsports do not. As a result, it is clear that a game exists for players but not for triflers, cheats, and spoilsports. From this observation it appears obvious that Schneider and Butcher's (1997) interpretation of the Grasshopper's theory of games is incorrect and that their fundamental assumption, that chess per se (in the absence of a lusory attitude) is properly referred to as a *game*, is false.

Schneider and Butcher's (1997) deduction that either chess is not a game or the Grasshopper's account of games is flawed is logically correct. In this either/or situation, they accept the commonplace assumption that chess is a game (indeed, chess is a game for the Grasshopper although not as characterized by Schneider and Butcher), rendering them committed to the conclusion that the Grasshopper's theory of games is problematic. Of course, challenging to their position is the fact that they have not argued that their characterization of chess is a game at all. Instead they have merely taken it for granted. It is important to recognize that what my colleagues have done is critiqued the Grasshopper's theory with an example that fails to conform to his definition in the first place! The consequence of this is that when faced with the same either/or situation, one may legitimately retain one's alliance with the Grasshopper by accepting the fact that chess (in the absence of a lusory attitude as characterized by my colleagues) is not a game at all.

The Institution of Chess versus a Game of Chess

Paralleling what I have argued to be a difference between the idea of chess and a game of chess is the Grasshopper's position on a game (an instance or instantiation) versus the institution of a game. The Grasshopper, as correctly observed by Schneider and Butcher (1997, 41), fails to specifically define the meaning of the institution of chess so as to more accurately contrast it with a game of chess. In response, Schneider and Butcher suggest that the Grasshopper's distinction is really one "between *the* game of chess and *a* game of chess" (1997, 41). In contrast, I am suggesting that the distinction is more accurately conveyed as that between *a game of chess* and *the idea of chess* (not the idea of the game of chess).

On Schneider and Butcher's view, the Grasshopper's theory requires the acceptance of checkmate as the prelusory goal of any *instantiation* of the game of chess due to the fact that it can be described prior to such an instantiation. If this is the case, then "one achieves the prelusory goal of *the* game of chess without playing *a* game of chess" (1997, 42). So, the Grasshopper has not provided a definition of *games* but rather a definition of particular *instantiations of games.* But the Grasshopper's notion of a prelusory goal for each individual instantiation of a game of chess is dependent upon the context provided by the institution of the game of chess (that is, *the* game of chess) which necessarily forces a shift in attention from the instantiation to the institution. With this shift, the question becomes whether or not the *institution* of the game of chess has a prelusory goal. Of course, the answer is no, because *checkmate* has no meaning beyond that which the institution gives it. This leaves the Grasshopper in a quandary: *A game of chess* (an instantiation of chess) cannot be played unless *the game of chess* (the institution of chess) already exists—which it doesn't, since chess is not a game at all but only particular examples of chess (Schneider and Butcher 1997, 42).

Suits points out that Schneider and Butcher might have easily taken this critique further to more sharply demonstrate the "grip of infinite regress" (Suits 2006, 3), which goes something like this: If the institution of chess is itself a kind of game, then it must have its own prelusory goal. But a prelusory goal is something identifiable independently of the game of which it is a part. Therefore, the prelusory goal of the institution of chess must also be identifiable independently of the institution of chess. So, the institution of chess must also have its own institution . . . and so on without end. Whoa, something must be wrong here!

Let's see if the rationale can be unraveled. In my assessment, Schneider and Butcher's interpretation of the Grasshopper's distinction between a game of chess (*a game* of chess) and its institution (*the game* of chess) can be charged with the fallacy of circular reasoning. In other words, the authors' argument is invalid, as it assumes the conclusion within its premises and then uses this assumption as proof for the conclusion. In essence, question-begging occurs as *chess* is automatically granted the status of *game.* As a result, it should not be surprising at all that if *a game* is dependent upon *the game*, and *the game* does not have a context within which to provide meaning, that *a game* cannot exist at all. Stated alternatively, it is no shocker that if a game of chess is dependent upon its institution and the institution does not have a context within which to provide it with meaning that no game of chess dependant upon the institution can exist at all. Of course, if the idea of a prelusory goal is situated in *a game* and *a game* is dependant upon *the game* (that is, its institution) as a nonexistent entity, then the idea of a prelusory goal is incoherent altogether. This cannot be what the Grasshopper intended!

So what did the Grasshopper have in mind with his distinction? It is instructive at this point to revisit the difference between *a game of chess* and *the institution of chess* (not *the institution of the game of chess* as Schneider and Butcher propose) so as to offer an alternative to Schneider and Butcher's circular account. On my interpretation, *the idea of chess* earlier described is effective in shedding light on the meaning intended by the Grasshopper for the *institution of chess*. Although the Grasshopper does not specifically define the institution of a game, this meaning is suggested within his characterization of foot racing wherein the elements central to it must serve as conceivable ideas that exist before or prior to any actual foot race: "[The] difference between foot racing and chess is less sharp than at first appears to be the case. For if no one had ever used his feet before the invention of foot racing, then foot racing would require the invention of running, and so pacing, sprinting, and passing would be as much instituted moves as are the moves in chess" (Suits 1978, 47). This assertion is further supported by Suits's recent clarification of the matter in "Games and Their Institutions in *The Grasshopper*": "The institution of game *x* is *a body of diverse meanings and practices* that all derive their meaning (that is, they are what they are) by being related, in one way or another, to game *x*" (Suits 2006, 4; italics added). That is, "there are a number of things that are lusory not simply by being *instances* of games but by being related to games" (5) and it is these kinds of things taken together that constitute a game's institution.

Within this context, we can equate the *idea* of a game with the Grasshopper's *institution* of a game. Nevertheless, it might be useful to distinguish between the two, and I think we can look to another of Suits's writings for some assistance. In, "The Elements of Sport" (1995) Suits describes a game of "Sweat Bead" (originally created by Kierkegaard):

> A high ranking official at my university has the constitutional peculiar-
> ity that when angry his anger is manifested solely by the appearance
> of a bead of perspiration at the centre of his forehead which then rolls
> slowly down his nose, clings for an instant to its tip, and finally falls.
> If the official's ire continues or recurs, the same steps are repeated.
> Whenever I have a conference with him I adopt as a pre-lusory goal
> that state of affairs wherein three separate beads of perspiration shall
> have progressed through their appointed stages inside of fifteen min-
> utes. And I adopt the constitutive rule that I will refrain from employ-
> ing as a means to this goal either threats of violence against the person
> of the official or aspersions on his personal and professional reputa-
> tion. (Suits 1995, 13).

Suits characterizes this game as being quite personal and private
and therefore unlikely to enjoy a wide following. It is also true that
Sweat Bead represents a game that has not enjoyed any degree of
stability whatsoever so as to persist through time. Sweat Bead does
not possess a governing body of experts, nor an official rulebook
intended to streamline the activity for mass participation. If it did,
Sweat Bead would be arguably characterized as *institutionalized*.
Paralleling this discussion I suggest that the term *institution* be utilized to capture an *idea* that has endured through time such that it
enjoys a higher degree of formalization and codification as well as
a more widespread following in contrast to more recently invented
or modified games as well as spontaneous games. Chess is institutionalized as an idea, Sweat Bead is not.

From this perspective, the *institution* of chess is really equivalent to an *idea* of chess that happens to have stood the test of time.
Of course, if this position on the institution of chess is feasible, it
is clear that it too is capable of serving only as a set of concepts
and ideas. The *idea* of chess, whether institutionalized or not, cannot be properly recognized as an *activity* or *game* of chess
because the lusory attitude is absent. As emphasized, a *game* of
chess exists if and only if the lusory attitude (that is, definitionally
compounded upon chess's prelusory goal, lusory means, and constitutive rules) is adopted and maintained. In contrast, the *idea* or
institution of chess is not at all dependent upon an attitude or
stance.

To summarize, chess is defined by one specifically achievable
state of affairs (perhaps checkmate and/or immobilization of one's
opponent's king) and one set of rules that specifies the lusory and
illusory moves for bringing about that state of affairs. As defined,

this represents an idea only (or a set of ideas), not an activity and not a game, which necessarily involve action and participation. In the sense that chess has become increasingly codified, regulated, and formalized over time, it provides the substance of the current institution of chess. Whether institutionalized or not, the idea of chess must always exist before or prior to any particular game of chess which involves this idea plus the participatory stance projected in the lusory attitude.

Prelusory Goals for Games: A Gambit Reclaimed

It is my position that the Grasshopper intended for the concept of a prelusory goal to be a defining feature of any game or activity but not a "defining" facet of its idea or institution. What this means is that the concept is intelligible as prelusory within the context of a game alone. In chess, for example, checkmate (and/or immobilization of the opponent's king) is identified as the specifically achievable state of affairs that chess participants aim to bring about during all games characterized by lusory attitude adoption. Within the context of one such game instantiation, this specifically achievable state of affairs is appropriately characterized as *pre*lusory because it can be described before or prior to that game. Of course, this also holds true for the states of affairs identified as touchdown and capture of the Golden Snitch by the Seeker: Touchdown (described as a football being carried into the opponent's endzone) represents a concept central to the idea of football just as Seeker and Golden Snitch serve as notions essential to the idea of Quidditch. While it is true that these same specifically achievable states of affairs are referenced within the idea of a game, each is completely unintelligible as before or prior to that idea. If the idea of a game, whether institutionalized or not, were itself a game, then it would also require an additional idea in order to make its prelusory goal intelligible. But the idea of a game is simply not a game at all, and therefore cannot itself be required to have a prelusory goal. The idea of a game only refers to the prelusory goal (in making it a requirement of the game), but to say that the idea itself has to have a prelusory goal is simply inappropriate, as it treats a set of requirements as though it were itself a game.

So, within the context of a *game* of chess, it is true that the state of affairs recognized as checkmate can be described (Suits suggests that "identified" may represent a more appropriate term [2006, 8]) beforehand and therefore independently of that game. However, within the context of the idea or institution of chess this is impossible. Fortunately, the Grasshopper's definition of game is located squarely in particular instantiations and not at all within ideas or institutions providing the context and conditions relevant to these instantiations. If a game of chess is necessarily dependent upon the context provided by the idea of chess and the specification of the prelusory goal is recognized to be referenced within this idea, this logical dependence in no way requires that the prelusory goal be describable (or identifiable) before or independently of the idea of chess. Prelusory suggests before or prior to the game not before or prior to the idea of that game. Of course, the condition of being identifiable before or prior to the game is satisfied if the idea of that game precedes its instantiation and the definition of that game is equivalent to its instantiation alone.

Conclusion

Schneider and Butcher argue the following: The Grasshopper's theory of games requires that all games possess a prelusory goal understood as a state of affairs that can be described independently of the game itself; chess does not possess such a goal; therefore either chess is not a game or the Grasshopper's account of games including the notion of a prelusory goal is problematic and incoherent. In this either/or situation, my colleagues assume that chess is a game and conclude that the Grasshopper's theory is flawed and that "prelusory goals should be abandoned for what they are, a failed gambit in the practice of philosophy of sport" (1997, 45).

Challenging the assumption of Schneider and Butcher, this chapter demonstrates that chess is not a game per se. Chess is a game only in the context of participation infused with the necessary lusory attitude. What the authors have done is inappropriately equivocated the idea of chess with an actual game of chess. In the alternative, I suggest that the idea of chess involves (at least minimally) the identification of a goal coupled with a set of means-limiting rules. Moreover, this idea of chess is distinct from a game of chess insofar as it fails to involve a lusory attitude.

Contrary to Schneider and Butcher's interpretation (1997), I suggest that the Grasshopper's theory is one specifically intended to discern the nature of games as activities, not as concepts or ideas. The problem with my colleagues' argument is that it inappropriately ascribes the idea of a game the status of a game as an activity and then offers an evaluation of the transformed position as a critique of the Grasshopper's account. In this respect, their argument is both invalid and unsound and therefore cannot be accepted as grounds for abandonment of the Grasshopper's theory of games. The idea of a prelusory goal is perfectly intelligible as a specifically achievable state of affairs that can be identified or described independently of any game of which it is or may come to be a part. There is no one game of chess but rather an infinite number of game instantiations each properly referred to as a game of chess. Nevertheless, there is only one idea or institution of chess.[6] The fact that the *idea* of chess precedes any and all *games* of chess makes it possible to identify and comprehend each of the requirements of chess (including its goal) independently of, before, and prior to any game. In other words, it is logically possible to understand the idea of chess and its subcomponents without ever participating in an activity or game of chess via lusory attitude adoption.

At the onset of this chapter I asked whether the existence of chess as a game is grounded in the understanding of chess or in the participatory experience itself. I am now in a position to respond. Because I have never played a game of chess via the adoption of the lusory attitude, I am forced to conclude that chess has never existed as a *game* for me. Instead, my experience with chess is limited to its idea or institution. This scenario parallels my experience with Quidditch. Because I will never actually be able to employ the lusory means toward goal attainment, it is impossible for me to adopt the lusory attitude required for Quidditch to *be* a game. Unfortunately, my definitional lack of knack for broom flying guarantees that Quidditch can never *exist* for me in the form of a *game* (except perhaps in my dreams!).

To conclude, I suggest that the Grasshopper's account of games, including the concept of a prelusory goal, be once again embraced by the philosophy community. To be clear, this suggestion requires that future discussions within this area include careful attention to the distinction between a game, as defined by a prelusory goal, lusory means, constitutive rules, and a lusory attitude, and the idea or institution of that game which is capable only of reference to and/or description of the elements central to any game foundational upon it.

NOTES

I would like to thank Bernard Suits and Robert Simon for their input into this chapter. Their encouraging comments and suggestions proved invaluable in its revision.

1. Quidditch is a game played by students enrolled in Hogwarts School of Witchcraft and Wizardry. The game is played in a stadium which is constructed fifty feet in the air. It is played at extremely high speeds on broomsticks and involves two teams of seven players (one Keeper, one Seeker, two Beaters, and three Chasers on each team) with each team seeking to score more points than the opposing team via the use four moving balls (one Golden Snitch, two Bludgers, and one Quaffle). The Golden Snitch is about the size of a golf ball and has silver wings allowing it to travel at great speed. Bludgers are hit by Beaters in attempts to knock opponents of their broomsticks. Finally, the Quaffle is about the size of a small basketball and is used to score points. The role of the Keeper is to try to prevent the opposing team from scoring a goal between one of the three golden goal hoops with the Quaffle. The Seeker's sole objective is to catch the Golden Snitch. The Beaters use wooden sticks to hit the Bludgers in an effort to knock opponents from their broomsticks and prevent their teammates from being knocked off. Finally, Chasers are expected to try to score goals with the Quaffle. The objective of the game is to score more goals than one's opponent. Generally, this involves the strategy of avoiding being hit with a Bludger while trying to score as many goals as possible with the Quaffle so as to have a higher score that the opposing team when the Golden Snitch is caught. A Quaffle goal is worth 10 points and the catching of the Golden Snitch is worth 150 points. The game begins when the referee blows his or her whistle and ends only when a Seeker is successful in catching the Golden Snitch. The winning team is that with the most points when the game is over (Rowling 1998).

2. In the original passage, the Grasshopper suggests that the prelusory goal "can be described before, or independently of, any game of which it may be, or come to be, a part" (Suits 1978, 37). In their citation, Schneider and Butcher, without the use of the customary ellipses of ". . . ," omit the option of *may be a part* and instead focus their paper on the alternative *may come to be a part*. Bernard Suits drew my attention to the omission during the early phases of writing this chapter. He also writes about this error in his own refutation of Schneider and Butcher's critique (2006, 8).

3. In my opinion, Schneider and Butcher's list of four possibilities for the prelusory goal of chess could easily be simplified to two. More specifically, I believe that the options of *arranging tokens in a pattern* as well as *immobilizing the king* can be safely omitted. My reason is that both options appear to conflate the idea of ends and means within a game.

According to the Grasshopper's definition, a goal is something that involves a state of affairs and the tasks of *arranging* and *immobilizing* cannot serve this purpose. The error made by Schneider and Butcher is to entertain *arranging* tokens in a pattern rather than the potential *arrangement* itself as well as *immobilizing* the king rather than the state of *immobilization*. It seems more legitimate to consider tokens as arranged in a pattern as well as king immobilization as potential options. However, this shift results in the equating of options insofar as *tokens arranged in a pattern* becomes equivalent to *checkmate spatiotemporally defined* and *immobilization of the king* equates to *checkmate conceptually defined*.

4 Schneider 2001 makes the same assumption.

5. In "Fruits, Apples, and Category Mistakes: On Sport, Games, and Play" (2001), Schneider charges Suits (1988) with a category mistake in his characterization of the interrelationship between play, game, and sport. The basis of her argument stems from the observation that games and sport represent *activities* whereas play is properly referred to as an *attitude* or "a mode of performing actions rather than a type of action" (2001, 153). On her view, the structural or conceptual level "where a practice is a sport [or game] if it meets certain observable criteria" (2001, 153) is logically inconsistent with and independent of the attitudinal level.

6. This statement is simplistic in that it assumes only one version of chess (that is, one specifically achievable state of affairs and one set of constitutive rules). In reality there are numerous chess variations each of which are *called* chess. Although modified games are beyond the scope of this paper, my position is that each modification to the original set of concepts associated with chess, a new *idea* of (modified) chess (chess[a], chess[b], chess[c], etcetera) arises, each of which offers the opportunity for a game of (modified) chess via adoption of the unique lusory attitude associated with each idea.

REFERENCES

McBride, Frank. 1979. "A Critique of Mr. Suits' Definition of Game Playing." *Journal of the Philosophy of Sport* 6:59–65.

Rowling, J. K. 1998. *Harry Potter and the Sorceror's Stone*. New York: A. A. Levine Books.

Schneider, Angela J. 2001. "Fruits, Apples, and Category Mistakes: On Sport, Games, and Play." *Journal of the Philosophy of Sport* 28:151–59.

Schneider, Angela J., and Robert B. Butcher. 1977. "Pre-lusory Goals for Games: A Gambit Declined." *Journal of the Philosophy of Sport* 24:38–46.

Suits, Bernard. 1978. *The Grasshopper: Games, Life and Utopia*. Toronto: University of Toronto Press.

———. 1988a. "On McBride on the Definition of Games." In *Philosophic Inquiry in Sport*, edited by William J. Morgan and Klaus V. Meier, 55–62. Champaign, IL: Human Kinetics.

———. 1988b. "Tricky Triad: Games, Play, Sport." *Journal of the Philosophy of Sport* 15:1–9.

———. 1995. "The Elements of Sport." In *Philosophic Inquiry in Sport*, edited by William J. Morgan and Klaus V. Meier, 8–15. Champaign, IL: Human Kinetics.

———. 2004. "Venn and the Art of Category Maintenance." *Journal of the Philosophy of Sport* 31:1–14.

———. 2006. "Games and Their Institutions in *The Grasshopper*." *Journal of the Philosophy of Sport* 33:1–8.

Vossen, Deborah. 2004. "The Nature and Classification of Games. *AVANTE* 10:53–68.

12

The Reviled Art

STUART RACHELS

If chess is an art, it is hardly treated as such in the United States. Imagine what it would be like if music were as little known or appreciated. Suppose no self-respecting university would offer credit courses in music, and the National Endowment for the Arts refused to pay for any of it. A few enthusiasts might compose sonatas, and study and admire one another's efforts, but they would largely be ignored. Once in a while a Mozart might capture the public imagination, and like Bobby Fischer get written about in *Newsweek*. But the general attitude would be that, while this playing with sound might be clever, and a great passion for those who care about it, still in the end it signifies nothing very important.

—JAMES RACHELS

Bragging and Whining

When I was eleven, I became the youngest chess master in American history. It was great fun. My picture was put on the cover of *Chess Life*; I appeared on Shelby Lyman's nationally syndicated chess show; complete strangers asked me if I was a genius; I got compared to my idol, Bobby Fischer (who was not a master until he was thirteen); and I generally enjoyed the head-swelling experience of being treated like a king, as a kid among adults. When I wasn't getting bullied at school, I felt special. And the fact that I was from Alabama, oozing a slow Southern drawl, must have increased my mystique, since many northeastern players assumed that I lived on a farm, and who plays chess out there?

In my teens, I had some wonderful experiences. I represented the United States in world youth championships in France and Israel (both times finishing a forgettable fifth); twice I played the great Garry Kasparov in small simultaneous exhibitions (both times, he threw temper tantrums); I went to England, where the eighteen-year-old Nigel Short showed me around the Tower of London and the seventy-three-year-old Miguel Najdorf affectionately roughed up my hair; and I played Bobby Fischer's rival, Boris Spassky—I was so in awe of him that I almost resigned just looking at him.[1] However, I had neither the killer instinct nor the work ethic to make it to the top. I almost retired from chess a complete failure, in my own eyes, but I did manage one "adult" success. By winning the U.S. Junior Championship in 1988—my sole victory in seven attempts—I earned an invitation to the *real* national championship, to be held in Long Beach, California. My opponents would mostly be Soviet-born Grandmasters, and everyone but me would be a professional player. I was expected to get clobbered. Instead, I tied for first, and for the last time I could be compared to Bobby Fischer, since, at twenty, I was the youngest U.S. Champion since Fischer's phenomenal victory at fourteen.

So much for the bragging; now for the whining.

When I was twelve, I thought I was famous. But as I grew up, I gradually realized that a chess celebrity is not a celebrity. In fact, I learned that what I did was neither respected nor admired by the general public. My proudest moment—winning the U.S. Championship—brought me satisfaction but no glory. By then I knew that my victory was not a national news story, but I was disappointed to discover that it was not even considered *local* news. In Atlanta, where I was then a college student, the *Atlanta Journal-Constitution* declined to run a story about the tournament, while my college newspaper ran a story on page thirteen, devoting its front page to the minor accomplishments of a Division III college swimmer. In Birmingham, where I had grown up, the chess club president (a salesman for Skoal chewing tobacco) repeatedly phoned the NBC affiliate, trying to get them to mention my name on the local news. Finally, they told him they would, but at the crucial moment they instead ran a story about the evils of tobacco.

I retired from competitive chess in 1993, and since then I can't remember even once being asked to explain how I won a national championship, nor what it was like to have played world champions. In 1998 I used to dine weekly at an Italian restaurant in Syracuse, New York, with a retired British chess master. After the food and wine, we'd bring out the board for a few games. Perhaps to embarrass me, my friend would always tell our server, "He was the United States Chess Champion, you know!" Servers want to get good tips, so they usually feign interest in anything you say. Chess, however, seemed to be the exception. No server or manager ever took the slightest interest in the fact that a national champion was having a game of chess in their restaurant against an accomplished British master. I guess we just looked nerdy.

Chess in American Society

Some variant of this vain and self-pitying tale could be told by any successful American player. There is always the vanity, because people are vain and want to be recognized for their accomplishments. But there is also the self-pity, because chess players all know that Americans are indifferent to, if not scornful of, the royal game.

Consider how chess is portrayed in our culture. If you want to define a character as a nerd, mention that he's a chess player. If you want a movie, book, or play to do badly, even a *good* one, center it around chess. *Searching for Bobby Fischer* (1993) was an excellent movie, but its box-office sales were poor. Since then, I can name only one movie in which chess was prominently featured.[2] Tim Rice's musical *Chess* was wonderful, but back in the '80s it lasted only eight weeks on Broadway. If there has been another play about chess since then, I can't name it. The book you now hold in your hands was accepted by Open Court Publishing Company but rejected for their "Popular Culture and Philosophy" series, presumably because they thought it would not sell as well as a book on Harley-Davidson and Philosophy, or on the Atkins Diet and Philosophy, or on Buffy the Vampire Slayer and Philosophy. And probably they were right. As for television, that most ubiquitous form of American media, chess is a nonentity. You might catch Sam Farha playing Texas Hold'em on ESPN, but you will never see Viswanathan Anand displaying his more impressive craft. Perhaps one day there will be a hit TV series called *Checkmate in Precinct 13: Philosopher by Day, Chess Master by Night*. If that ever happens, I'd be happy to work as a consultant.

For a brief moment, chess had a chance in the States. The 1972 Fischer-Spassky match riveted Americans like no other chess event. Fischer's face graced the covers of *Life*, *Newsweek* and *Time*; chess diagrams appeared in mainstream magazines; housewives who didn't know the moves watched Shelby Lyman's PBS coverage of the match; and Lyman himself—a rather uncharismatic ex-sociology instructor—was stopped in public by Dustin Hoffman, who recognized him, but whom he didn't recognize. Bobby Fischer almost became our Arnold Palmer; he almost put chess on the map. But after beating Spassky, Bobby's mental health declined, and he became a recluse. When Fischer disappeared, so did chess from the public consciousness. *Searching for Bobby Fischer* effectively conveys the feeling of loss and isolation that pervaded American chess circles after Fischer left. What finally ended the Fischer era was not the passage of time so much as the rise of Garry Kasparov. By 1989, the world could see that Kasparov was an even better player than Fischer had been in his prime.

Part of this story, however, is not quite right. The Fischer-Spassky frenzy was about a Cold War clash, and about the public's interest in Fischer himself; it had little to do with chess. If Bobby had kept playing, it would have been great. Professional chess players might now make a decent living in America. The U.S. Chess Federation might have as many members as the American Contract Bridge League (USCF: 90,000; ACBL: 160,000). But Fischer could not have made chess popular in the United States. There are three reasons for this.

The first, peculiar to the U.S.A., is our country's deeply engrained anti-intellectualism. In America, chess is regarded as the premier strategy game,[3] but this accolade earns the game little respect. In Western Europe, where George W. Bush could not have become the president of anything, the chess professional enjoys a higher status.

The second reason is that chess is an antisocial activity—or rather, tournament chess is. Casual games can be social affairs, but serious chess is quiet and solitary. Tournament games typically last for hours, and though you are playing against a human being, you do not speak to him, and you are not working with him—you are trying to beat him. Not many people want to spend hours alone with their own thoughts.[4]

The third reason Fischer couldn't have made chess as popular as golf or tennis is that the game's beauty is invisible to those who haven't labored over a chessboard for untold hours. I'll discuss that idea later.

Beauty in Chess

The *New York Times* honors two games with regular columns: chess and bridge. I have now been playing bridge obsessively for four and a half years (I played for four hours earlier today), so I could prattle on about its virtues. However, my father's attitude still seems justified to me. My dad played chess and bridge for over forty years. Late in life, when he wanted to simplify his library, he threw out all of his bridge books. However, he could not bear to throw away all of his chess books. "Throwing away Fischer's games," he said, "would be like throwing away Shakespeare's plays."

Great chess games are breathtaking works of art. What does their beauty consist in? Some facets of a game's beauty can be grasped only by considering the game as a whole. For example, an entire game can embody the flawless execution of a plan (as when, in a Queen's Gambit Declined, White launches a minority attack on the queenside, creates a weak black pawn on c6, organizes his forces around that pawn, wins it, and displays good endgame technique). Or, the protracted struggle of a long game, with its tensions, its clash of styles, and its shifting fortunes, can have aesthetic merit. Or, a whole game can be satisfying because the victor made no detectable errors; reflecting on the game as a whole, we can see that the victor's performance was unspoiled.

Perfect play, however, cannot guarantee a beautiful game. For one thing, it is not enough that you play perfectly; your opponent must also play well.[5] A master who has just crushed a weak player—a "fish," "patzer," "weakie" or "woodpusher"—will rarely keep the scoresheet; routine demolitions need not be preserved. This principle holds true for most other competitive activities, such as boxing. Muhammad Ali's defeat of George Foreman in the "Rumble in the Jungle" in Zaire was beautiful only because Foreman's power posed enormous problems for Ali; a fight between Ali and Howard Cosell would have been downright ugly. But even a game played perfectly by *both* sides can be dull, if both players lack ambition. For example, there is a line in the Petroff Defense that sucks all the life out of the game, even though it involves no "mistakes."[6] Or even worse, consider Huebner-Rogoff, Graz 1972: 1. c4 draw agreed.[7] There's no beauty in that, just as there is no beauty in a boxing match if neither fighter leaves his corner.[8]

Although whole games can have aesthetic virtues, the main aesthetic units in chess are smaller: an idea, a plan, a position, a move, a theme, a clever sequence of moves, and so on.[9] Most of a game's beauty derives from these smaller units. The fan's favorite is the tactical combination—a sequence of forceful moves that usually results in either checkmate or a decisive material gain. If a combination is spectacular enough, even the quiet tournament hall can come to life. Mikhail Tal, arguably the greatest tactician ever, said that he *liked* noise in the playing hall—a remarkable statement from a chess player—because it showed that the audience was riveted by his work-in-progress.[10] And legend has it that when Frank Marshall, the great American attacker of the early twentieth century, played his most spectacular move ever, the spectators showered the board with gold coins. This legend is probably true, although the real story might be that the onlookers had bet on Marshall's opponent, so now they were paying up.

What is it about these smaller units—the tactical shots, the motifs, the positional sacrifices—that accounts for their aesthetic value? The answer will depend on the example, but here are some typical explanations: "look at the coordination of White's queen and knight"; "I would never consider that move in a million years!"; "every black piece participates in the attack;" "zugzwang[11] in the middlegame—unbelievable!" One overarching theme is that chess is like humor: the unexpected can have special value.

Explanations of beauty, however, ring hollow in chess, much as they do elsewhere. In the end, the beauty of chess is something you grasp visually, if you grasp it at all. The move, the combination, the final position, *look* beautiful. You *see* it. Even when a Grandmaster thinks about a beautiful move while he's watching a dull movie, he "sees" the board in his mind.[12]

Chess Perception

Chess cognition is mostly unconscious. In studying a position, a master may quickly understand that there are three viable possibilities for the player on move. But how his brain has determined this, he has no idea. And even when he is deliberating among the viable options, there is typically little inner dialogue. Chess thinking is rarely linguistic.[13] Also, chess cognition bears little or no resemblance to computer number-crunching. Contrary to popular belief, great chess players usually don't think many moves ahead,[14] and judgment is more important than calculation.

Chess provides a striking example of how knowledge can influence perception. When a novice and a master look at a position, there is a profound difference in their experience. The master *sees* the power of the pieces: he immediately knows which squares the bishop attacks; no conscious thought is required. More complicated matters can also be perceptual. A master can immediately perceive that a square is weak, a bishop is bad, a pawn is backward, and a queen is pinned. He can perceive all this in one or two seconds of scanning the board, while the novice has only taken in the fact that chess is being played on the board rather than checkers. As Thomas Kuhn might say, the master and the novice look at the same board but inhabit two different worlds.[15] They "inhabit two different worlds" because, not only is the novice unable to perceive the board as the master does, but the master cannot perceive the board as the novice does. A master cannot see the bishop on e3 as a chunk of dead wood, any more than you can look at your best friend's face and see a meaningless matrix of colors and shapes. The master *once* saw the board like this, but now there is no going back (unless there is some unfortunate neurological event). The best a master can do to understand a novice's perspective is to look at a board on which the pieces have been haphazardly placed, without any regard for chess rules or chess strategy. Such a pile of pieces will resemble a "blooming, buzzing confusion,"[16] even to a master.[17]

As a player gets better, his perception matures. After a while, he can perform tasks of perception and memory that seem amazing to others, though trivial to him. Here are some examples:

- *The colors of the squares.* There are sixty-four squares on a chessboard—thirty-two white and thirty-two black.[18] In algebraic notation, they each have a name: a1, a2, a3, and so forth. If you name a square, I can immediately tell you what color it is. I don't need to think; I just *see* the square in my mind: a3 *looks* black; h7 *looks* white, and so forth. A good player is intimately familiar with *each* of the sixty-four squares.[19]

- *Blindfold chess.* A Grandmaster can beat you blindfolded, take the blindfold off, and then show you the game you've

just played. Playing without sight of the board requires concentration (it is not trivial, like naming the colors of the
squares), but any strong player can do it. Remembering the
game afterwards is about as easy as remembering the details
of a gripping story right after you hear it. A reasonably played
chess game fits together like a novel.

- *Simultaneous exhibitions.* A master can easily play forty or
  fifty games at once by circling the inner perimeter of an
  enclosed group of tables, making one move at each board
  each time around. The hardest thing about giving simuls is all
  the walking involved. I could play a thousand games at once,
  for as long as I could stay awake, if only I could sit still while
  my opponents passed by on a conveyor belt.

Once, when I was giving a thirty-five-board simul, I noticed at one
board that a piece had been moved to a different square while I
was concentrating on other games. My opponent immediately apol-
ogized and put the piece back, blaming the error on his small child,
who was watching. This was not a matter of "memorization"—I do
not have a trick memory—the position just didn't make sense with
the piece misplaced.

When Bobby Fischer was preparing to play Spassky in 1972, he
studied Spassky's games in "the red book"—a book published in
German, so-called because of its cover.[20] Back then, there were no
databases, and Fischer was lucky that this book containing 353 of
Spassky's games existed and was in his possession.[21] A friend of
Fischer's told me that you could give Bobby any number between
1 and 353, and he could tell you: all the moves to that game; the
analysis of the game given in the book; and Fischer's own
improved analysis. This is the most amazing feat of memory I have
ever heard attributed to a chess player.[22]

Changes in chess perception are typically gradual. Sometimes,
however, you can experience rapid shifts. In the last round of the
1987 U.S. Open, I accepted an early draw offer from Grandmaster
Lev Alburt. The position was dead equal, we were about to swap
some pieces, and I did not expect to beat my famous opponent.[23]
Afterwards, when I looked at the final position with my trainer,
Boris Kogan, Boris said, "Of course you are a little worse here."
"Why?" I asked. "Because your b-pawn is weak." "No, it isn't."
So we played it out. Twenty moves later, Boris had captured my

b-pawn with his knight, and I was sure to lose. So we played it out again, and the same thing happened (except this time, he captured my pawn with his *king*). Boris had convinced me he was right, but more amazingly, he had changed my perception of the position. The black pawn now *looked* weak to me. I could now see what Boris had seen.

When art lovers talk about what they "see" in a painting, I usually don't believe them. I usually think they're just being pretentious. If you suspect this of me, please know this: any chess expert can confirm what I've said about chess perception. And there is no issue about determining who the experts are. In chess, the experts are the ones who win. In other artistic areas, experts are harder to discern, and so claims about perception and beauty are harder to verify.

Perception and Popularity

Most of the fun in chess comes from appreciating the game's beauty.[24] This requires being able to see it. And being able to see it requires time and effort: it takes most people years to develop a competent perception of the board. This is the main reason why chess will never become popular in America—it's too hard. And this is why Fischer could not have been Caïssa's[25] Arnold Palmer.

Of course, you don't need to be a Grandmaster to appreciate chess. Weaker players can enjoy the game, and it doesn't take years to become weak.[26] Different things *are* enjoyed at a lower level than at a higher level. For example, a novice might get excited by a simple knight fork, which a stronger player would find routine. But this is enjoyment nonetheless. Thus, chess fans need not possess expert perception; and so, perhaps chess can become more popular than I have suggested.

The fact remains, however, that even a rudimentary understanding of chess takes time to develop, and until it is developed, chess seems utterly dull. This is the curse of chess. Until you know a good bit about chess, you don't even possess the *illusion* of understanding it. Most other activities are not like this. I know nearly nothing about poker, opera, football, piano, and surrealist art, but this doesn't stop me from enjoying them occasionally. By contrast, someone who does not play chess will never enjoy looking at a great chess game. And if you know only a little bit about chess, looking at a game can be downright irritating, because you're frustrated by your partial understanding, and because you realize that, to understand more, you'd have to do something tedious: you'd have to figure out where all the pieces on the board can move to, in each position. And even if you do that, you may grasp a few particulars about the position, but the position as a whole will get lost like a forest for the trees, and the game will be a blur.

Chess Compositions

The composed problem is the highest form of art in chess. A problem consists of a position, a task, and a solution. Typically, the task is for White to force checkmate, or to arrive at an obviously winning position, or to force a draw from a starting point that appears hopeless. There are also more esoteric tasks. In "helpmate" problems, both sides cooperate to checkmate Black as quickly as possible. In "selfmate" problems, White forces Black to checkmate him (naturally, Black is not allowed to resign!). "Retrograde" problems have us discern something about the past—for example, what Black's last move was.[27] Since problems are composed, they can be crafted to perfection. By contrast, "studylike themes" arise rarely in play, and almost never in pristine form. In a game, the most thrilling variations tend to occur, not on the board, but in the notes. A beautiful variation can be thwarted not only by an opponent who wishes to avoid it, but also by an opponent who resigns. Thus, Fischer once described Robert Byrne's resignation as "a bitter disappointment."[28]

When I was ten years old I invented a variation on the helpmate idea. Consider any possible chess move—for example, Qe6. The problem is to find the shortest game ending with that move as checkmate. With Qe6, I discovered that mate can be accomplished in five moves. One solution I especially liked.[29] However, the problem is flawed, since there are other solutions.[30] In the jargon of compositions, the Qe6 problem is "cooked," since there is more than one "key" (a "key" is the first move of a solution). Grandmaster Pal Benko did not self-consciously work on this type of problem, but a wonderful problem he composed can be described as "find the quickest possible mate with gxf6." Benko did it in six.[31] You now know everything that is known about this type of problem, since I have forgotten anything else I might have discovered twenty-six years ago.[32] I encourage you to compose some problems of this type.

Sam Loyd (1841–1911), Alexei Troitsky (1866–1942), and Genrikh Kasparyan (1910–1995) are three towering geniuses of chess composition. Like most composers, Loyd, Troitsky, and Kasparyan are not remembered as players. And Grandmasters rarely compose. If a Grandmaster does, it is usually as a solace, late in life, when he despairs of achieving any more over-the-board successes. Grandmaster Jan Timman and former Champion of the World Vasily Smyslov have turned to problem-composing in recent years. Benko, one of the finest living composers, composed the least when he played the most.[33]

I cannot exaggerate how marvelous chess problems are. There are *thousands upon thousands* of gloriously beautiful problems. They are awesome, fantastic, stunning. Yet, if chess players are ignored and shunned by American society, problemists are even more isolated and unappreciated—not only in America, but around the world. Just as American culture is indifferent or hostile to chess, chess players themselves are indifferent or hostile to chess compositions. Why is that?

If you show a chess player the starting position to a problem, he is liable to sneer, "*That* position would never occur in a game!" And, indeed, chess problems tend to be "unrealistic" (except for endgame studies). The impracticality of problems might explain why many players are indifferent to them: many players are indifferent to *anything* that does not directly improve their game (for example, food, water, air, a date for Friday night, and so on). However, the mere fact that problems are unrealistic can't explain the irritated disdain that a great many players have for them.

That irritation is explained by the other thing players often say about problems: "They're too difficult." Most problems are way too hard for most players. (Mate-in-two problems are the exception, since they can be solved fairly quickly by mechanical means, but that's no fun.) Most problems stump me too, so I conceive of the time I spend looking at them as time spent preparing to appreciate their solutions—not as time spent trying to solve them.[34]

Problems are hard for tournament players partly because composers delight in the counterintuitive, where "counterintuitive" refers to the intuitions of the seasoned tournament player. Ideally, a key move should not be a capture or a check, because those are "obvious" moves—that is, moves that an expert might consciously consider.[35] Here is an example of a problem that trades on the unexpected. White begins the game with 1. f3; his next moves will be 2. Kf2, 3. Kg3 and 4. Kh4. Black must play so that these moves will all be legal. In reply to 4. Kh4, Black will deliver checkmate. But how? I'll put the solution in an endnote.[36]

Remarkably, problems tend to be harder when they involve fewer pieces, because the mind has less to latch onto. As an illustration, consider the pawnless endgame of two bishops versus one knight. Human beings used to think it was drawn with perfect play, but computers have now proved that the two bishops win. The proof, however, is of no use to human players, since it consists in long, massively branching, unmemorizable lines of analysis that employ no known strategic principles. If this endgame occurred between two top Grandmasters, they would be on their own, and you could get an even-money bet as to whether the bishops would win.

The world of chess compositions is like the chess world writ smaller. Society ignores chess players; chess players ignore composers. Chess players don't like problems for the same reason that greengrocers don't like chess: because it strains the brain. Humans can grasp a lot about chess, but most people don't want to; chess players can grasp a lot about problems, but most aren't interested. The chess composer is a tragic figure, even compared to the chess player. Kasparov and Fischer enjoy fame, and even players who haven't penetrated the public consciousness are renowned in chess circles. Yet the Kasparovs and Fischers of the composing world are largely unknown even to chess players. In America, Sam Loyd's name might elicit a tinge of recognition, but ninety-nine tournament players out of a hundred will not have heard of Kasparyan or Troitsky, much less of Leonid Kubbel, Kenneth Howard, Eugene Cook, William Shinkman, Henri Rinck, or Godfrey Heathcote. These geniuses remain obscure, even among the pushers of pawns. Is there any greater injustice in the world of art?

Pride and Sorrow in Chess

Chess writers often refer to chess as a sport.[37] One can understand why they want it to be a sport. Many sports are popular. Sports stars get rich. They sign autographs and appear on TV. Movies and books lionize them. They are allowed to perform at the Olympics. They are mobbed by admirers. Chess players would be happy if just one of these things were true of them.

When chess players call chess a sport, this strikes me not only as false, but as pathetic. It's pathetic in the same way it's pathetic to ask someone out on a date who said no the last three times you asked. American culture has rejected chess. For the chess player to insist that chess is a sport is a way of not taking the hint.

Of course, chess has a lot in common with sports—they're both competitive activities. But chess is not a sport, because physical exertion is inessential to chess.[38] A great chess player could be paralyzed his whole life, but a sports star could not be. Note that sports practitioners are called *athletes*, but no one ever calls chess players athletes, presumably because "athlete"—even more than "sport"—connotes physical acumen.

What is chess, if not a sport? Chess is a strategy game. It is also, I believe, an art. Chess compositions are artistic creations in the fullest sense of the term. However, you might think that calling a chess *game* a work of art is dubious. Chess games are more about winning than creating; chess is a battle that resembles war more than painting. Yet this is a false dichotomy. A battle can *produce* objects of aesthetic value.[39] Chess is a game, an art, and a competitive struggle. That is nothing to be ashamed of, is it?

NOTES

The epigraph to this chapter is drawn from James Rachels 1984–85, 106–7.

1. During our game, Spassky asked my trainer, "Why is Stuart so nervous?" When I heard about this later, I was embarrassed. But I also thought that Spassky had asked a stupid question—who wouldn't be nervous, playing against Boris Spassky?

2. *The Luzhin Defence* (2000). Like most people, I never saw it.

3. I have heard it said that the Asian game of *go* is even more difficult than chess. In my opinion, chess is harder than bridge.

4. Chess's antisocial nature might help explain why so few women play chess. Bridge—a partnership game—attracts significantly more females.

5. This is a pun on the adage: "It is not enough to be a good player; you must also play well." This adage has been attributed to the German Grandmaster Siegbert Tarrasch (1862–1934) since at least 1898—see Armin Friedmann writing for the *American Chess Magazine*, August 1898. The adage might sound better in German, which uses the same word ("gut") for both "good" and "well." ("Es ist nicht genug, dass man ein guter Spieler ist, man mussß auch gut spielen.")

6. I have in mind a game that begins 1. e4 e5 2. Nf3 Nf6 3. Nxe5 d6 4. Nf3 Nxe4 5. Qe2 Qe7 6. d3 Nf6 7. Bg5 Qxe2+ 8. Bxe2 Be7 and then snores its way to a draw, without either side slipping up. In practice, the derision would be hurled on White, who has made no attempt to win despite having the advantage of the first move.

7. Admittedly, 1. c4 draw agreed is a better-played game than 1. c4 Black resigns (Fischer-Panno, Palma de Mallorca 1970). Panno resigned in order to protest having to play at a special time due to Fischer's religious beliefs. And actually, the arbiters refused to accept Huebner and Rogoff's one-move draw. They instructed the players to go back and play a few serious moves before splitting the point. Instead, Huebner and Rogoff went back and played a ludicrous, even whimsical, game in which both sides hung pieces and made unnatural moves. The arbiters also refused to accept that game. Eventually, Rogoff was declared the winner because Huebner refused to do anything else.

8. In this paragraph, I do not mean to suggest that the notion of perfect play is unproblematic. Since the goal of chess is to win, the "best" move in any position may be defined as the move most likely to lead to victory. (Or more accurately, the best move will have the highest expected utility, where a victory = 1, a draw = 1/2, and a loss = 0.) *Which* move is most likely to win may depend on the abilities of one's opponent. The best move against one player might be third-best against another. This is why Emanuel Lasker and Viktor Korchnoi "play the opponent, not the board." Suppose you must choose between two moves, each of which should lead to a draw. Are the two moves therefore equally good? No, because one move might present your opponent with more practical difficulties. Paradoxically, a losing move might even be better than a winning move. Suppose you must either accept your opponent's piece sacrifice (and thus endure an attack on your king) or else make your own sacrifice (and thus launch your own attack). It's possible that neither attack should work, and so, "objectively," you should accept the sacrifice. But since it's easier to attack than to defend, it may be that, in practice, both attacks are likely to work. In such a scenario, perfect play against a human opponent might be disastrous against God.

9. If architecture is frozen music, then chess is half-frozen music, since there is beauty in both static positions and lively sequences of moves. (Incidentally, the phrase "frozen music" is usually attributed to Goethe but is probably due to Schelling's student, Henry Crabb Robinson; see Pascha 2004.)

10. Tal 1976, 173.

11. *Zugzwang* is a German word meaning "the compulsion to move." When you're in zugzwang, every legal move hurts your position. The bridge equivalent is being endplayed. A remarkable fact in chess is that the endgame of king and rook versus lone king—a trivial win for the

stronger side—relies on zugzwang. If it were legal to "pass" in chess, then the king and rook could never checkmate the king. That fact would have profound implications for chess. Winning would become harder.

12. Forgive my use of the male pronoun to refer to chess Grandmasters. I do so because 99 percent of Grandmasters are male. Once I submitted an article to *Inside Chess* in which I alternated uses of "she" and "he," but the editors got rid of all of my "she's."

13. Individual players do, however, have their little habits. Ben Finegold, a professional player from Michigan, once told me that, when it is his move, he always thinks, "Should I offer a draw?" even when he is crushing a weak player. I used to do the following. If I was debating between two moves—the move I wanted to play, and the move I feared was better—I would deliver a silent lecture on why the move I preferred was superior, to see if I could convince myself.

14. Upon being asked, "How far do you see ahead?" Al Jaffe replied, "I see only one move ahead, but always the best move." Jaffe had reason to crow, since he had just defeated the great Capablanca. (This was reported by Al Horowitz, *Chess Review*, May 1946, 34.)

15. Kuhn says this about scientists who are looking at the same world but operating under different theoretical paradigms. See Kuhn 1970. Kuhn clarifies what he means by "paradigm" in the postscript.

16. This colorful expression comes from William James (1981, 462).

17. Similar remarks are true of bridge. I was a bridge novice twenty years after becoming a chess master, so my memories of being bad at bridge are clearer. The biggest change in my bridge perception came when I learned to think of the hand in terms of suits. A bridge expert will instantly see four different battles looming, in clubs, diamonds, hearts, and spades. Until you can see that much, bridge hands are very confusing.

18. Actually, the squares are usually not black and white, but they're always *called* black and white. When I was a kid, I once heard an elderly gentleman at the Birmingham chess club look at his position and complain, "I'm weak on the buff-colored squares." We laughed about that remark for weeks.

19. A good friend of mine is in prison. When I visit him, I can't bring in a chess set, but I can bring in pocket change to use in the vending machines in the visiting yard. Sometimes we use the change as chess pieces. We don't have a board, so we play on a solid brown table. As we're playing, my friend can point to any spot on "the board," and I can immediately tell him whether it's white or black.

20. The "red book" is actually *Weltgeschichte des Schachs*, vol. 27, edited by Eduard Wildhagen (1972). Edward Winter pointed out that although the book contains 353 numbered games (plus Spassky-Fischer, Siegen 1970), the book's title page boasts of 355 games.

21. Fischer's great book—*My 60 Memorable Games*—was published three years before his match with Spassky. Fischer's friends have told me that Bobby was reluctant to publish the book, since he knew it would help the Russians prepare for him. But Bobby went ahead with publication, telling his friends, "What does it matter? The world is going to end soon anyway." As it turned out, the apocalypse Fischer believed in did not occur, but this did not help Spassky.

22. Allen Kaufman is the friend of Fischer's who told me about this. Some people will be even more impressed by George Koltanowski's blindfold simultaneous exhibitions.

23. The moves were 1. d4 Nf6 2. Nf3 e6 3. g3 d5 4. Bg2 Be7 5. 0-0 0-0 6. c4 dxc4 7. Qc2 a6 8. Qxc4 b5 9. Qc2 Bb7 10. Bd2 Be4 11. Qc1 Bb7 12. Rd1 Qc8 13. a4 c5 14. axb5 draw agreed (Alburt–Rachels, Portland 1987). The game should continue 14. . . . axb5 15. Rxa8 Bxa8 16. dxc5 and then Black can recapture the pawn in either of two ways.

24. The rest of the fun comes from winning (or, as Fischer put it, crushing the other guy's ego).

25. Caïssa is the goddess of chess.

26. I most enjoyed the game, not at the height of my powers, but when my learning curve was most steep. Improving was the most fun.

27. See Smullyan 1979 and Bernd Graefrath's chapt. 1 in this volume.

28. Fischer 1969, 301.

29. 1. c4 f5 2. Qa4 Nf6 3. Qxd7+ Kf7 4. Qxc8 Kg8 5. Qe6 mate.

30. For example, 1. e4 d5 2. exd5 Nf6 3. Qh5 Kd7 4. Qxf7 Ne8 5. Qe6 mate.

31. 1. e4 e5 2. Qh5 Nc6 3. g4 d6 4. g5 Kd7 5. Bh3+ f5 6. gxf6 mate (Benko 1982). Benko formulates the problem as "White (who moves first) Helpmates in six via *en passant* discovered mate." See Benko and Silman 2003, 654.

32. Aside from Qe6, the only other move I remember working on is Bab1. To play "Bab1 mate" requires promoting a pawn to a bishop, since there must be two white bishops that can move to b1 (the bishop on a2, plus one more light-squared bishop). Note that moving the other bishop to b1 must also be mate, or else one wouldn't need to specify that it was the a-bishop whose movement ended the game (the move would just be "Bb1 mate"). This condition can be satisfied when both Bb1 moves uncover an attack on the black king by a rook or queen. I might have achieved Bab1 mate in 15 moves, but I'm not sure.

33. Benko and Silman 2003, 567. Richard Reti was also a great composer, and John Nunn is a great problem-solver.

34. I suppose this is a variant of "Can't win, don't try." My version is, "Can't win, tell yourself you're not trying."

35. "My theory of a key move was always to make it just the reverse of what a player in 999 cases out of 1000 would look for." —Sam Loyd, as reported in *Lasker's Chess Magazine*, December 1904, 84.

36. 1. f3 e6 2. Kf2 Qf6 3. Kg3 Qxf3+! 4. Kh4 Be7 mate. This problem is almost impossibly difficult because Qxf3+ is such a horrible move by normal chess standards; it is hard for a competent player to consciously consider it. We no longer know who composed this problem. There can be some disagreement as to whether it's flawed, because Black's first move can be either e6 or e5. In general, "cooked" problems are flawed, but here I find it natural to say that the problem has just one solution, with two trivially different variants. Qxf3+ is the real point of the composition.

37. Bridge writers also like to refer to bridge as a sport. The discussion that follows about chess applies equally to bridge. (By the way, the title of this section—"Pride and Sorrow in Chess"—pays homage to David Lawson's 1976 book *Paul Morphy: The Pride and Sorry of Chess.*)

38. Physical exertion does become important when the time control speeds up. A "specialist" at one-minute chess can make more than sixty moves in a minute, a feat that owes as much to dexterity as brainpower. Fast enough chess games might constitute sporting events. But whether they deserve to be in the Olympics is another matter.

39. Compare Rachels 1984–85, 109.

REFERENCES

Benko, Pal, and Jeremy Silman. 2003. *Pal Benko: My Life, Games and Compositions.* Los Angeles: Siles Press.

Fischer, Bobby. 1969. *My 60 Memorable Games.* New York: Simon and Schuster.

James, William. 1981. *The Principles of Psychology.* Cambridge, MA: Harvard University Press.

Kuhn, Thomas. 1970. *The Structure of Scientific Revolutions.* 2nd ed. Chicago: University of Chicago Press.

Lawson, David. 1976. *Paul Morphy: The Pride and Sorry of Chess.* New York: McKay.

Pascha, Khaled Sale. 2004. "Gefrorene Musik." Berlin: Technische Universität.

Rachels, James. 1984–85. "Chess as Art: Reflections on Richard Reti." *Philosophic Exchange* 15 and 16.

Smullyan, Raymond M. 1979. *The Chess Mysteries of Sherlock Holmes.* New York: Knopf.

Tal, Mikhail. 1976. *The Life and Games of Mikhail Tal.* USA: RHM Press.

Wildhagen, Eduard, ed. 1972. *Weltgeschichte des Schachs.* Vol. 27. Hamburg: Verlag Dr E. Wildhagen.

Contributors

Tama Coutts is a philosopher, chess player, and chess coach. He works on the philosophy of Donald Davidson and completed his masters degree in philosophy at the University of Melbourne in 2008. He is also in the top hundred chess players in Australia, and has won a number of grand prix tournaments, including the Gold Coast Classic; in that event he was involved in a four-way tie for first with IM Solomon, (then) IM Zhao and GM Rogers.

Tommy J. Curry is currently an Africana Research Center Post-Doctoral Fellow at Penn State University. His research interests are Critical Race Theory, Africana philosophy, and the newly emergent themes of cultur-alogics. Following the work of his dissertation, Curry is interested in investigating the philosophical implications of the various manifestations of a people's historical consciousness and how that historical consciousness actively modifies (contours) the social entities confronted in racialized experience.

Chess has been a long time love of Curry's. Though he does not have an official USCF chess rating, he has amassed an interesting recreational record—drawing a grandmaster in correspondence chess, publishing several theoretical novelties on Chesspublishing.com, and beating various National and International Masters in Blitz games. His interest in this project was largely rooted in his attempt to popularize the philosophical consequences of the research in Black psychology and contemporary African worldview analysis on aesthetics.

Bernd Graefrath was born in Bonn, Germany, and has studied philosophy and English literature at the University of Muenster, the University of

Arizona, the University of Konstanz, and the University of Pittburgh. He earned his PhD in philosophy in 1989 at the University of Konstanz and his Habilitation in philosophy in 1996 at the University of Essen. Currently he is a lecturer in philosophy at the University of Duisburg-Essen, Germany. He is a former correspondence chess player (ICCF, Higher Class), a composer of chess problems, a judge in composing tourneys for retro problems, and a researcher of chess history (especially concerning Emanuel Lasker).

Benjamin Hale is Assistant Professor of Philosophy and Environmental Studies at the University of Colorado at Boulder. For two years he was the Director of the Center for Values and Social Policy in the Philosophy Department, where he focused on expanding the reach and approachability of applied philosophy. Though he no longer directs the Center, he maintains a strong and ongoing connection to it. He is also an Affiliate Fellow in the Center for Science and Technology Policy Research at CIRES (the Cooperative Institute for Research in the Environmental Sciences) where he focuses on research at the intersection of ethics, science and technology policy, particularly as related to the environment.

Hale holds a PhD in philosophy, with a specialization in environmental ethics, and an MPA. in natural resource policy. He has published peer-reviewed articles in journals such as *Metaphilosophy*, *Think! Philosophy for Everyone*, the *American Journal of Bioethics*, the *Journal of Medical Ethics*, the *Journal of Agricultural and Environmental Ethics* and *Ethics, Place, and Environment*, as well as given papers at numerous conferences, related to the need for applied ethics to respond to concrete policy and science concerns in a way palatable to a nonphilosophy audience. In his pedagogical capacities, he has taught environmental ethics, politics, and policy to varying levels of graduate and undergraduate students at the University of Colorado at Boulder, New York University, Columbia University, Hofstra University, and Stony Brook University. Through it all, he has struggled mightily with an addiction to chess.

John Hartmann is a doctoral student in philosophy at Southern Illinois University at Carbondale, specializing in contemporary Continental philosophy, American philosophy, and philosophy of science and technology. More importantly, he is a chess player.

Hartmann's chess career began at the tender age of fourteen, when he played in his first tournaments at the Nassau Chess Club in New York. His grandfather supported his chess habit by sending him the *New York Times* chess column without fail, and by procuring him a subscription to the greatest chess periodical in the history of the world—Yasser Seirawan's now-defunct *Inside Chess*.

While Hartmann has more or less progressed beyond the rank of patzer, he sports an (obviously outdated!) USCF rating of 1468. He has also been a member of the Internet Chess Club since it went commercial in 1995.

Bill Martin is Professor of Philosophy at DePaul University in Chicago. He is the author of numerous books, including *Humanism and Its Aftermath*, *Music of Yes*, and, most recently, *Ethical Marxism: The Categorical Imperative of Liberation*. He is also a musician and avid bicyclist and chess player. At DePaul he teaches a course called "Chess/Culture."

Andy Miah is Reader in New Media and Bioethics in the School of Media, Language and Music at the University of the West of Scotland, Fellow of the Institute for Ethics and Emerging Technologies, USA, and Fellow for Human Futures at the Foundation for Art and Creative Technology, UK. He has a PhD in Bioethics and Cultural Studies and a master's degree in Medical Law. He is author of *Genetically Modified Athletes* (Routledge, 2004), co-author with Dr. Emma Rich of *The Medicalization of Cyberspace* (2008, Routledge), and co-editor with Mike Stubbs and Laura Sillars of *Human Futures* (2008, Liverpool University Press). Miah's research discusses the intersections of art, ethics, technology, and culture and he has published broadly in areas of emerging technologies, particularly related to human enhancement.

Peter Morriss teaches in the Department of Political Science and Sociology, in the National University of Ireland, Galway. He teaches mainly political philosophy, but also a course on Korea. He is the author of *Power: A Philosophical Analysis* (second edition, 2002), and many articles on power, political philosophy, and Korean politics. More recently, he has written articles on whether there should be legal recognition of marriage, and on the history of the law on abortion in Ireland and England.

Peter wasted much of his teens playing chess, not very well. He then succeeded in giving the game up for nearly thirty years, before being drawn back into it, a few years ago, while on a sabbatical in Australia. He now plays at roughly U.S. expert strength, and is captain of the Galway chess team.

Ahti-Veikko Pietarinen is University Lecturer and Adjunct Professor in Theoretical Philosophy in the Department of Philosophy at the University of Helsinki, Finland. He received a PhD in philosophy in 2002 and a master's degree in computer science in 1997. He is author of *Signs of Logic: Peircean Themes on the Philosophy of Language, Games, and Communication* (Springer, 2006), and editor of and contributor to *Game Theory and Linguistic Meaning* (Elsevier, 2007). Pietarinen's research involves philosophy of logic and mathematics, philosophy of language, game theory, pragmatism, and semiotics.

Stuart Rachels is a professional philosopher and former United States Chess Champion. In chess, he became the youngest master in U.S. history in 1981 at age eleven; he won the 1988 U.S. Junior Championship at age eighteen; and at age twenty he tied for first in the 1989 U.S. Championship, thus becoming an International Master. In philosophy, Rachels received degrees from Emory University, the University of Oxford (where he was a Marshall Scholar), and Syracuse University. His father, James Rachels (1941–2003), was a well-known philosopher. Since James Rachels's death, Stuart Rachels has revised some of his books, including *The Elements of Moral Philosophy* and *Problems from Philosophy*. He lives in Tuscaloosa, Alabama, where he is Associate Professor of Philosophy at the University of Alabama. His website is www.jamesrachels.org/stuart/.

Evan Selinger is Assistant Professor of Philosophy at Rochester Institute of Technology. He has written many articles and edited or co-edited several books about issues raised in the philosophies of technology and science, phenomenology, and science and technology studies. He's currently completing a monograph entitled *Embodying Technoscience.*

Deborah P. Vossen is Associate Professor of Human Kinetics at St. Francis Xavier University. She received her PhD from the University of Western Ontario where she specialized in the philosophy of sport. Her research is grounded in metaphysical questions relevant to sport and physical activity and includes queries such as what is the essential nature of these activities, what is the nature of human participation in them, and what is the meaning and significance of this participation? Although grounded in metaphysics, her primary area of research interest is sport ethics and involves the development of foundational principles for action therein.

Index

Aagaard, Jacob, 55–56
absurdity, philosophy on, 94–95
Achterhuis, Hans, 49
African psychology, 153n8
Alburt, Lev, 216
Alekhine, Alexander, 176
Ali, Muhammad, 213
Allen, Woody
    "Death Knocks," 68
Anand, Viswanathan, 57, 211
Apel, Karl-Otto, 158
Aramil, William, 138
Aristotle, 173
    Ars Obligatoria, 120
    Topics, 120
artificial general intelligence (AGI),
    21
artificial intelligence (AI)
    and chess, ix, 14–15, 19, 22
    and game playing, 20–22
    and game theory, 14
    philosophy of, 13–14
        bias in, 15
    research in, critique of, 19–20
    and speciesism, 14
    storytelling test for, 20
    storytelling view of, 17–18, 25
    weak view of, 17–18, 25
Artificial Life (AL) research, 19–20
Aschwanden, Reto, 10
Ashley, Maurice, 109, 138, 141–42

Augustine, Saint, 112, 125
Avni, Amatzia, 70

Benko, Pal, 218, 219
Bergman, Ingmar, x, 66, 67, 70–71,
    81
Beth, Evert W., 129
blindfold chess, 215
blitz chess, 98
    and the absurd, 98–99
Borel, Yannick, 121, 125
Botvinnik, Mikhail, 142
Boudy, Julio, 47
Braswell, Isaac M., 138
Bringsjord, Selmer, 19, 20
Brouwer, L. E. J., 120, 129
Bush, George W., 212
Butcher, Robert, 193–94
    critique of, 195–96, 198–200,
        204
Byrne, Robert, 218

Caillaud, Michel, 10
Caïssa, 89, 217
calculation, and creativity, 112
Callois, Roger, 92
care ethics, 175
Carnap, Rudolf, 8
casuistry, xii, 172–75
    expertise in, 181–82
    history of, 173–74

probabilist school of, 173
skill in, 180
slippery slope in, 183–84
weakness of, for ethics, 170,
        182–83
chess. *See also* blindfold chess; blitz
        chess; chess problems; chess
        software; chess technology;
        lightning chess
and the absurd, 93–94, 97–100,
        103, 107
and African worldview, 142, 150,
        151
in American society, 211–12
analogical thinking in, 177, 178,
        180
and anomalies, 103–4
beauty in, 93, 107, 213–14, 217
and body language, 79
calculation vs. wiliness in, 104–5
and casuistry, 177–84
and chance, 104
cognition in, 214–17
and cognitive limits, 70
cultural embodiment in, 66–67, 80
and culturalogics, 151
and culture, 146
and deviousness, 92
and dynamic advantage, 141–42
and embodiment, 71, 77
and ethics, differences between,
        179, 182
and game theory, 159
and Go, comparing, 90
and hip hop, 138–40
and human singularity, 68–69
idea of, 199, 202, 203, 204
institution of vs. game of,
        199–203, 205
and intelligence, 15
and intentional stance, 165–66
as interaction, 165
and intersubjectivity, 109–110
and the irrational, 106
and language, 133
and logic, 140–43
lusory attitude in, 202
and material advantage, 141

as *memento mori*, 71
mistaken depictions of, 90
modern, 53–56, 138
and moral considerability, 159
and narrative myths, 143–44, 146
as not a game, 195, 199
and the Other, 164–65
and philosophy, 89–90, 113–14
and philosophy of language, 120
and prelusory goal, question of,
        194–95, 200, 203
and psychoanalysis, 143
and psychologics, 146
rule-independence in, 55
and sports, 220–21
and strategic reason, 160
as symbolic motif, 68
and theodicy, 101–3, 111
traditional theory of, 143
and underdetermination, 102–10
and women, 78–79
Chess (musical), 211
ChessBase, x, 41, 44, 45, 56
chess narratives, 65–66
chess-playing computers, ix, 177–78.
        See also Deep Blue; KAISSA
as brute calculators, 72
chess problems/compositions,
        95–96, 218–20
and the absurd, 99
retrograde analysis of, viii–ix, 2, 3
insights from, 9
and theodicy, 96, 98
chess rationality, 93
chess software, 40–41
chess technology, 41–42
fetishization of, 42
influence of, 56–58
judicious use of, 44–48
Chinese room argument, 16–17, 25,
        29
and chess, 32–35
and intentionality, 30–32
responses to, 29–30
robot reply, 30–31
systems reply, 30
cognitive optimism, ix, 9
Collins, Harry, 76

communicative interaction,
pragmatics of, 161–62
compatibilism, 113
Cook, David, 18
Cosell, Howard, 213
Crafty clones, 42, 48
Crease, Robert, 78
Csikszentmihalyi, Mihaly, 75
Cupitt, Don, 94
cyborg, 52

Davidson, Donald, 90, 94, 167–68
on triangulation, 96, 99–100
Davis, Martin, 111–12
Deep Blue, x, 15, 18, 19, 20, 22,
39–40, 56, 71, 72, 79, 83, 166,
178
Deep Junior, 57
de Groot, Adriaan, 175–76, 179, 180
Deleuze, Gilles
A Thousand Plateaus, 90–91
Dennett, Daniel, 71, 89, 165
Derrida, Jacques, 93
Dewey, John, 94
discourse ethics, xii, 162
discourse theory, 158, 160, 163
Dreyfus, Hubert, x–xi, 39–40, 66
on chess, human/computer
differences in, 73–74
on chess-playing computers,
71–72
critique of, 66–67, 71, 76–81, 83
on embodiment, 76–77
on Grandmasters, 75, 76, 81–82,
85n12
Dreyfus, Stuart, 72, 82
Dummett, Michael
The Game of Tarot, 1

Eeden, Frederik van, 129
Ellul, Jacques, 42
ethical intuitions, critique of, 181,
182
ethics, and question of principles,
171–72
Euwe, Max, 176
exact proof games, 10
existentialism, 94

existential phenomenology, 67

Farha, Sam, 211
Fine, Reuben, 79, 176
Fischer, Bobby, 60n10, 209, 210,
212, 213, 216, 217, 218
Flexner, Abraham, 125
Flohr, Salomon, 176
"flow," 74
Foreman, George, 213
Frankfurt School, 160
Freeman, Walter, 76
Frege, Gottlob, 124
Friedel, Frederic, 56
Fritz, 41, 48
interactionalist view of, 51–52

Gadamer, Hans-Georg, xi, 112
on chess, 91, 97
and the absurd, 95
and theodicy, 89, 93, 100
critique of, 100–101, 103, 113
on fusion of horizons, 96
game metaphors, in philosophy,
119–20
game-playing behavior, 21
game(s)
conditions for, 192
and constitutive rules, 192
idea of, 203
and intelligence, 22
and language, 132
lusory attitude in, 192, 196–99
philosophy on, 119–20
prelusory goal in, 203–4
game theory, 128, 131–32, 159–60
and economics, 125–26
and language, 126–27
Girard, Jean-Yves, 122
Gladwell, Malcolm
Blink, 77
Gödel, Kurt, 9
Graefrath, Bernd, 164
Grandmasters, 180
and choice-of-move problems,
181
and "flow," 74
method of play of, 176–77

Grice, H. Paul, 126–28
  on cooperation, 128
Guattari, Felix
  A Thousand Plateaus, 90–91
Gufeld, Eduard, 92
Gurevich, Mikhail, 53
GZA, 139

Habermas, Jürgen, 120, 158, 167
  communication/strategy
      distinction in, 130–31, 160
  on linguistic competence, 131
  Theory of Communicative Action,
      161
Haraway, Donna
  "A Cyborg Manifesto," 52
Harré, Rom, 132
Heidegger, Martin, 43–44, 69
  on technology, 43, 48–49, 50
hermeneutics, 95
Hilbert, David, 122, 129
Hintikka, Jaakko, 127
hip hop, 138–40
  and chess, 138–40
Hjartarson, Johann, 165
Hjelmslev, Louis, 123
Hoffman, Dustin, 212
Holmes, Sherlock, 2
Huizinga, Johan, 92
  Homo Ludens, 20
human/animal distinction, 69
human/animal interaction, and
      intentional stance, 166–69
human/nonhuman, blurring line of,
      52
Husserl, Edmund, 120, 123, 124, 129
  game-meaning in, 122
  Logical Investigations, 122

Ihde, Don, 50, 52
intentionality, 30
intentional stance, 165–66

Jakobson, Roman, 123
James, William, 94, 113
Jaspers, Karl, 42
Jay-Z, 139, 153n4
Jonsen, A. R., 174

The Abuse of Casuistry, 172

KAISSA, 178
Kant, Immanuel, 119, 171
Kaplan, Julio, 75
Karavis, Andreas, 92
Karjakin, Sergey, 60n10
Karpov, Anatoly, 102, 108–9
Kasimdzhanov, Rustam, 57
Kasparov, Garry, x, 18, 19, 39, 40,
      41, 56, 71, 77, 83, 102, 108–9,
      110, 178, 210, 212
  and chess technology, influence
      of, 56–58
  as cyborg, 56
Kasparyan, Ghenrikh, 219
Kelly, Sean, 74
Keres, Paul, 176
Kierkegaard, Søren, 201
Knuth, Donald E.
  *Things a Computer Scientist
      Rarely Talks About*, 106
Kogan, Boris, 216–17
Kotik, Jack, 2
Kramnik, Vladimir, 57
Kroker, Arthur, 18
Kuhn, Thomas, 215

Lamb, Charles, 183
language, 128
  and chess, 133
  and games, 132
Latour, Bruno, 50
Lee, Mark H., 14
Lehrer, Jim, 71
Leibniz, G. W., 111–12
lightning chess, 75, 146
logical positivism, 11n1
Lorenzen, Paul, 129
Loyd, Sam, 3, 219
lusory attitude, 192, 196
Lyman, Shelby, 209, 212

Mannoury, Gerrit, 129
Marshall, Frank, 214
Martin, Bill
  Avant rock, 91
McBride, Frank, 197

Mead, George Herbert, 94
Mill, J. S., 179
Mirabile, Tim, x, 45–49, 51–52
Moore, G. E., 11
moral considerability, 159
Moravec, Hans, 18, 19
Morgenstern, Oskar
   The Theory of Games and
      Economic Behavior, 121, 126
Mumford, Lewis, 42

Najdorf, Miguel, 210
National Rifle Association, 49
Negritude, 149
Nietzsche, Friedrich, 119
nonhuman agency, 51
Novikov, Igor, 45–48
Nunn, John, 53, 54

Paethz, Elizabeth, 79
Palmer, Arnold, 212, 217
Pascal, Blaise
   Provincial Letters, 174, 183
Peirce, Charles S., 126, 129, 130, 131
   chess in, 120–21, 133
Plato, 95, 119
Platonism, 95
Polgar, Judit, 60n10
Polgar, Susan, 79
Pollan, Michael, 43
pragmatism, 94
prelusory goal, 191, 192, 193–94
   critique of idea of, 193–94
principle of verifiability, 11n2
prisoner's dilemma, 160

Quidditch, 191, 206n1

Rachels, James, xiii
Rice, Tim, 211
right and wrong, principles of, 171
Rorty, Richard, 94
Rowling, J. K., 191
Rowson, Jonathan, 138, 142–43

Saussure, Ferdinand de, 120, 123,
   127
Schiller, Eric

Unorthodox Chess Openings, 102
Schiller, Friedrich, 129
   Aesthetische Briefe, 121
Schneider, Angela, 193–94
   critique of, 195–96, 198–200, 204
Schopenhauer, Arthur, 9
Scott-Heron, Gil, xi
Searching for Bobby Fischer (film),
   107, 211, 212
Searle, John, ix, 13, 16–17, 18, 25
   on computers and cognition, 26,
      28
   on intentionality, 30–31
Senghor, Leopold Sedar, 149–50
The Seventh Seal (film), 66
   chess symbolism in, 67–68, 70–71
Shabalov, Alexander, 80
Shahade, Jennifer, 42, 44, 79, 80, 81
   Chess Bitch, 78
Shakespeare, William, 213
Shirov, Alexei, 56
Short, Nigel, 210
Shubik, Martin, 132
   Game Theory in the Social
      Sciences, 114
significians, 128–29
silicon seconds, 41
Silman, Jeremy, 141
simultaneous exhibitions, 216
Smullyan, Raymond, ix
   antiverificationism of, 7
   best retro problem of, 4–7
   The Chess Mysteries of the
      Arabian Nights, 1
   The Chess Mysteries of Sherlock
      Holmes, 1
   Forever Undecided, 1
   on religion, 8–9
   Some Interesting Memories, 1, 7
   The Tao Is Silent, 1, 9
Smyslov, Vasily, 219
Socrates, 70
Solway, David, 91–92
   Chess Pieces, 91
   hoax of, 91–92
Spassky, Boris, 210, 212, 216
Spielbedeutung, 122
Stohl, Igor, 54, 56, 57

Suits, Bernard, ix, 198, 200, 201, 202, 203
 The Grasshopper, xiii, xiv, 21, 191
surd, etymology of, 93
Sutton-Smith, Brian, 92

Tal, Mikhail, 141, 157, 165, 166, 214
Tarkatower, Savielly, 176
technology
 "empirical turn" on, 49–50
 instrumental view of, 43
 interactionalist view of, 49, 50–51
 philosophers on, 42–43
Tevis, Walter
 The Queen's Gambit, 90
theodicy, 89, 110
 and determinism, 111–13
 superficial, 101
Tinman, Jan, 219
Tisdall, Jonathan, 109
Toulmin, Stephen, 174
 The Abuse of Casuistry, 172
Troitsky, Alexei, 219
Turing, Alan, ix, 13, 16, 18–21, 36n1
Turing machines, 15, 26–27
 and understanding, 33
Turing test, 16

Ulam, Stanislaw, 120

Van Meegeren, Hans, 183
Vermeer, Johannes, 183
Vienna Circle, 126
von Neumann, John, 121, 125
 The Theory of Games and Economic Behavior, 121

Waitzkin, Fred
 Mortal Games, 108
 Searching for Bobby Fischer, 108
Waitzkin, Josh, 107
Watson, John, 53–55
 Chess Strategy in Action, 55
Welby, Victoria, 129
Williams, Bernard, 183
Wittgenstein, Ludwig, 89, 92, 120, 122, 129
 chess in, 122
 on games, 124–25
 on language games, 124, 126, 128
 Nachlass, 126
 Philosophical Investigations, 124, 125, 126
 Tractatus, 111
 Zettel, 126

Zermelo, Ernst, 121
Ziyatdinov, Rashid, 140–41
Zugzwang, 222n11